CHIEF DESIGN OFFICERS AT WORK

INSIGHTS AND STRATEGIES FROM CDOS ON THE FRONTLINES OF INNOVATION

Jaleh Afshar

Apress®

Chief Design Officers at Work: Insights and Strategies from CDOs on the Frontlines of Innovation

Jaleh Afshar
Menlo Park, CA, USA

ISBN-13 (pbk): 979-8-8688-1136-4 ISBN-13 (electronic): 979-8-8688-1137-1
https://doi.org/10.1007/979-8-8688-1137-1

Copyright © 2025 by Jaleh Afshar

This work is subject to copyright. All rights are reserved by the Publisher, whether the whole or part of the material is concerned, specifically the rights of translation, reprinting, reuse of illustrations, recitation, broadcasting, reproduction on microfilms or in any other physical way, and transmission or information storage and retrieval, electronic adaptation, computer software, or by similar or dissimilar methodology now known or hereafter developed.

Trademarked names, logos, and images may appear in this book. Rather than use a trademark symbol with every occurrence of a trademarked name, logo, or image we use the names, logos, and images only in an editorial fashion and to the benefit of the trademark owner, with no intention of infringement of the trademark.

The use in this publication of trade names, trademarks, service marks, and similar terms, even if they are not identified as such, is not to be taken as an expression of opinion as to whether or not they are subject to proprietary rights.

While the advice and information in this book are believed to be true and accurate at the date of publication, neither the authors nor the editors nor the publisher can accept any legal responsibility for any errors or omissions that may be made. The publisher makes no warranty, express or implied, with respect to the material contained herein.

    Managing Director, Apress Media LLC: Welmoed Spahr
    Acquisitions Editor: Shivangi Ramachandran
    Development Editor: James Markham
    Project Manager: Jessica Vakili

Distributed to the book trade worldwide by Springer Science+Business Media New York, 1 New York Plaza, New York, NY 10004. Phone 1-800-SPRINGER, fax (201) 348-4505, e-mail orders-ny@springer-sbm.com, or visit www.springeronline.com. Apress Media, LLC is a California LLC and the sole member (owner) is Springer Science + Business Media Finance Inc (SSBM Finance Inc). SSBM Finance Inc is a **Delaware** corporation.

For information on translations, please e-mail booktranslations@springernature.com; for reprint, paperback, or audio rights, please e-mail bookpermissions@springernature.com.

Apress titles may be purchased in bulk for academic, corporate, or promotional use. eBook versions and licenses are also available for most titles. For more information, reference our Print and eBook Bulk Sales web page at http://www.apress.com/bulk-sales.

If disposing of this product, please recycle the paper.

Contents

About the Author v

Introduction vii

Chapter 1: Anand Jha, *Miko* — 1
Chapter 2: Andrea Mangini, *Shopify* — 13
Chapter 3: Anita Patwardhan Butler, *Strava* — 25
Chapter 4: Baylie Brenner-Bruzgis, *Twitch* — 35
Chapter 5: Bernadette Irizarry, *Sony Pictures Entertainment* — 45
Chapter 6: Chooake Wongwattanasilpa, *Bank of Singapore* — 55
Chapter 7: Chris No, *Demand.io* — 61
Chapter 8: Christie Fremon, *Asana* — 69
Chapter 9: Courtney Allison Brown, *CarMax* — 79
Chapter 10: Daisuke Sakai, *teamLab* — 85
Chapter 11: Geunbae "GB" Lee, *Statsig* — 91
Chapter 12: Gianluca Brugnoli, *TomTom* — 99
Chapter 13: Helena Seo, *DoorDash* — 107
Chapter 14: Joann Wu, *Uber* — 123
Chapter 15: Josh Mahoney, *Breadfast* — 133
Chapter 16: Linda Sum, *Samsung Electronics America* — 141
Chapter 17: Lissette Sotelo Parr, *Personio* — 151
Chapter 18: Michael Nitsopoulos, *Thentia* — 159
Chapter 19: Mig Reyes, *Duolingo* — 167
Chapter 20: Mohammed Adib, *Intercon* — 173
Chapter 21: Olatunji Saliu, *Interswitch* — 177
Chapter 22: Payam Tabrizian, *Unity* — 183
Chapter 23: Ruchi Batra, *IBM* — 191
Chapter 24: Rufei Fan, *PicnicHealth* — 199

Chapter 25: Ryan Leffel, *Priceline* — 209
Chapter 26: Saurabh Soni, *Razorpay* — 219
Chapter 27: Temilola Oyenuga, *Spazio Ideale* — 225
Chapter 28: Uday Shankar, *Perforce* — 235
Chapter 29: Wendy Owen, *Meta* — 247
Acknowledgments — 253

Index — 255

About the Author

For over 18 years, **Jaleh Afshar** has been responsible for shipping large-scale mobile, web, voice, and AR experiences and leading product design teams. Currently a Director of Design at Meta, she has taught courses, led workshops, and published on various creative industry topics. She lives in Menlo Park, California.

Introduction

Join me in uncovering behind-the-scenes stories from prolific design executives, who have each woven the fabric of design through the essence of their organizations. This collection of interviews, completed over the last two years, transcends the boundaries of industries, company size, location, management styles, and backgrounds, presenting a diverse view of design leadership. Each discussion was approached in a candid, transparent way, with minimal editorializing of the insights shared live in the conversation.

As you'll discover, what differentiates these leaders is not simply their aesthetic eye. Expertise in pioneering innovation, developing high performing teams, setting clear vision, and proficiency in infusing creativity into business strategy are just a few examples of the ways they've amplified the success of their companies.

Whether you're a seasoned executive, aspiring professional, or simply curious about the lessons learned in the trenches of design leadership, there is something here for you. Expect to be inspired, educated, and entertained at these insights, and most importantly, see the world through the eyes of those who dare to apply the transformative power of design. Let the conversations begin!

—Jaleh Afshar

CHAPTER

1

Anand Jha
Miko

As the Chief Design Officer at Miko, Anand Jha leads the product, design, gaming, and content verticals for the Mumbai-based companion robot company that creates enriching experiences for children. Anand has over 16 years of experience in design and product leadership, with expertise in user research, design systems, product launch planning, and user-centered design.

In previous roles, Anand led design for products and services across various domains, including e-commerce, healthcare, media, and automotive. He resides in Delhi, India.

Jaleh Afshar: How did you discover design as a career path?

Anand Jha: I grew up in a place that had very little exposure to design as a profession. I was exposed to other creative activities like writing and theater, and I felt seen and understood in these settings. I also liked making stuff, and I liked it when people responded well to it. However, it never sort of struck me or my family as something I could take up as a vocation.

So, sticking with what felt like a safe career direction, I pursued my undergrad in mechanical engineering. That was when I discovered that I was a complete lab rat. I loved making things in the foundry. I enjoyed forging workshops in the robotics lab. Just making things by hand is what gave me a lot of pleasure, and that stayed with me.

© Jaleh Afshar 2025
J. Afshar, *Chief Design Officers at Work*,
https://doi.org/10.1007/979-8-8688-1137-1_1

Once I graduated, I wanted to do something about this... feeling, whatever it was. Could I make a living out of making things? So, after graduating, I remember going into my master's exam for design, fairly uninitiated. I was barely informed by what it takes to enter a design school and what would make a good portfolio. I put in anything which I felt could be interesting to them, and oddly I got in! I had the most wonderful time studying.

Even taking the master's entry exam for design was such fun; I had such a great time writing the exam answers and that gave me a lot of validation. I felt like I had come home. It felt close to my heart and I knew I had to pursue this further.

Design school was a great experience. It was unlike anything else that I'd seen before; these were very self-driven people. They were happy to collaborate. They were happy to give more. There was very little competition. People were taking their own time, their own pace. The whole thing felt very different from the way I had studied previously. I felt this was going to be what I'd do for the rest of my life, and I'm happy that it really ended up happening.

Afshar: At Miko, you lead a team that designs both software and robotics hardware. What are some unique challenges of physical product development?

Jha: I started my career with General Motors, designing cars and vehicle HMI systems. That gave me my first 'phy-gital' product learning. Making a car is a massive process, and a lot of those practices were ironed to perfection with years of investment and motivation behind them. It became a good training ground to understand how physical products were built.

Another stint at Siemens R&D, where I worked on market requirements for cardiology and ultrasound machines, helped me connect the product development process to demand side in the market. These weren't objects sold for their aesthetics, but artifacts solely built for precision and usefulness and my learnings here were to connect craft to business realities.

Now at Miko, I bring these learnings and make them work in a very volatile business environment. There are new variables that keep emerging frequently and design has to respond to it. For instance, one of the first challenges we worked through was the chip shortage during Covid. Our component procurement was experiencing volatility, which meant redesigning the circuit board layout frequently, which can affect the design of the overall form. You might need to use other tooling, or swap components. These variables will bring constraints from which you'll have to operate. So, I have a deep appreciation for designers who can operate through constraints, understand the implications of choices they make, and do all of that in a very short cycle.

Our products operate in a fairly high technical complexity landscape, with physical interactions, Wi-Fi, connections with other micro devices, and more. That has a lot of impact on the role design gets to play in the phygital world.

The design language is important to get right; however, the luxury of time is not always available for us as a startup. So we have to figure out how to move much faster, using trade fairs as a way of quickly validating concepts. CES, Nuremberg Toy Fair, etc., are all helpful to get feedback from retailers to drive our decision-making. This feedback can lead to iterations on all aspects of the design, every single joinery, material choice, each curve and detail, user journey experiences, etc. And, of course, on the leadership side, ensuring that these design decisions are aligned with the business decisions and the interest of all stakeholders.

There is an ideal process, but that ideal process functions in an ideal setup. That means realistically, there's not an ideal process to anything. Building that elasticity as a professional, and working with what space you are afforded is key. If you are working in spaces that have their own economics governing them, for instance, in retail, when we must hit the stores at a certain point in time, this creates a certain set of operational constraints. The process we create for our teams has to be able to accommodate or to work with those operational constraints. It also means letting go of some changes that you may have wanted to make because there is simply not enough time in this iteration. You might need to come back to those things next year or the year after. For physical products, sometimes it's a gradual journey.

Of course, we do embrace ways of doing faster iterations. For example, 3D printing and quick mockups allow for early testing and faster movement toward a concept. And bringing all your stakeholders on board early, even if they might not give you the most textbookish perfect design feedback, the early feedback is still so valuable. It's important to figure out a way to take generic feedback and break it down to specifics. So, when I speak to, say, someone in sales they might say, "this is not looking bright enough" or "this is not speaking to me." It may not be actionable feedback for the designer, so I need to take that and translate it into something tangible. Having the conversation to uncover what they *actually* mean is that the contrast in the colors need to increase, or the curvatures in the shape need to be more uniformly rounded. Now *that* is actionable!

Some people ask why can't we go back to our stakeholders and say, "why can't you give me specific feedback?" Well, they won't be able to. Because your technical physical product design language is not something to be expected of people outside of your role. So you'll have to step back and look at the bigger view, and build the capacity to translate high-level feedback to a very specific direction for your team. If you give the same feedback verbatim from the stakeholder directly to your design team, your team might not be able to address it.

Afshar: Miko's flagship products are created for kids. What are unique design challenges when creating for this audience?

Jha: There are definitely many unexpected challenges. When I first started in this sector, I thought that because I'm a designer, I'll probably automatically be disposed to working with an audience who understands play, which is not the case.

Children do not use products as intended! When we started doing user research, we built a small usability lab in the office and got our first set of kids to try out our prototypes. These were kids aged four to seven. In the research lab, you're so used to the standard procedure. You have a protocol, you have a debriefer, you have the prototype in front of the user.

None of that works with kids! They would barely stay in one place. They won't sit. And they're happy! They're jumping, they're moving around, they're doing other things. I also realized how the children needed a sense of connection and space to really come around and engage.

I spoke to a friend who's an actor. I said, "my first session doing research with kids has been a complete disaster." And he told me that children are very fluid. They move. Their bodies move. Their heads move. They move around objects. They move around things. They go inside the furniture. They'll get up and climb something else. If they don't see you doing something similar, they will not trust you. You'll have to play with them for like 20, 25, 30 minutes, doing all those things. And if they don't trust you, they will not engage with the product meaningfully. I remember there was this one child who got fascinated with a white board that we had kept in the meeting room. He'd flip it around and around, and started calling my name from one side of the white board. So then I would go on the other side and start calling him back. And then you do this for 20 minutes and the kids are having fun, and then they want to try out the thing that the research team has prepared.

We've also had this dialogue internally about the effectiveness of the research. Many of the team members didn't have kids nor worked with kids before, and their experience was from very different backgrounds selling only to different audiences whether it was e-commerce or digital media. They're extremely data-driven, and all of us geek on data a lot.

So imagine all of us coming to a play space like this. It doesn't intuitively come together in the most logical way possible. If there is a cart abandoned in an e-commerce company, or there's a drop-off on the funnel in a content platform, you would be able to do your research, form a clear hypothesis, test it in some form, and be able to do something around it. Here, the hypothesis that we form and how children behave may not be completely in sync. It was because we were taking a lot of understanding from the products meant for adults and trying to impose it here. Kids don't function like that. How they get motivated, how they get engaged is very different.

Another thing happens with kids is they grow very fast and become different people very fast. With adults, it doesn't happen so much. You're not really differentiating between an adult who is, say, 35 and an adult who is 38. They're all grown-ups in the same larger bracket for you, demographically. With kids, it's not the case. A child who's four years of age, a child who's seven, and a child who's nine, they're very different people. They have very different expectations of a product.

Those are the learnings I've taken away so far. It's still a work in progress and I think it's an audience that's extremely complicated to crack.

Afshar: In your current role, your team has begun creating artificial intelligence (AI) powered devices. Would love to hear your take on the future of AI.

Jha: AI embedding across our daily lives is something that is at the back of our heads constantly as we're building products in this space. Users are diverse. There's a lot of subjectivity in what they want. Effective AI is not like industrial automation where something has to simply execute a standard process, so traditional robotics is not much of a help here.

Once AI gains more momentum, the larger question would be what happens between the idea of a human and labor. These AI-powered solutions are going to move with a certain degree of autonomy. That debate is definitely going to shape what becomes the next evolution for us as humans. What do we take up next? What is it that we're thinking about next as a species?

Because, and I'm just extrapolating, let's say AI "brains" become more understanding of human complexities and nuances over a period of time. When it learns with more complex data, it is able to accommodate more complex use cases. At that point, I think what it is to be a human might need to be conceptualized in a different way.

Our understanding of being a human is also very institutionalized. We come into the world, we celebrate our birthdays, we study, then we take up a job, and then we might have kids, find a place to live, find a vocation. All of these constructs are part of what shapes our idea of being a human. Some of this will start getting blurred. For example, there will be a massive shift for society at large when a vocation might not be one's identity.

When I ask people I meet to tell me something about themselves, typically the first thing they start with is, "I work for this company, I work as an analyst." But if there is someone else who's analyzing data, doing the job you are doing today, and that someone is not human, then what is your identity? We will probably be grappling with things way more existential as this thing grows up. That is one shift that I see.

The countries that are linked to some form of global capital will probably start living similarly and functioning similarly. So, for example, the most modernized neighborhood in New Delhi is not much different from Washington. But there's a huge gap between the lifestyle in that same neighborhood in New Delhi to, say, a village just 200 kilometers away from it. There's certainly uniformity in terms of what kind of lives people live and how people function. Those are bigger change vectors that will come in.

And AI and related concepts that humans are now exploring will be at the forefront of working through these lifestyle changes, and modifying this journey in some form. It could be regulators. It could probably be large communities of people with a shared goal. The biggest forces shaping AI might not only be tech players. We'll need to understand what AI-powered journeys are valuable to society at large. How that decision will be made is yet to be seen.

Afshar: How do you balance creative freedom with practical business constraints?

Jha: I still personally struggle with this sometimes, and I've come to the understanding that there are three variables that you're constantly optimizing as a creative practitioner.

First is your craft. What is the ideal way of doing things and the vocabulary around that? So if you understand forms, you'll be able to understand how forms function together, how they compose together, and so on. If you understand two-dimensional form, you can understand grids, typography, colors, and so on and so forth. This knowledge builds technical depth. This is your craft.

Then there is expression, which is why many designers ended up in this profession in the first place. Very few of us became designers because we solely wanted to make things for other people. Many of us originally wanted to be artists, who then became designers, and then in the process ended up—if I'm being honest—making things for other people. So there is this need to express yourself creatively. The need to express gets compromised at times from the previous variable. Expression gets compromised from the principles of craft in that expression doesn't always want to obey a set of rules. Ideally, expression can be completely explorative and not take any frameworks that are given to force one to function a certain way.

And third is the market, which brings its own set of variables. Acknowledging market constraints can also feel like a compromise against the first two variables. You might want to do concepts that are not really grounded in physics or in manufacturing cost reduction or in supply chain realities.

The role of the designer is our ability to acknowledge that this conflict exists. And, for a design team leader, being able to build safe places for designers to express themselves and develop a greater engagement with their craft but also understanding that there are other stakeholders in the picture. Each stakeholder is looking at their area of deliverables with the same degree of depth that you as a designer might be looking at your own work. As a designer, when we speak to other people, different parts of these variables will come into play. For example, designers speaking with their managers might focus on craft. Or if they are speaking with sales, maybe the market discussion will come more into play.

In those conversations, that means you'll have to move a little bit away from your position and you'll have to move closer to other people's positions, where you can better see their viewpoint. It doesn't mean that your position wasn't valid. It doesn't mean that your position is not of value, but that's a personal value that you'll acknowledge within yourself.

So, as a designer, when you are exploring, the first person you show your work to is yourself. You establish comfort and honor in what you've made. However, sometimes when you take your work to market, sometimes the market doesn't acknowledge it, and that can create a lot of self-doubt. We as creative people are in constant dialogue with other people, and we're putting a lot of our own vulnerability out there. When we envision a concept and we make something very creatively, we don't want it desecrated with a million external opinions of this or that, right? It can become very personal, very sort of…hurtful at times.

In those cases, what we have to do is honor the fact that we created something. So I tell people that if you're *expressing*, that is sacred. Keep that feeling and acknowledge it. And then, if the thing you made is going through changes or modifications, it is because it has to accommodate goals that weren't what your creation was originally meant to stretch to, right? But doesn't mean that your original creation is not of value.

So the first dialogue that has to occur is that conversation has to happen somewhere.

This acknowledgement is very important for designers newer to the fold. They come with a lot of fresh ideas. I don't want them to shut down that part of themselves and become people who only follow cookie cutter templates. That takes away from the individuality of who they are and why they came into the profession in the first place. Creative explorations have to be done in a space where they're completely unleashed. Because the moment it goes out into the rest of the team and starts interacting with other variables, those variables will shape it.

So, helping designers understand that process will happen. The craft is its own beast. And the market is also its own beast. And those variables will come and inform whatever it is you're building. A design can't be devoid of this. So, allow for that journey to happen.

And at some point in this process, learn how to start building an objective distance from your work, where you are able to see that the greater creation that is being built is a function of other people's labor as well. It is not just about one designer but a collaboration that is shaped by many authors. And that is the beauty of it, seeing how a creative idea becomes a collective thing.

Afshar: You've had a distinguished career in design across India, having held executive roles at multiple companies across various sectors. From your perspective, how has the role of design evolved in the business landscape?

Jha: In India, and perhaps the whole southeastern continent in Asia, design is still growing and evolving. People here understand art, they get the role of an artist. However, they don't necessarily get a designer. So when they meet a designer, they want to place them in some quadrant that is familiar. And the closest proximity they have is art.

At some companies, you may have functions who have worked with designers before, such as product management or marketing. But say, sales may not have worked with designers, or supply chain folks wouldn't have worked with designers. So when I started my career, I think a lot of industrial designers were seen as applied artists. User experience as a profession was just coming up. We didn't have a vocabulary for it. People were called applied artists, and the combination of art and logic was even somewhat looked down upon. "You're creative people, why are you thinking logically?"

I think that gradually started changing as the profession matured and as more and more executives came into the space. There is now more value placed on design. I don't think it's very clear across the board though as to what is the end business value that we bring. If I were to ask, what does design do in terms of the top line on the balance sheet? Very few people would be able to put a finger on it and clearly articulate an answer. That is where there's still a long way to go for us to build value and clearly communicate.

In India, that awareness has been building through cross-border services. Awareness gets built when a software architect or a business analyst would go to some other country to bid for projects. And the client might say, who's designing this? Do you have a designer? The response might be, why do we need a designer? And then the value would be explained, and that analyst might come home and look for someone to fill that role.

The level of scale in India has been great for building those digital skills in this region. With ecommerce happening here, hyper-local products, and other startups, there is good demand for designers to come in. But I think we still have two journeys to take.

One is, how does a designer add value to the business of the company and get direct attribution for that value add? I think that has yet to be established and universally understood very clearly.

And the second one is, understanding a designer's role backward from the final artifact to the initial concept, which is where design and research have struggled. Companies can be quick to fund a design team, but then shut them down in the times where the company might not be doing well. They are the first set of people that are considered to be let go in many organizations. In that sense, there is also a lot of growth that's needed to advance the reputation of design.

Afshar: How have you adapted your leadership approach in light of these preconceived notions about design's role?

Jha: I've had multiple experiments around how to approach this at various companies, and they've been met with different results. To begin with, the conversations I have between designers to communicate our values are approached in a more codified way. It might be using our jargon to focus on design principles, which is helpful to do in conversations with people who already have a certain level of understanding of your discipline. In fact, being deeply specific in your discussion with other designers can bring a lot of credibility to your leadership reputation.

But the moment I speak to outside stakeholders, coded conversations don't help. Like, if you approach a non-designer with why the typography in a certain logotype isn't ideal or why kerning on a design isn't optimal, they generally won't sit down and geek out with you. Instead, what's worked well for me is moving and trying to understand various functions and their vocabularies, and tying design concepts together to the stakeholder's key concerns with the business. This means, to some degree, I'm able to read balance sheets and income statements. I can understand supply chain functions and manufacturing constraints my colleagues are operating with.

As designers, we constantly talk about user empathy, but there also has to be empathy for the business and for the immediate stakeholders. Because design as a function gets somewhat protected from the daily onslaught of the market. Meanwhile, those immediate stakeholders are the functions who face that instead. The sales team, the marketing team, they go through a lot of volatility that is directly subjected toward them. One day they are able to ride the waves, the next day they come crashing. Most of those functions' remunerations are tied to how the markets behave at any immediate point in time. So comparatively, design as a function is a relatively safer environment, where we can work within our innovation spaces to some extent.

As a design team, if we are able to empathize with those other functions, if we are able to empathize with what it is that they're trying to do or solve, we would be able to bring better alignment with the rest of the organization. When that starts happening, when you start becoming meaningful to other functions, then you are able to solve their problems. And as a result, those functions are more willing to come back to you later and listen to your problems in return.

I think leaders on top need to be able to do that a lot more, that is, being able to open up a little bit and become a generalist once again. After being in one field for 15 or 20 years, it's natural to become a specialist. But for the next level of leadership growth, you'll have to move up from that head space to some degree and start seeing how other functions are collectively orchestrated and synchronized to grow an organization at large. And then, show up in whatever capacity you can contribute whether that's officially "design" or not. If you can do that to your own set of stakeholders, you will eventually be able to do that to the broader company. You earn that possibility of being able to create a more user-centered organization.

Afshar: You've spoken about your philosophy on leading a creative life. Could you tell our readers more about that?

Jha: Creativity is something that you experience, it's a life force, it's a disposition. Just like you have the ability to smell or you have ability to see, you're also given this ability to, or itch to, make stuff constantly. It's a close personal part of who you are. It's a spiritual life force.

Once we start linking this creative urge to the market though, we start linking the joy of making things to selling things to other people for their usage, that part goes through a certain transformation. And we'll have to figure out what that transformation means for all of us. What is our personal relationship with that change? How do you foreground that relationship with your own creative self?

Not every creative outlet needs to necessarily link it to a professional position. You could play music, but not be a musician. You could paint, but not be an artist. You could act, but not be an actor. When you do these life-force-generating activities and unlink them from a professional position, these life forces continue to be life forces. You can continue finding fulfillment and gratification in doing these things on a daily basis, not because it's on a to-do list or it's on a Trello board, but because it comes naturally to you.

A person doesn't have to be a professional artist to live a creative life. I've seen some people who do futures trading to be excellent doodlers. There's no link with their job, and they are happy that they're doing it. When they come back to their homes every night and they get that half an hour of quiet somewhere and they'll take a pen and paper and doodle. It makes them feel alive again. So I think the sense of being creative and feeling alive are being anchored in that act, which is very personal.

That habit though needs to be nurtured. I don't know how it is in the United States, but across the Indian subcontinent, many of us end up thinking about everything in professional terms. If you paint, you have to be a painter. If you write, you have to be a writer. The societal expectation is to not do anything that doesn't look or feel productive in a career sense. Living one's creative life has to be something that takes you away from that expectation.

Doing things that are simply about expressing yourself in some form and showcasing individuality, that is what it means to be human. That sense of creative life is what it means to be human. It's an act that doesn't need to "scale," it's about acknowledging oneself.

I could have the best possible gadget to create food for me. But when I go into my kitchen, pick my favorite ingredients, put them together and cook myself a meal, light a candle next to it, and eat that meal in peace—now that feels human.

In the times where you are overexposed to so much external stimuli, these ways to express your creative self becomes a tool for centering yourself in the chaos every single day. A way to be able to ground yourself.

At General Motors, many of us used to do this. We'd be in the meeting rooms and we'd constantly be sketching cars. There might have even been a meeting happening, but we were much better listeners when we were sketching in our notebooks. It was part of our muscle memory. And I realized that's a grounding force. We do it so that we can feel in the moment. It centers us in some form. I think just being able to acknowledge that humans are wired this way is something to celebrate. Living a creative life is beautiful. It can be a part of your daily existence. I hope we can all think more actively about living creatively.

CHAPTER 2

Andrea Mangini
Shopify

As Vice President of UX & Creative at Shopify, Andrea directly oversees Merchant Solutions, Growth, Retail, and Shop businesses for Shopify, and also owns both the UX & Creative disciplines across the company. Prior to her time at Shopify, Andrea has led and practiced Product Design at companies including Netflix, Autodesk, and Adobe.

Jaleh Afshar: What makes a good designer?

Andrea Mangini: I love this question. I honestly only started thinking deeply about this around 2012, when I took on my first role as a leader of other designers. This is when I was at Autodesk—which is a company really full of very deep thinkers. They had a fascinating framework about learning and mastery that was introduced by our CTO's office. The concept was that acquiring mastery involves three key components: the toolset, skillset, and mindset. So I applied that to thinking about what I should look for in a great designer.

Mastery in design starts with the toolset—having the right tools and a dedication to mastering them. This is a continual journey for designers—especially in user experience, where the tools we use are constantly co-evolving with the mediums we design for.

© Jaleh Afshar 2025
J. Afshar, *Chief Design Officers at Work*,
https://doi.org/10.1007/979-8-8688-1137-1_2

Next, the skillset—which involves figuring out how to apply the toolset effectively. This consists of identifying and leveraging opportunities to enhance people's lives and making the world more enjoyable and user-friendly.

However, the *mindset* is perhaps the most crucial element. A designer needs a blend of optimism and dissatisfaction to truly excel. The best designers I know are often dissatisfied with the world as it is, driving them to want to improve it, yet they remain optimistic about their ability to make positive changes. This belief fuels their willingness to apply their skills and tools daily to make incremental improvements.

Let's say someone has strong mastery over the tools, and the skills to know how and when to apply them—but the mindset balance is off. Some may not be critical enough and become disillusioned when they realize how challenging it is to effect change, while others might be so focused on the negatives that they struggle to find the motivation and inspiration to drive improvement.

This concept of the three key components particularly resonates with me when I think about design. Finding the right balance of optimism and critical thinking is essential—it's the engine that keeps designers striving to make things a little better every single day.

Afshar: Being a leader of a large organization, do you find yourself in a position where you must measure the value of design itself (as compared to engineering, product, sales, etc)?

Mangini: It's an interesting question. I'm not sure I "measure" the value. As in, I worry that the question sets up a presumption that design's impact is in doubt and therefore needs to be defended or adjudicated. In places where I think design has been most successful, that isn't a question. I almost wonder, if one has to ask that question in an organization, if there's something else we have to talk about first.

Are you unclear on the value your customer places on your product?

Are you unclear on how your competition may disrupt you with a more delightful, usable, accessible, or durable product?

I find that designers end up in the coal mine mode sometimes in organizations. For example, when the organization is at odds with its market, or at odds with its customers. Designers will often intuit that, but then intuit that in a way that manifests in their perception that design is not being valued.

Ultimately, it's not really a conversation about how to make design more *valuable*, it's actually a conversation about whether or not that business is at odds with its customers.

When you're in a mission-driven business or you're in a business where your product's purpose and your business model requires humans to align with what it is you're offering them, design's value is very self-evident and nobody has to ask that question.

Afshar: What's your assessment of the current state of the industry when it comes to design as an executive function?

Mangini: Earlier in my career, I often thought that when design was in the executive suite, the company would become design-led, and it would become obvious that design would help transform the way a company would run.

What I would say now though is, in the executive space, much more about how a company operates fiscally, operationally, technically, and legally is discussed over how design manifests, through either brand, storytelling, or executional craft. It's not always obvious how design influences executive spaces.

Of course, there's the obvious role as a design executive, where you are responsible for managing the designers, design work output, and the design practice within the company. But sometimes the best executive move is to limit the space for design, because it may be that design actually isn't the most critical function to push a business critical outcome.

An example of this might be deciding that it makes more sense to have, let's say, more engineers working on infrastructure and performance than investing in designers working on crafting the expression of a product, because at the end of the day, the right user experience for that particular product is going to be one that's incredibly performant, regardless of how it might be styled or shaped in a workflow.

It could be that the best and most "designerly" outcome for another product is to harden the security model, so that people's personal information is secured and prevented from being accessed by malicious actors.

Those would be "designerly" acts, as in, those would be acts of compassion for your customer, but they wouldn't manifest in the way that designers often think about their work.

So I think that's the main puzzle for how design should show up in executive spaces. In many cases, deciding that designers don't have the primary role in solving a problem, and underwriting an investment of company resources in other functions to solve a problem, means you are still landing a human-centered vision of making the company better for people, better for its users, and better for its customers.

Afshar: Does every organization need a head of design?

Mangini: I think product companies do.

I do want to clarify that a "head of design" and executive functions aren't always the same. The altitude at which a design leader might be needed can be different, depending on the type of company you might be.

If you're a company that needs to speak to the world and shape a narrative about what you're about and why people should choose to partner with you or use your products, if you're a company that creates products that people have to engage with, if you're a company whose products impacts human beings in some meaningful way, then it's important to have design oversight and to coordinate outcomes with a lens toward humans.

Now, sometimes that's called head of design.

Sometimes that's called customer success.

Sometimes that's called head of product.

Sometimes that might be called head of marketing.

So I think design instincts—and you could replace the word "design" with human-centered instincts or customer-centered instincts—have a place and need to have a place in any enterprise that's impacting humans. But does that need to be a single function? Maybe, maybe not. Does that need to come from the function of graphic design, user interface design, user experience, or craft instead of customer success or product management or support or marketing? Maybe, maybe not. It really depends on the company and what it does. But I do believe humans, customers, and users need champions in every company.

And I think that does also contribute for some people to that concept of *our company isn't design-led because we don't have a head of design*, but it's really what's the driving principles and practices behind what's prioritized for the product, not necessarily the literal job title in this case.

Acknowledging the flip side though, I will say, having a seat, having an office of *something* within a company signals what the company cares about.

So when a company has a head of technology, it's clear to its employees as well as its investors and customers and shareholders that the company values technology. Same with a head of security, a head of operations, head of sustainability and so on. An investor may look at that and feel confident that the company is on top of reducing waste and creating efficiency. If there's a CFO in office then people may feel like the company is more reliable as it has someone predictable leading fiscal discipline.

I do think it says something to your company and to the world around your company, based on what type of offices you create. When you have a company that doesn't enshrine a role with real authority around it, to care for and focus on the outcomes for humans, it is easy to assume that the company's priority is not humans.

Is it always absolutely necessary? No. Is it a strong signal that your company cares about its customers, cares about the impact your company has on its users, and both directly and indirectly invests in human-centered thinking? Frankly, if you have a product that's consumer, that humans use, and you care about how craft and usability bring utility to that product, then having named design leaders says a lot. It's a smart thing for companies to have. I don't think it's the only possible way that companies can practice and achieve good design, but it can help.

Afshar: You're currently at Shopify, a leader in the e-commerce platform space. Can you share any common misconceptions about designing and building for e-commerce?

Mangini: I didn't know a ton about the commerce space when I first joined Shopify..

I've always been interested in innovations that democratize access to something for people who otherwise couldn't access it without specialized skills or training or a certain amount of money. Almost every place I've worked in my career, I've had the privilege of working on some type of version of that, democratizing access to creative tools and publishing through Adobe, democratizing access to industrial design and manufacturing at Autodesk, democratizing access to telling the world's stories and accessing them broadly at Netflix.

And now, at Shopify, it is democratizing access to being able to start and launch and maintain one's own business without having access to specialized business and technical skills, not needing a ton of capital up front, and lowering the ramp so more people can step onto the platform of entrepreneurship and try to take hold of their own destiny from a commercial perspective and financial perspective.

That's been the throughline of why I chose certain career opportunities. Anytime I have the chance to use design to bridge that gap, that's kind of my sweet spot. That's what I love to do.

Getting more specific though, what I thought about e-commerce was that it was largely about making websites. What I've learned though is that the "e" in e-commerce isn't very important because, at this point, the world is Internet accessible. Whether you're running a brick-and-mortar business or your business has an online component or you're selling B2B to another business that's re-merchandising their products or you're a content creator using tools to help build your network and get paid with product and affiliate merchandising.

So, in reality, commerce is "e". There is no e-commerce. That's the first myth. The myth is that there is "regular" commerce and e-commerce. There's only one kind. It's the Internet. The Internet is in all of it. Unless you're cash on the barrelhead transaction and you can't accept a credit card at all, you're "e". All payments run over the Internet.

The other important realization is that commerce has such deep roots in culture. I don't think I totally understood this before. Going back to Shopify as a mission-driven company, it's still led by its original creator and founder, and it really has a mission which is to make commerce better and more accessible for everyone. In particular, people at their first stages of entrepreneurship and tiny businesses that might not believe they could make the jump, might not otherwise *be able* to do it without technical support and a platform like ours. That caused me to think deeply about what better looks like. What isn't good about commerce? What does commerce even mean to people?

Commerce is one of those deep human activities, right? It's down there with the creation of language and sharing of stories which is how culture moves. The creation of tools, which is how we extend our reach and our agency beyond what we can do independently with our own teeth and fingernails effectively. And next comes the exchange of goods. The exchange of goods is a really interesting way for societies to have access to food at all times while still remaining planted in a place where they otherwise couldn't grow that food or move their cultural artifacts around. A big part of history is based in trade and commerce. It's quite interesting as the initial core of civilizational development is trade and commerce.

When you think about things that are not good about commerce today, one is that commerce today is rather inaccessible for lots of people. There may be many people who have a good, a skill, an idea, a trade, but for some set of reasons in today's society it is not clear at all how it is they would bring that trade or good or skill to market, how they would manage the regulatory and technical aspects of providing that for sale, how they would acquire customers, how they are expected to address those customers.

And then on the customer side, how many things do you see that you question. *Is this online shop valid, is this merchant trying to steal my information, is this a real product, will I receive it on time, is this the right price I should pay, is this a real brand, is this a real person behind this brand?*

And so on both sides of this equation, there's a lot built up to make that really direct person-to-person, brand-to-buyer exchange more difficult, less reliable, and more expensive. There are reasons for that of course. There's huge companies involved. But I think part of what we'd like to get back to is a more direct consumer-to-buyer version of commerce.

So back to your question on what are the misconceptions. Many of the myths today are that commerce belongs to marketplaces, commerce belongs to banks, commerce belongs to places where the maker of the thing and the user of the thing never meet each other in any meaningful way, don't even know of each other's existence and that purchasing means you go to some giant mart on the Internet or mart in real life, and that's supposedly how commerce works best.

Shopify's vision is to offer an alternate view of that, that commerce works better when brands and buyers can connect to one another, when a buyer can connect to the story and the humanity and the real people behind a brand.

Right now, in many cases, the convenience aspect of commerce is locked to huge marketplaces with anonymous tiles of products. We're trying to change that and give people the convenience of one-touch purchasing and quick checkout and rapid returns, without having to only use these big marts. You can still have all those things that you might expect without using powers of extreme aggregation to get leverage over that scale. You can still have that as a buyer, and you can still offer that as a seller.

You don't actually have to sacrifice that direct relationship that you as a brand have with your buyer. Your buyer can still have a real connection with you. I observe that people enjoy certain brands because they actually connect to them. For example, when I wear a piece of clothing from a particular provider, I enjoy it more when I know who made it, and I know what their values are. I can talk to other people about it, and if they like it, I can make that recommendation to them, and then that's a way for me to move the story into my world. It's a conversation. It's a part of culture.

With these big, anonymous markets people have lost, to some extent, what it means to make a specifically personal choice, not just on the basis of price, but also on the basis of a story or a cultural moment that I can make some meaning around. I don't make any meaning when I'm throwing things in a shopping cart. I make meaning when I think about who made an object, why they made it, what it says about them, what that says about me, and why I choose that provider. And I find it more emotionally and culturally enriching to participate in commerce that way.

So I would say that's the biggest misconception, that e-commerce has to be big marketplace-type experiences and can't be something that is deeper and more connected. And that you can connect a buyer to a brand without losing all of that scaled benefit the Internet brings.

Afshar: You have an impressive track record with over two decades in the design field, leading teams at many well-known companies including Netflix and Autodesk. Over the course of your time in this space, how has design evolved?

Mangini: I'm older than the dinosaurs basically! I started practicing design in the late 1990s. The words we use to describe what we do as designers have evolved throughout the software and Internet era. One of the interesting changes I've witnessed is that design for digital spaces has been reinventing itself right alongside the technologies and tooling platforms that we design *within*. Our medium is incredibly volatile and evolutionary.

What we call ourselves and how we practice our craft had to continue evolving right alongside technology. Humans don't evolve nearly as fast as technology evolves.

On the one hand, there's this sort of stable set of truths around human behavior, human psychology, and human culture. That's important grounding for our work. But graphic design, commercial art, UI, UX, front-end coding, web design, information architecture, content strategy, pick your poison—that's ever evolving. We've been trying to solidify an idea of what this profession is, and translate the possibilities of technology into value for humans for the entire space of my career. Evolution will always be ongoing. I don't think it's going to settle down.

We're entering the applied AI era, and as far as I can tell this means we're going to have to talk about linguistics because these are computers you can speak to, and they speak English, French, Hindi… whatever language you speak. So what is the role of translator between humans and technology when technology itself has its own translation layer that speaks a human language? I don't know how much that's going to rely on the traditional aspects of design, like visual balance and layout and hierarchy or even knowing about front-end coding or knowing about information architecture. The future of design is a thing for us to re-discover.

Each of those steps in recent design history, from designing desktop software, to designing websites, to designing software to publish to websites, to designing for mobile spaces, to working in design systems because we're now designing at scale and with ecosystems… all of those things share certain characteristics, those core design skill sets and mindsets. But now what I think is true is that we have to accept that evolution is always on, in everything we do.

We are tied to a rapidly moving rocket ship, and so we should probably give up trying to pin it down and just accept that we're on this ride. What we should always be doing is learning. We should be incredibly tool-hungry, trying to learn the cutting edge of whatever tool it is going to best help us talk to the technology on behalf of the people. We should always be reinvesting in our understanding and curiosity about the humanity that we're attempting to bridge technology into.

For me what's evolved is I see design less as a subset craft. Like previously there's architecture, they design buildings, there's industrial design, they design products, there's digital UI, they design interfaces and software. Now, I think we're more like translators. It won't be long before digital platforms like AI start to enable physical experiences to become programmable. What happens when physical experiences can morph and interact and change the way that they present themselves to an individual person?

I'm not sure what we call ourselves anymore. Is it user experience? Maybe. But is it user experience when we're not even talking about only human users? Increasingly, we are not talking about a traditional user anymore, we're talking about the interplay between people and technology with sometimes aligned incentives, and sometimes misaligned incentives. You're addressing interactions, not just between an individual user and a fixed piece of technology, you're addressing interactions within a system that people and their incentives participate in. These technologies are not fixed. They are themselves evolutionary and responsive, and are participating in society. We're attempting to adjudicate the transactions and interfaces between those participants in a way that still centers human need and human benefit.

Afshar: What's your approach to building high-performing and diverse teams?

Mangini: Another word for diversity is variety. Variety is good. It challenges you and forces growth, and as a result produces more resilient, creative, productive teams. It's just generally a good practice to seek variety. I don't think that in any way means you compromise on hard skills, on quality, on competence, on requirements of excellence…it means you demand all these things in how you assemble a team—but you intentionally complement that with mix of viewpoints, personal styles, skillsets, life experiences…and you get something really additive.

I also want to be very clear here, since there is such a politically charged dialogue around diversity as a buzzword these days. I don't believe it is the role of private companies to use their hiring practices to address historical inequities or social ills as a form of charity, or corporate responsibility. I disagree strongly with hiring quotas of people from certain backgrounds or with certain characteristics. I disagree with putting people into the position of being seen as the "diversity hire" on a team. This is very cringe and generally results in a negative experience—most especially for that person.

That said, when we have teams that bring together a diverse mix of highly skilled and motivated people, these teams tend to create products that better address the needs of a broader set of users.

I'm working currently at a company whose mission is to *make commerce better for everyone*. Everyone is *everyone*. Everyone is not just people who look like me, who come from the same background I come from, who went to the schools that are likely to be places where I might recruit people from, or who have had the same cultural experiences I've had. With diverse creatives together in a team, we challenge each other on more dimensions, we bring richer thinking to the process, and create more excellent products as a result.

Afshar: To wrap up, let's get a glimpse of your earliest moments in this industry. What sparked your interest in design?

Mangini: I grew up in the San Francisco Bay Area. It was a privilege to grow up in that area and have access to the earliest personal computers and video game consoles. When I was 10, I started learning to program little things and play with things like Mac Paint. At 14, I had access to early versions of Photoshop and desktop publishing software.

Chapter 2 | Andrea Mangini, Shopify

I always wanted to make things. I wanted to be an artist. I got a camera early on as my dad had done some amateur film photography and he got me interested in it. I wanted to tinker with things and explore the world by trying to capture it and see what it looked like once I developed film or once I translated it into a drawing or a painting. My dad also was an engineer and a tinkerer and so I fell in love with tearing things apart to learn how they work to put them back together again. These were the things that I grew up with.

My actual interest though was people. I went to school for sociology, I wanted to be an academic sociologist, mostly because I was kind of awkward and I thought, man if I study people maybe I'll make more friends, maybe I'll be able to go on dates. I just didn't think I could be popular unless I studied people. Seriously, I was a big nerd. Being into computers, video games, and thinking maybe I could study people so one day I could make friends. I was this dorky, artsy kid, lucky enough to grow up in what turned out to be like this incredible incubator that was the Bay Area.

So, I got into school, and realized that sociology was much harder than I had given it credit for. Not that the academic work of sociology was hard, but that the academic work wasn't rigorous. Sociology is an exciting question with very incomplete answers available. These were the days before Meta or Google could easily run a test on 100 million people. Understanding social behavior across the world's people is largely much more instrumented in 2024 than it was in the 1990s. Sociology in the 1990s was still focused on arguing philosophy and politics. It was masquerading as science without the data. I was dissatisfied with sociology as a science. It didn't seem like it was going to get us any closer to understanding humanity, and it felt a bit circular.

I appreciated the size of the challenge of understanding humans, particularly humans in groups, and how humans in groups perceive one another and act in groups. So I completed my degree in sociology, but I didn't pursue an academic career because I was quite frankly depressed and disheartened by the whole enterprise.

On the side, I had been working in art and photography, and at that point, digital photography started to be a thing. I was working with Photoshop a bit more and was starting to play with digital art. I had done a little bit of side work and built a small business doing some digital publishing. Meanwhile, a friend of mine worked as a software tester at Adobe. She was on the Photoshop team when QA was not considered a technical job. It was a role where companies would hire people to use the product and tell them if a feature worked. This friend of mine convinced me to come and work at Adobe.

After a while, the team got grouchy with how I would leave feedback on these QA tasks. A good friend of mine, who's now at Netflix, said, you're not logging bugs. You're writing design specs. I kept writing what I thought the feature should do. How it would be more useful to me as somebody who does photography. Through this, I worked my way up from within to an accidental ux design job.

At Adobe I was designing for designers. If you're designing for people who use Photoshop, and people use Illustrator, and people use Premiere, you're designing for designers. I got to know the industry from within, and then realized that there was a space for sociology there. I had to actually question, well, how do people see this work? How do people work together on a project? How do people interact with technology? And thus I found a place for my sociological interest to come to life.

I also found a place for my artistic inclination to come to life. Because let's face it, I'm not the type of artist that could ever make a living in art. Very few people are. And those passions came together in an incredible moment of fortune and privilege, in my working at the beginnings of technology at one of the great early companies in the Valley.

So I grew up with design. I fell in love with it because designers were my users. I fell in love with it because it was a way my three interests in my early life—art, technology, and sociology—all offered themselves up to me as useful tools, skills, and mindsets. Once I realized that this was the thing I was going to do, I just threw myself into it.

I started to really study design, really study designers—I'm self-taught. I grew up with it, grew up with the industry, and consider myself and my journey a ridiculous backdoor miracle. It's ridiculous. I'm so fortunate.

For anyone out there who is entering the field, being curious, courageous, and skill hungry—literally skill hoarding is an important thing. Sometimes we in design spend a lot of time arguing about the skills we *shouldn't* need to have. I remember how there was a very long and boring part of UX design history where we were fighting about whether we should learn how to code.

I would just say, ditch all of that bullshit at the door. None of that serves you. If we can do with one set of hands things that used to take ten different specialties, that's a miracle and embrace it. If AI changes it so that we don't need to code it all anymore, and we can speak our intent into systems that can represent it back to us, that's a miracle, embrace it.

We have to really embrace the fluidity of the medium that we work in, which is technology. When technology threatens a thing that we have spent time developing, we need to accept that and move on and start grabbing hold of the next skill. So, be tool hungry, be skill hungry, and be curious and courageous because technology is not going to let us build castles around ourselves.

It is fascinating just to see a lot of this self-imposed gatekeeping. It's a limitation that otherwise would not be there, yet it prevails in this ongoing narrative. Instead, embrace the reality. There were a lot of professional photographers that Photoshop threatened. There were a lot of commercial artists and print publishers that InDesign and Illustrator threatened.

The Internet creates entire industries and destroys others. You can't be a designer in this era and be fundamentally against technological progress, even if that technological progress threatens the basis upon which your unique leverage has been based. Staying close to what is right for humans, now *that* is durable. Technology is changing a ton. But what humans need is not changing very much. So being focused on how to continually interpret, shape, guide, and utilize technology is our role.

Also, a lot of the world has not gotten the benefit of most of what design does. Most of what designers have done so far in history has touched only the richest and most privileged part of the world. So what happens when software writes itself? What happens when design is so much easier to practice? Sure, maybe the number of jobs for unique designers servicing only the rich world shrinks a bit. But there's a lot of world out there. There's a lot of space for design and software and technology to bring goodness into entire industries. Imagine healthcare, imagine education, imagine transportation.

Imagine so much of the world having access to the types of tools and technology that right now are so expensive to make that only the richest part of the world can access it. That's where we as designers need to go when we realize that some of our skills aren't as rare and special as we thought we were because the tools we used to rely on are easier to access now. Use that information to inspire and empower you to do more of what you do, but now in places and spaces that used to not be able to afford you. Bring design everywhere, for everyone.

CHAPTER 3

Anita Patwardhan Butler
Strava

As CDO, Anita Patwardhan Butler leads the entirety of Strava's design organizations, including brand and marketing design, product design, research, content design, and design operations. In this role, she shapes how the product and brand inspires movement for active people in over 190 countries globally.

With over 15 years of experience, Anita was previously Vice President of Product Design at Twitter and held several senior design positions at Meta, Ancestry, Sephora, Walmart, and Hotwire.

Jaleh Afshar: Did you always want to be a designer?

Anita Patwardhan Butler: I did not grow up thinking I wanted to be a designer. In fact, when I was younger, my parents really wanted me to be a doctor. My parents are doctors, my sister is a doctor. Almost everyone in my

© Jaleh Afshar 2025
J. Afshar, *Chief Design Officers at Work*,
https://doi.org/10.1007/979-8-8688-1137-1_3

family is in some sort of medical profession. And so, I went to university for pre-med for a couple years in college. However, I did not like it and always wanted to do the arts and, at the time, specifically something to do with writing.

In sophomore year, I dropped the pre-med classes and my mom was really upset. She was the one who really envisioned a family of four doctors. Now, while I knew I didn't want to be a doctor, I also wasn't yet sure how to make a career out of my passions. So I thought, maybe I'll be a lawyer! I changed my major and I graduated with a BA in international relations, as I was deeply interested in political science, foreign policy and at that point, what I wanted to do was become a diplomat. Spending some time in D.C. though, I realized that life in politics was very different from what I thought it would be. I kind of bailed on that too, and then I was kind of lost. I didn't know what to do.

It was the late 1990s and this thing, this "Internet" was happening. You'd hear of people starting to use the Internet, and a lot of websites were popping up. It was still early days and I thought that this could be a path for how I could be artistic. In my heart, I am a maker. I wanted to build something that was useful to people. So, after moving to Boston, I started learning how to code HTML and JavaScript. I was much more interested on the front-end side, so I started doing more design and writing through small jobs where I was hired to work on various companies' websites. I truly enjoyed this work. However, not a lot of cutting-edge work was happening in tech where I was, so after a couple of years, I felt the need to move to California. I figured, if I plant myself there, hopefully I'll meet people and I'll be able to figure it out.

Luckily one of my best friends out in Boston was from the Bay Area. She was moving back to California and I decided to get an apartment with her. The first year I was out in San Francisco, I was taking design classes and worked as an executive assistant to pay the bills because I could not get a full-time design job. Finally, I got a job at Sharper Image, a catalog retail company that wanted to move into selling on the web. The guy who interviewed me asked me if I could get the "New" banner to blink on the website, *"If you can make that thing animate, I will hire you."* To be honest, I didn't know how to do that, but I said I could, because I was sure I could figure it out. So he hired me.

And I remember going home in a panic and thinking, *oh my God, I need to figure this out!* I learned by reading books and copying other designers' work to build my rendering skills, and used tools like Photoshop, Illustrator, Adobe ImageReady, and GifBuilder. The boyfriend of my friend (who I moved out here with) was a designer, and he taught me a lot as well. And that's how I got into design.

Afshar: How did you transition into design management roles?

Butler: Much of my early career in design was marketing because I could code HTML emails. Emails used to be text-only, but once the email clients were able to render HTML, you could put images in the email and really make them unique. I later worked at agency.com where we had a lot of clients who wanted their website built or an email campaign or digital ads. I worked on the marketing and creative direction side for years, culminating at Walmart, where I was a creative director leading a team of 50 people. Through this role, and even the role I had prior at Bank of America, I started building the muscle of making marketing more personalized and relevant.

At Walmart, we would work with the Bentonville, Arkansas headquarters and across the various stores, coming up with store signage, digital marketing, and retail campaigns like back to school, seasonal initiatives, or holidays. Mobile was on the horizon. We'd approach the web aspects with tailored user experience in mind, for instance, showing different content based on what we thought you liked. That approach was still pretty new back then.

We also worked on integrating the purchase experience from site to store. For example, you could buy something on your phone and it would be ready for you in the store. Again, for the time this was quite new. One challenge was, while the digital aspect of this was working well, problem would arise when customers would get to the store and their order wouldn't be ready. Store operations hadn't kept up. This was a good eye-opener to start learning multi-channel and how these experiences manifest in a retail environment.

We also worked on the delivery side, which covered the experience from the moment you went on the website to order, to designing the trucks, driver uniforms, even the bags the orders would come in. Here, I really learned a lot as this work was more complex and truly end-to-end. After building my skills there, I did, however, realize I didn't want to work in marketing anymore. I wanted to move away from pure product sales and go back to the original reason why I got into design: to build a product that was useful to people, and not be as focused on selling and marketing. I wanted to move to the product side of design.

I connected with the woman who had hired me at Bank of America, Sara Ortloff. She had lots of colleagues in the area and one of them, Sarah Bernard, was looking for a UX director at Expedia at Hotwire, which was a subsidiary of Expedia. I interviewed with her and she said she liked me, but that I didn't have a product design background. She continued her search for a few months.

At the time I was in a panic. I really wanted to move into product design and it was hard for me to look for a job or create a portfolio while managing such a big team. After talking to my husband, he was like, why don't you quit? Take a few months off?

And so I quit Walmart…and then a week later found out I was pregnant! Literally, in that time period between me interviewing, quitting Walmart, and Expedia still searching, I got pregnant with my second child.

Then Sarah Bernard came back to me. She said that Sara Ortloff gave a high enough recommendation that she would bet on me. By the time I was offered the job at Hotwire, I was three months pregnant. I told her, and she was very cool about it. That was my first time moving into product design. I learned a lot and it was a small enough company where I felt like I could cut my teeth on product design and not feel stressed. I had some major imposter syndrome, especially working with product managers and engineers in a way that I hadn't before. I'd worked with them on the marketing side, but in real product development, things were different. I really enjoyed my time at Hotwire. Sarah Bernard was a great leader and I learned a lot from her, not only about product but also about the Agile dev process and leadership.

After that, I went to Sephora, which interested me since they were one of the retailers that was breaking a lot of boundaries between digital and store experiences. Buying a product online without knowing what it would look like on your own skin is risky. Color is so important and makeup wearers are definitely looking for a certain look, and needed to know if a product would look good on them. I worked on Sephora Virtual Artist, an augmented reality tool where people could try on makeup virtually. For this product, I worked with a third party and the internal team on how you could apply makeup virtually so you could see if lipstick, foundation, or eye makeup looked the way you expected on your face.

It was my first time working with AR, and what I loved improving on this product is ensuring it worked for all skin types. Being a person of color with a darker skin palette, we did a lot of testing on not just me but many other women of all skin tones. This needed to work on all people.

In addition, I also worked on the Beauty Insider rewards program and we reworked the whole sephora.com website navigation. There was also no Android app when I got there and we designed and built the whole Android app using Material Design, building and shipping it in nine months. This work shows the power of a great design system and true partnership with engineering.

After this role, I didn't want to work in e-commerce anymore. I didn't want to work on a product that helps sell another product. I wanted to work at a fully tech-focused company, not tech-adjacent. That's when I moved over to Ancestry and worked on their DNA products.

This was a time when consumer DNA products were just coming out, like 23andMe, and Ancestry was trying to get into the DNA space because what they were finding was younger people were not building family trees. Most of the family tree subscribers were 65 years and older, and these people started building their family trees as an artifact for their families to view their legacy. The data showed us that people in their 30s or younger were not interested in building a family tree, which is time-consuming. They were much more willing to spit into a tube to get their DNA analyzed and to understand their ancestry that way.

The product which I would consider the most innovative in my time at Ancestry was taking these millions of DNA samples and merging it with family tree data. We could accurately tell if you were German and Irish, or tell you who your ancestors were and how they migrated. The other piece that was quite interesting was health predictions. We worked with geneticists and epidemiologists and population scientists. This was really fun and I learned a lot because most product folks don't usually get to work with talent like that.

For example, the aspiration was that if we could see Alzheimer's or BRCA in fourth or fifth cousins, we could predict it could be a genetic trait for you. Or letting someone know if they had a predisposition for a certain disease, and the aim was to help people live longer and have a healthier life by understanding these things about yourself from a simple $100 DNA test.

Unfortunately, when I was there, we never shipped anything on the health side because of FDA regulation. What we were able to ship are other trait observations, like "you have dark eyes" or "you have curly hair," which wasn't as valuable to people because they told us, hey, I can see that in the mirror. But what was valuable is we could also tell you wellness information: like if you have a caffeine sensitivity or you're lactose intolerant or cilantro tastes bad to you.

Through that process, it was really interesting to see how people connect and what people consider as important family data. Family circumstances, like adoption where people may not know their ancestral roots, were definitely top of the list. But also people wanting to know their history, their background and culture. And so we were trying to get people to engage with their distant cousins, but nobody wanted to do that. Most people would say, *I don't want to talk to random cousins*. It made me start to think, why do people connect and share? Which is why I moved to Meta, and then Twitter after that. I was really interested in understanding why people share and what people try to do online in a way that they can't achieve IRL.

That's a long way of sharing my journey, but that's the real deal of how I got into design management. It was very circuitous, but definitely rewarding.

Afshar: You've had quite a prolific career across many business sectors. How has that influenced the way you approach leading teams today?

Butler: One thing it taught me is how design should drive business results.

When you're in an e-commerce environment, your goal is to help people purchase something, whatever that thing is, it could be lipstick, it could be a hotel, it could be a fleece jacket or lettuce. A lot of my early learning in marketing was around how design drives purchase rate and how design drives an end result—a tangible business goal.

When you get into tech and product development, a lot of times you can lose sight of that because it becomes easy to get distracted by, *what's the coolest thing we can build?* And then it's about the "cool" factor or leveraging emerging technology, and not the actual value to the person interacting with it. It's a combined effort, having impact not just by using the latest technology, but providing customer and business value. The goal is to make people's lives better while also contributing to the bottom line.

That's really important for the design discipline, as we are a function that is just starting to be represented in the C-level. There are many organizations where design is still a service to product or to engineering or marketing. You'll see org structures where a head of design will still report into a CPO, CTO, or CMO, even at very design-forward companies.

And so, how to move design out of a service organization is to actually prove how design can truly drive business, and how design can bring a different point of view to the table that a product manager or an engineering leader may not see from a customer perspective.

Even at Ancestry, when we were doing what I would consider the nascent product work, ultimately the goals we had to hit were getting people to either buy more kits, or subscribe to get continual insights about their genetic selves. And if all the fancy design work didn't get somebody to buy a kit or to come back and check their traits report, then why bother doing it? After all, we are a business. I aim to help my team understand that their work can't simply be a cool thing as a design artifact, it has to have tangible impact for people, for the customer and the business. Design also has to ensure that you are building a product that drives customer value—that makes people's lives better somehow. And at times, that means we are the "canary in the coal mine." If you only focus on metrics impact, you can lose sight of the customer. It's our job to drive for the balance bw the business and the customer. If you do it right, all boats rise.

Afshar: Any memorable activities or company traditions that had a positive impact on how you think about building team culture?

Butler: There was one particular activity that they had leaders do at Meta that had a long-lasting impression on me. It was focused on shedding light on privilege and how that can impact our everyday actions and how we should be aware of our own privilege when hiring for our teams.

The activity was focused around a set of questions like: *Have you ever felt that you wore the wrong outfit to work? Have you ever had someone misinterpret your job in the office? Have you ever lied about something in your personal background?* Then the moderator would read out each question and if you answered yes, you had to take a step back. If you answered no, you could take a step forward. At the end of the questions, it was illuminating to see who was in the back of the room and who was not. And it was also illuminating to better understand how different types of privilege play out both in your personal and professional life.

This had a very positive impact on how I think about building team culture. First, you never know where or under what circumstances someone is coming from. Taking the time to ask the questions and to listen to your team is critical. Being observant and a strong listener can reveal so much about the mindset of your team: what they have gone through, their challenges, their joys and where they are coming from. If you know even a little of that, it helps in building a culture that is relevant to their backgrounds and perspectives. I hold monthly Listening Sessions so that I am always talking to the team and understanding their excitement and anxieties at any given time. I remember this particular exercise at Meta because I learned so much about my colleagues. I realized that I had made assumptions about a few of them that were just straight-up wrong. This exercise reinforced that it's important to get to know the individual, and not make assumptions about anyone.

Afshar: How does your role operate at Strava?

Butler: I report directly to the CEO. That was a decision I made when leaving Twitter. I was running the consumer design team and I reported into a GM, I did not report into product or engineering.

And that distinction is important because not only did I have a good relationship and energy with the GM, I was able to have my voice heard directly vs. having to go through another person/discipline. So when I was interviewing after Twitter, I was looking for a role where I would report into a GM or a CEO, not a product or tech lead. Design has much more influence and can better advocate for the customer because of that reporting structure.

A big goal for me has been how to have that level of influence and show what the power of design is. I feel like we've made inroads in my one year at Strava. My first year at Strava was focusing on table stakes improvements. For example, they didn't do portfolio reviews when they would interview designers, and there were no career ladders. There was limited rigor around how we interviewed or handled promotions. And there was no design review or crit culture so designers didn't get regular feedback on their work. We didn't have a design system. My first year was establishing those processes and foundations. Now this coming year is where we can make even more product impact and brand improvements. It's great and I enjoy all of this so much.

Another aspect of the CDO role at Strava is I oversee the creative side along with the product. Half of my team works closely with the Chief Business Officer on TV, film, photoshoots, advertising, and more. I also oversee product research and this is the team that helps the company deeply understand our customer needs through constant inquiry and focus groups with our customers.

Afshar: When you joined Strava, what was the design strategy and how have you shifted it up until today?

Butler: When I join a new team, I try to take the first 30 days to learn and observe the organization. I literally met with everybody and asked them some version of the same three questions: *What's working? What's not? If you were me, what would you focus on?*

Through these one-on-one meetings, I was able to kind of get a sense of the org more quickly. Within the first 90 days, I started deeply understanding the challenge and understanding where we had gaps, and also better understanding the strategic shifts we needed to make going forward.

So with Strava, what we're trying to do is we're trying to build for *her*. We see there's a lot of inequity in sport. I'm always looking for that—the ways we can make this for everyone. Running and especially cycling are very male-dominated. Women, through our research and talking to a lot of elite athletes, have stated that it's just not very inclusive. This is the other reason we need to build for *her*. And by doing so, I hope that we support women in sports that are hard for them to currently enter. In addition to evolving the product for her needs, we also want to change the brand expression to be more accessible, to showcase *her* in our brand expression, to showcase powerful women athletes working together to achieve their goals.

Through our research, we've learned that women also want to be part of a community that helps them and motivates them. When I was looking at the brand, when I was looking at the product and the features within the product, there were some significant gaps. In order to build the right skill sets on my team to get this work done, I hired an Executive Creative Director (ECD), the former global head of creative for Airbnb. On the product side, I invested in finding deep systems thinkers, product builders, and folks who have more of a social platform background, because we wanted to bring more of a community aspect to Strava.

The former CDO at Twitter, Dantley Davis, said to me: *"if your team doesn't 100% have the skills you need, go get that talent."* As a manager, your influence is through the talent on your team. If you don't feel like you have the right team, you are responsible to change it.

Afshar: You've shared in past articles how you overcame opposition (cultural, familial, societal) and found success. What advice do you have for those who may be facing these challenges today?

Butler: Persistence and resilience in light of failure. I have fallen down a lot for a variety of reasons. I never thought about it at the time, but I always got back up. Even in the moments where I wanted to quit, I never did. I think that is it.

The people who can come back from failure, learn from it, and keep persisting—they will succeed.

There's a lot of my career that's not the sexiest. I clawed my way through it to a certain degree until finally building the reputation and or network to help.

There's a lot of folks who get really upset because the industry or the world is not the way it should be. I agree with them. However, don't allow this to defeat you. This will hamper you. My goal is how can we make things better and more equitable, while also understanding that fairness isn't something that can be counted on.

I have this sign here in my office. It says "die trying." If you keep trying, it will happen. I do believe most people who have been successful are like a dog with a bone. They just keep chasing.

Another aspect of success is I've had great mentors, and at different points in my career, I've had people bet on me. That's really important to acknowledge. I don't think I'd be where I am today if I didn't have people who said, "*I'm going to give you this chance.*" Of course there is an aspect of unfairness, because some people get chances more often than others. I've definitely felt that when I've seen people rise in their career much faster than me.

I was talking to this junior designer recently, who is still looking for a job. It's really hard for people early in their career right now, because the market's so rough. I was telling her I was an admin for a year of my life, and that many times, I was unemployed, couldn't find a job, felt like a failure. A lot of people don't see those low points in others who they perceive are successful. I don't know anybody who I would consider authentically successful in design who hasn't had these things happen to them. And if they're saying it hasn't happened, I'm pretty sure they're lying.

Sometimes the grunt work is also part of leveling up. I had someone tell me that they wouldn't take a job for a company whose values didn't align with them. And I thought, well that's very privileged of you, because I've certainly taken jobs that I wasn't passionate for to learn the skills I needed. Sometimes you have to take a job because that's what you get, so instead of being choosy about the company, see what kind of learning you can gain from the opportunities that are right in front of you.

CHAPTER 4

Baylie Brenner-Bruzgis
Twitch

Baylie Brenner-Bruzgis is the Head of UX Operations at Twitch, an interactive livestreaming service for content spanning gaming, entertainment, sports, music, and more. Prior to Twitch, Baylie was the Head of Design Operations & Delivery at Disney Streaming Services where she was responsible for the Design Operations space serving a team of over 150 UX designers, researchers, and prototypers and execution of design through Design Systems. She has additionally held roles at Chase, as Vice President of DesignOps, and Merrill Lynch, as Director of Strategic Program and Change Management.

Jaleh Afshar: For those who might not be as familiar with the field of User Experience (UX) Operations, can you explain the essence of this role?

Baylie Brenner-Bruzgis: The saying "People, Process, and Tools" is a summary of core responsibilities. UX Operations or Design Operations typically involve a blend of scalable processes and frameworks. These frameworks can range from work or execution-related aspects, governance and systems, to team function, career progression, or learning series frameworks. These are usually driven by a Design Program Manager or an Operations sub-team.

I typically establish and maintain regular communications within and outside the team by organizing meaningful meetings and routines, managing budgets, overseeing organizational design and resource balancing programs, and developing strategies for implementation, release planning, and cross-organizational engagement. This might include finding solutions through the right teams in the right places or scaling efforts, such as creating broad planning and roadmapping rituals for the entire Product/Digital organization since Design/UX often acts as a bridge.

This role can also involve strategizing, planning, and executing a design system, which includes full governance, communications, and bringing the entire organization along for buy-in. Additionally, it encompasses design delivery, measurement, and finally, accessibility—ensuring subject matter experts can execute plans, develop training materials, galvanize the organization around doing the right thing, conduct bug bashes, and establish design and engineering best practices.

In some organizations, these operations remain very internal to the design team. However, in my experience, it's less insular and involves significant stakeholder management, especially concerning the process aspect alone.

As Dwight D. Eisenhower said, "Plans are nothing; planning is everything."

Afshar: In the context of your current company, where is UX Operations positioned organizationally?

Brenner-Bruzgis: I currently serve as a department head working in sync with our Chief Design Officer (CDO) and the head of User Experience Research (UXR) & Data Analytics. This position allows me to effectively launch end-to-end processes where our team considers user problems from exploration through execution, with access to studies, data, systems, and the proper tooling.

Our UX organization is composed of designers, animators, front-end engineers, researchers, and analysts, as well as my team of program managers and accessibility subject matter experts. We work closely with our CDO, Jacob Woodsey, who is also one of the company's founders. The CDO, as part of the C-suite and Head of UX, could be seen as our direct superior, yet we collaborate as department heads.

In this structure, operations align with the CDO, the head of research, and data and analytics. Despite changes within my team—formerly overseeing platform and operations—I'm still recognized as a department head responsible for driving roadmaps, setting strategies, and supporting various teams across the organization. I often serve as a proxy in high-profile projects, acting as a Chief of Staff when needed. This role includes managing mobile redesigns and other critical initiatives, requiring me to adapt my responsibilities while maintaining my department head status.

Regarding the positioning of operations in the industry more broadly, I've observed that in some organizations, the Chief Design Officer, whether a VP or SVP, may elevate their Operations lead to a similar title due to the significant influence and responsibilities they hold. Title recognition is crucial for ensuring that operations leaders are viewed with the appropriate level of seniority and influence, enabling them to work effectively with HR partners, leadership in other areas such as tech, and the CTO.

Afshar: How do you work with other departments, like engineering, product management, sales, or marketing?

Brenner-Bruzgis: I am deeply engaged in various aspects of the organization, particularly where there is significant overlap and opportunity to enhance visibility and communication. This effort is aimed at driving efficiencies and creating better experiences—not just within Marketing and Brand, but also across product and engineering. These areas are a given, as we frequently collaborate on high-profile projects, either directly or as stakeholders in processes and programs I develop, such as our remediation efforts ahead of the European Accessibility Act (EAA) deadline.

My design program managers, while primarily focused on internal operations, also collaborate with their EPD (Engineering, Product, and Design) partners on smaller projects. They regularly interface with creative teams and other departments, depending on the product or future area they are supporting. This often involves a lot of cross-functional work, bringing together different teams to achieve our goals effectively.

In addition to working with product and engineering, I have historically collaborated with legal and communications teams. This collaboration is essential, especially as the current team, though smaller in headcount, maintains the same scope of work.

Our Head of Accessibility, for instance, works with the entire organization regularly. Interestingly, design and research are not our primary concerns; instead, our focus is on engineering and influencing individuals who may not have prioritized accessibility in the past. With significant regulatory changes on the horizon, this has become a critical area of influence for her. She leverages legal resources and works closely with our legal partners to ensure compliance and alignment across the broader organization.

Afshar: Can you describe a time when you identified a surprising operational inefficiency? What was the solution?

Brenner-Bruzgis: My current engagement spans various levels of operations, from very tactical issues like managing multiple projects in JIRA without clear reporting methods, to larger strategic initiatives involving multiple orgs and even external regulation.

One of my key contributions has been establishing steering routines and frameworks beyond the UX org, where none previously existed, which ultimately trickles down to making decisioning and execution a lot easier and more efficient for our IC's.

I've also focused on cost-saving measures, like consolidating teams onto enterprise agreements. This effort has led to significant savings, sometimes amounting to millions of dollars, especially when managing contracts that are at different stages of maturity and where new offers or pricing ramps might be overlooked—such as in a font agreement.

Networking plays a crucial role in driving operational efficiency. By building connections and understanding who is responsible for what, I've created channels that save time and enable more effective problem-solving. For instance, knowing the right people allows me to address challenges within the organization, whether it's handling one-off artwork requests or establishing a systematic approach to briefs and requests.

At a very basic level, the dividends paid by setting these foundational processes—like standardizing the use of JIRA—are significant. JIRA, despite its reputation, is a tool we all must embrace. Ensuring that everyone is on the same project and adhering to a unified process is a simple fix that yields substantial benefits, such as better resource allocation, capacity analysis, and team velocity tracking.

Additionally, changing how we use tools like JIRA to better serve design needs rather than adhering strictly to their traditional engineering structures has been a key focus. I've successfully implemented end-to-end processes within JIRA that make sense for designers, allowing them to track their work by meetings, artifacts, and activities rather than breaking it down into disparate pieces of functionality. Or in cases of process documentation, I collaborated with a designer to integrate documentation, how-to's, presentation templates, and design system integration into the tools the team was already using, effectively creating a quick-reference template that streamlines their work.

Routines are another critical aspect of operational efficiency. I've encountered many organizations that believe they have the right routines in place, but they often aren't sequenced properly. Simple adjustments, like aligning sprint planning with leadership reporting schedules, can ensure that by the time we meet with our executive teams, we have a comprehensive view of the organization's activities. These operational improvements range from the tactical—like optimizing routines—to the strategic, such as shipping products on accelerated timelines.

When I begin work with a new team, I start by meeting with every individual, even as a department head. I view the individual contributors (ICs) as my constituents—they are the most important resources, and I prioritize protecting and supporting them. Understanding their strengths, needs, and what drives them is crucial for creating efficiencies.

In parallel, I conduct an audit of the team's meetings, routines, and rituals. I document every meeting, its purpose, and how it fits into the larger ecosystem. This allows me to identify redundancies, sequence improvements, and opportunities to streamline processes. For example, I've been able to consolidate meetings, eliminate unnecessary ones, and create blocks of uninterrupted time, such as a "no-meeting day." This kind of efficiency improvement not only benefits our team but also encourages other teams to adapt to the changes we're implementing.

Afshar: What sparked your interest in operations?

Brenner-Bruzgis: Looking back to my childhood, I can see the roots of this in my upbringing. I realize that I've always been drawn to fixing things, finding solutions, establishing routines, and helping people.

My father's side of the family was full of analytical minds—engineers, mechanics, even radar operators during World War II. My dad was the type of person who would sit down, write things out, and insist on thoroughly understanding how everything worked before taking any action. I vividly remember how he'd make me read the entire manual before setting up a stereo system. He instilled in me the importance of understanding the mechanics of everything around me.

My mother was highly academic, with multiple degrees, always sharp and intellectually curious. This blend of technical understanding from my father and the academic rigor from my mother shaped me into someone who is constantly seeking to understand, learn, and apply that knowledge to add value in any situation.

As a child, I was often the shortest person in the room, which made me more determined to prove myself and be taken seriously. I learned early on that understanding how things work, being helpful, and creating solutions were ways to add value. This mindset, combined with my parents' teachings, shaped me into someone who is very regimented, planning everything down to the minute and always seeking efficiencies, even in the smallest tasks, like brushing my teeth.

This natural inclination for organization and problem-solving translated well into my career. For instance, when the industry needed to transition from green screen and mainframe technology to web-based applications, I was able to step in, break down the problems, and help the team navigate the path forward. I've always been good at breaking down complex projects and identifying problems early in the implementation process and finding solutions to address them.

Interestingly, I didn't initially know what to do with these skills. I thought about studying law and was even set to go to law school, but I eventually realized it wasn't the right path for me. However, the skills I developed during that time—approaching problems methodically, analyzing legal systems, and researching past Supreme Court cases to find precedents—have been incredibly valuable in my career.

Additionally, the writing skills I honed, especially in crafting briefs, have played a significant role in my work. Writing briefs is similar to setting up thought leadership for an organization; both require clear, strategic communication. Over time, this combination of problem-solving, strategic thinking, and communication naturally led me into operations and strategy roles.

Afshar: Can you share some details about your career progression?

Brenner-Bruzgis: I feel like my career has been a natural progression to where I am now. My years of experience in Mergers & Acquisitions (M&A) required me to focus on parity requirements, which eventually pushed me into design, research, project management, system building, and business analysis.

My career spawned from a true tech background, having learned systems analysis and business analysis in the traditional GenX way. This included writing SQL statements, building databases, and addressing complex issues like surveillance on trading floors. I started from the position of a business analyst, which quickly led me to become a project and program owner. From there, I advanced to become the youngest project manager on two of the most significant mergers in Wall Street history. Following this, I joined Bank of America, where I delved into data analysis on surveillances and eventually built the first fully agile internal shop—quite a feat at the time.

For example, I once tackled a situation where bad actors were manipulating stock prices, requiring a deep dive into data to develop solutions for monitoring and identifying such behavior.

My career continued as I moved into change management, taking on strategic roles within the PMO on major regulatory initiatives. I also worked on behavioral wealth management, which gave me the opportunity to serve on executive teams and gain experience across various domains, from back-office operations to marketing and client advisory. This wide array of experiences eventually led me to design operations at JPMorgan Chase, where I had the privilege of working under the legendary Kristin Skinner. It was she who recognized my strengths and told me, "This is your job; this is what you do."

Despite my extensive experience, I was once turned down for a role due to a perceived lack of systems experience, even though I led a massive design program management team within a 400+ person design organization, including design system oversight both from a process and project management standpoint. This experience taught me resilience and to keep my head down looking for opportunities to prove myself and build my personal tool kit, knowing that someday the right path would present itself and it did.

This combined with the earlier conversation with Kristin as well as some soul-searching led me out of financial services and to Disney Streaming, where I was able to attain plenty of design system experience. In one project, we faced a "black hole" of a pattern library with no process or governance attached. A colleague, Davy, who was incredibly sharp and results-oriented, reached out for help and eventually joined my team. I seized the opportunity, knowing together we could make a difference. We prioritized launches, expanded the design system, hired more people, and consolidated multiple streaming platforms into one system. This effort like so many others in Operations was about building for both *future resilience*, or in some cases *future resistance* as my friend Donnie says, and investing in areas that would serve us long-term.

Throughout this journey, I learned a great deal from those around me and, in turn, shared my knowledge on organization, politics, messaging, and process. Understanding the end goals before starting any build is crucial. This ensures that our work serves all our customers—both within and outside the design organization—by connecting with other departments and securing buy-in from key stakeholders like the head of tech.

I've always believed in taking on more responsibilities, learning new skills wherever possible, and pushing myself to grow. On Wall Street, if you're smart and hungry, you'll find opportunities—I've made it a point to seize them wherever I am and whenever they come my way.

Afshar: You earned a degree from Rutgers University in Political Science and Government. How did (or didn't!) your academic background prepare you for a career in Operations?

Brenner-Bruzgis: The deeper analytical thinking required in my roles, combined with the need to memorize countless facts, details, and timelines, has always been a natural fit for me. My ability to retain and recall information has certainly been an asset. Additionally, the emphasis on writing—crafting detailed, precise documentation—has been a consistent part of my work.

One aspect that I've always valued is understanding the "why" behind everything, particularly from a historical standpoint. Context matters deeply to me. I believe that to make informed decisions and drive meaningful change, it's crucial to understand the historical context behind the issues and processes we're dealing with. This approach not only informs better solutions but also helps in communicating those solutions effectively to others.

Afshar: Earlier in your career, you worked at a number of financial-focused companies. In recent years, you've pivoted to consumer-focused companies like Disney Streaming Services and now Twitch. What inspired you to make a pivot in industries?

Brenner-Bruzgis: I'm always looking to add new skills to my toolkit, and when the opportunity with Disney came along, it seemed like the perfect fit. At the time, I was pregnant, and Disney had always been a significant part of my life, especially through my father's love for Mickey Mouse. Some of my earliest and fondest memories are tied to his childhood love of Disney. As he was battling ALS, the move to Disney felt like the right decision—it was both a personal and professional alignment.

At Disney, I dove into a completely different subject matter and product space—streaming. It was an exciting challenge, learning about an iconic brand that brings so much joy to people. Plus, it was Disney! It's hard not to be drawn to a company with such a profound impact on culture and entertainment.

Following that, I worked with Twitch, which was equally rewarding but in a different way. Twitch creates a sense of community for people who might not have that connection elsewhere. Both experiences were enriching, offering new perspectives and skills, and contributing to my growth both personally and professionally.

Afshar: What unique challenges or opportunities have you encountered in the media and gaming industry that differ from finance?

Brenner-Bruzgis: Honestly, I sometimes find myself longing for the days of regulatory rigor. There's something reassuring about the boundaries it creates, adding a level of seriousness when you're working on something as critical as people's entire retirement savings. That rigor still matters, even in different contexts.

I'm often the first to ask, "Are there any rules we need to worry about?" Whether it's ensuring the wording in our UX writing is correct, framing the content properly, or understanding the legal implications of our CTAs, these principles still apply. You have to talk to legal, make sure everything is compliant—it's just that the stakes are different when you're dealing with platforms like Twitch.

Of course, creators' livelihoods are tied to Twitch, and real money is involved, so it's still important even though it feels different than managing tooling for a full pension for an entire company. Different fields require different types of rigor, but having a framework to assess risk and ensure compliance is always crucial. It's something I've carried over from my time in financial services, and it's served me well in other industries too, even if it's not as obvious or prevalent.

Bringing that mindset into media and tech environments like Twitch has been valuable because it helps us get ahead of potential issues before they become problems. For example, with the EAA regulations on the horizon, having that kind of scaffolding in place is vital. It's something I learned from financial services, where boundaries were clear and necessary. It might not be the most glamorous part of the job, but it lays a strong foundation for your career.

Working in highly regulated environments forces you to think deeply about problems and come up with creative solutions within strict boundaries. It's not as simple as just choosing a color scheme—everything has to be accessible, and you might be limited in what you can use. But those constraints can actually foster creativity, pushing you to think harder and smarter about the solutions you develop.

People often perceive certain companies as being all about fun and creativity because of their products, but the reality is that laws and regulations apply to everyone, regardless of the industry. Designers, in particular, might struggle to proactively set those boundaries if they don't have the right background or mindset.

Laying a foundation for additional processes often gets a bad rap, but if it's done with firm intention and flexibility in implementation, it can be incredibly successful. Change might take time—sometimes a lot of time—but over the long run, it leads to better outcomes. You can see the difference between teams that have embraced these processes and those that haven't. It shows in the quality of collaboration, the effectiveness of the tools they set up, and ultimately, in the products they deliver.

CHAPTER 5

Bernadette Irizarry
Sony Pictures Entertainment

Bernadette Irizarry is the Vice President of Product & Design at Sony Pictures Entertainment. In this role, she leads the Platform Experience team serving B2B enterprise needs. Bernadette is also the Founder and Design Principal of Velvet Hammer Design, a consultancy dedicated to product and services development with a focus on strategic partnerships with C-suite and business leaders. She holds an editor role in the Advances in Information Architecture journal, is the founder of the Los Angeles Chapter of Ladies that UX, and acts as an advisor for the LA Design Festival.

Jaleh Afshar: You hold an executive role at a major media studio, and are active in advising for film festivals within your resident city of Los Angeles. Can you share the story behind your enthusiasm for the entertainment field?

Bernadette Irizarry: For me, it all started when I was younger. I watched so much television that it probably worried my parents! My mom would say, "It's going to rot your brain!" But it didn't. Instead, it sparked my love for storytelling, media, entertainment, and the creative process. My big break came when a friend invited me to Los Angeles. She was joining a startup—kind of like YouTube meets Project Greenlight—and asked me to come along.

I had been consulting during the dot-com boom, so I knew a bit about technology. When she asked me, "Do you have the guts to move to LA?" I was like, "I'm Puerto Rican, of course I do!" It was a no-brainer.

The startup was ahead of its time, merging technology and creativity. They took cube trucks around the country to meet creators and teach them how to digitize their films. They would upload those films online, and viewers could vote for their favorites. The winners got a first-look deal with HBO. This was back in 2000, long before YouTube existed. It was an incredible experience, pioneering the intersection of creativity and technology. From that moment, I knew LA was where I belonged.

I continued consulting because media was rapidly evolving. Eventually, I landed my first job at Sony Pictures, and it felt like a dream. I'd go to the studio lot and think, "This is so cool." For me, it's always been about being proud of the product I'm creating. When I tell people, "We make Spider-Man," I feel immense pride. There's this shared excitement around the work we do. It's not just about the individual; filmmaking is a collaborative art. That's what attracted me to it—the combination of creativity, collaboration, and the joy of seeing something come to life. And, of course, you can't help but get excited when you're surrounded by celebrities. It's hard not to feel energized by the environment.

Ultimately, I think the key to staying engaged in your job is loving what you do. If you're not passionate about the work you're producing, it's going to be hard to stick with it. That's not to say finance or other industries aren't engaging—I've worked on some great projects for companies like Intuit. But if the passion isn't there, it's time to move on. It's not healthy to stay in a space where you don't feel fulfilled.

Afshar: Along with your executive role at Sony Pictures Entertainment, you contribute to your local creative community and additionally operate as the head of your own design consultancy. Do you have any rituals or habits that help you manage your time effectively?

Irizarry: Honestly, it's tough to balance both a full-time job and a side hustle. I tried it for a while, but as things progressed, I realized I had to shift my focus. Eventually, I transitioned my side hustle into more of a consulting and creative guidance role, because trying to juggle all three—work, side hustle, and personal life—just wasn't sustainable.

When I had my own firm, I was consulting, doing a lot of community work, and managing my family, which required a lot of energy. So I reached a point where I had to ask myself, "What's my side thing going to be?" For me, family is non-negotiable; they come first. As my job grew—managing more people and taking on larger responsibilities—I had to make tough choices. Was my side thing going to be community work? Luckily, for a while, the Internet took some of that pressure off, though it's starting to pick back up. I'm still involved, doing things like serving on the LA Film Design Festival board, but you really have to be ruthless about prioritizing.

I remember Philip Rowley, the former CFO at Sony Pictures Entertainment, a truly great leader. He would tell us that our primary job, our core role should take about 70% of our time, leaving 30% for things that help us and our team grow. That really hit me. We often try to cram so much into our schedules that no one gets the optimal version of us. It reminds me of that Foo Fighters lyric, "Is someone getting the best of you?" The answer is usually no if we're stretched too thin. There were times in my career where that was exactly the case. The work suffered, I suffered, my family suffered. You end up doing everything halfway, and that's not a sustainable way to live.

So, to answer your question directly, my priorities are simple: family first, then my job, and finally, I set aside a good amount of time for creativity. The best part is when I can find overlap between these areas, especially when I can pick a community or activity that fuels my passion.

When I start to feel that itch to pick up another side hustle, I give myself personal projects to stay connected. For example, I've been working on a poetry book. I've been taking poetry classes, doing some editing, and screenwriting. Doing personal creative work, like writing my poetry or working on a script, is good for me. It keeps me grounded, and it ultimately benefits the team because I'm bringing that creative energy back into the work environment.

Afshar: How do you balance artistic vision with practical constraints in your projects?

Irizarry: I often hear people assume that creatives can't be structured, but I think that's a total myth. There's this romanticized idea that creatives wake up in the middle of the night with a brilliant, fully-formed idea and just start making something amazing from scratch. Sure, that might happen to some people—I did know a few in art school—but the reality for most is that the act of creation is highly structured and requires a lot of discipline. You don't just magically create the perfect piece of art on your first try every time. It takes multiple iterations to reach that final version.

You learn to respect deadlines. Whether it's a production deadline or a launch, you have to plan and structure your work to get there. So the way I manage my priorities, especially as my design role has evolved, is through a lot of strategy and product work. I use tools like Figma to create Gantt charts that project our timelines, and I build roadmaps to ensure we stay on track. I spend a lot of time thinking and planning, sometimes using sticky notes to map out ideas for myself.

For example, I literally map out sprints, figuring out what's needed to hit our goals by December, and planning backwards from there. It's not just about having the vision at 50,000 feet; it's about getting into the details and asking, "Is this deadline even feasible?" We don't operate on the happy path—things rarely go as smoothly as we anticipate (or hope.)

So, a lot of my process is about planning and vision-boarding for myself. Some days, I take time away from the usual hustle to strategize. It might look like a lot of boxes and arrows, and while it's not the most glamorous part of the job, it's crucial. The colorful diagrams I make allow me to communicate effectively with my team, ensuring we're all working toward the same goals—and it keeps me sane because I've mapped out a clear path to get there.

Of course, there are moments of creative spark, but those "happy accidents" occur because of the repetition and discipline you've put in. I've seen this with my team—sometimes they hit a creative block, and I tell them a story from my art school days. I studied sculpture, and during one of our first classes, everyone was hunched over their sketch pads, drawing in tiny, controlled strokes. Our instructor made us stand up and draw huge shapes on large pieces of paper taped to the walls, using our whole arms to move. It was about getting out of our heads and loosening up. For two months, we drew nothing but circles. So, when we were finally allowed to draw something more complex we were thrilled!

The point of that exercise in drawing circles was that discipline and repetition made us better, and it's the same in digital design today. You build that muscle memory through practice, and sometimes that leads to a creative breakthrough—an unexpected solution or "happy accident." It's about all the practice and thought you've put in leading up to that moment. You might move something around in your design, and suddenly, a visual idea clicks. That's where greatness comes from—repeated effort and refinement.

I also encourage my team to go out and seek inspiration. I tell them to visit museums, galleries, see films, and watch shows—even those unrelated to their craft. Inspiration comes from seeing things from a different perspective. I recently visited a Mark Rothko retrospective and saw the progression in his work. You could see the years he spent solving creative problems, experimenting and iterating. That's where creativity really happens—it's not just about waiting for a flash of inspiration. It's about thinking deeply and working through a problem for years. And yes, sometimes you really do get that spark of lightning that answers everything in a day, but that only happens because you've been laying the groundwork through years of practice and creative thinking.

Afshar: Your consultancy focuses on developing strategy with C-suite partners. Can you discuss an instance where your design strategy shaped a direct positive impact on business outcomes?

Irizarry: There are a couple of stories that come to mind, and they're from very different industries. I'll start with home improvement. I mentioned earlier how important it is to work on things you love. Well, two of my favorite clients were Ace Hardware and Behr, the paint company.

Growing up, I used to visit a store called Pergament Home Centers with my dad. My dad had four daughters, and I was his closest thing to a son, helping with carpentry and hands-on projects. As I grew older, I learned welding and sculpture, which I think made him pretty happy. But back to the story—let's talk about what happened with Ace and how that shaped their brand strategy.

Ace Hardware is a home improvement retailer, but depending on which location you visit, the experience can vary quite a bit. An Ace in a big city like Chicago is very different from a small-town Ace. That's because Ace operates as a franchise, meaning each store is independently owned, so you could have a "Bern's Ace" or "Jim's Ace," each with its own flavor.

After the 2008 recession, home improvement as a category started to bounce back, but Ace wasn't seeing the same growth as its competitors, like Home Depot and Lowe's. I had the privilege of working with a brilliant woman executive who recognized that a major growth driver in the industry was the paint department. Paint and lawn and garden are crucial for home improvement stores, and at the time I was consulting for them, Ace's paint section wasn't keeping pace.

If you've been to a big-box store lately, you'll notice that the paint section is all about selling a vision—capturing people's dreams for their home. So, we put together a strategy focused on attracting more female customers. The data showed that while men were often the ones doing the painting, women were the ones dictating color choices and making design decisions. Over the course of three years, my team worked to completely reinvigorate Ace's paint department. We helped them rebrand, create a new paint line, and design an entirely new in-store experience—the Paint Studio.

What made this project so successful was my client's commitment to research. We didn't just guess; we did everything from ethnographic interviews, visiting people's homes to observe their painting habits, to designing how they would select paint in the store. It was such a fulfilling project, and I was over the moon with its success.

What's more, my favorite Ace exec shared a piece of wisdom that stuck with me. We were working on a panel, and I asked her, "Why are we doing this research? You already know the answer. You already have the business sense for a strong direction." Her response was, "Because I could be wrong." That humility and willingness to discover new insights is what made this project, and Ace Hardware, truly exceptional.

Now, let me shift gears to another story—one of my most unexpected projects: toilets. Yes, toilets! I've worked on everything from high-end skincare to, well, toilets, and it was one of my favorite projects.

We were brought in to prototype a touchless actuator for toilets, and the idea was to cater to germaphobes who didn't want to touch anything in their bathrooms. So, we went into people's homes, and they let us into their restroom facilities—talk about getting personal! We thought people were looking for a germ-free solution, but what we discovered was at home, they weren't as concerned about germs. What they really wanted was a design that felt like an iPhone—sleek, modern, and easy to use.

We worked with the engineering team to prototype the product and eventually sold it to an original equipment manufacturer (OEM). It was such a collaborative process, and it was thrilling to see an idea go from research to physical product. There's nothing quite like seeing something you worked on out in the world.

I'll never forget when my sister called me and said, "I just saw your paint on TV!" It's such a rewarding feeling to see the things you've created being used and appreciated. The infectious energy that comes from making something together as a team is one of the best parts of this work. When it's done right, it's a great time.

Afshar: In past interviews, you've examined change management models and how leaders can manage challenging transitions creatively. Could you share more details about this approach with our readers?

Irizarry: Change management is an integral part of being a designer. When you're brought in to design something, your job is to create something new, something different—essentially, you're introducing change. Whether it's a product, a service, or even a new department, the change you're putting into the world affects multiple levels and people across an organization. So, how successfully that change takes root often comes down to a few key principles: How are you managing the transition? Do you understand the context? Have you enrolled your team and stakeholders in the process?

I've seen both sides of this. I've had incredible clients who made significant, impactful changes, but the moment they left the company, the change unraveled. It made me realize that sustainable change doesn't happen by accident—it must be built to last beyond the presence of a single individual. This was driven home for me when one of my clients left a company, and I watched as all the hard work we had done began to fall apart. As consultants, we often "jet in, do the work, and then jet out," like a Seal Team Six operation. But if you don't build internal champions to carry on the work after you're gone, the change likely won't stick, and that's incredibly disheartening.

This led me to focus more on making lasting change. How do you ensure that the work you've done continues after you're no longer involved? It comes down to recruiting people into the process from the start and empowering them to sustain the change. There's a book I love by William Bridges called *Managing Transitions*, and it really resonates with me because it focuses on the emotional and psychological aspects of change, especially during times of corporate downsizing or restructuring. His insights into how people react to change, and how to guide them through it, have shaped how I approach change management.

One of the key points Bridges makes is that, often, leaders are prepared for change long before their teams are. For example, in a company reorganization or product shift, the leadership team might have known for months that layoffs or changes were coming. By the time they inform the rest of the company, they've had time to process it and move on, but the employees are just hearing about it for the first time. The leadership may be ready to move forward, but the employees are still in shock, stuck in a stage of grief. If leadership doesn't acknowledge this emotional gap and help people transition, the change won't take root.

When I lead change management efforts—for example, when I've rolled out Agile transformations in corporations—a huge part of the process is storytelling and messaging. I tell people why the change is happening, and I keep reinforcing that message over time. You can't just drop the news and expect people to accept it. You need to build a bridge that takes them from where they are now to where you want them to be. It's about being honest, addressing concerns, and creating a narrative that helps people see the bigger picture. And crucially, it's about rooting out skepticism and converting those skeptics to champions of the change.

One of the things that made that Ace Hardware executive such an exceptional leader was her ability to be honest and direct about the need for change. When we worked with her on revitalizing Ace's paint department, she didn't sugarcoat the situation. She told the team, "Our competitors are doing well, but we're not. We need to fix this." Her honesty helped people accept the reality of the situation and motivated them to take action. That's a big part of successful change management—being transparent about the challenges and creating a shared sense of purpose.

Managing change, especially in design, is a lot of work. It involves constant communication, planning, and yes, plenty of slides and diagrams. But in the end, it's about ensuring that the change sticks—that the new product, process, or strategy becomes embedded in the culture and doesn't disappear the moment you step away.

Leadership, at its core, is about managing change. It's about getting people ready and willing to come along with you to the other side. Whether you're shifting a company's operating model or transitioning to a new product line, the change won't succeed if you don't invest time in managing its impact on people. You can have the best strategies and diagrams in the world, but if you don't address how the change will affect the individuals involved, you risk seeing it all fall to pieces.

Afshar: What's your perspective on storytelling and its impact for effective communication?

Irizarry: My love for storytelling started with my family. We were always telling stories—stories about my mother coming to the United States, about love, about loss, and everything in between. Storytelling was a part of our everyday life.

One thing I've come to realize, especially through studying the craft, is that people often underestimate the power of storytelling. It seems easy because it's everywhere—we tell stories at the kitchen table or with friends. But what many people don't realize is that storytelling is intrinsic to human evolution. There's a great book on this—*Wired for Story* by Lisa Cron—that explains how our brains are built to process stories as a survival mechanism. Think about the earliest humans sitting around a fire, telling stories to warn others about the dangers they'd encountered, like the lions lurking near a certain bush. Our brains evolved to absorb the emotional resonance of these stories so we could learn from others' experiences, like avoiding a certain lion-infested bush, without having to face the same dangers ourselves.

From an evolutionary perspective, stories helped us adapt and survive. But on a more practical level, understanding how our brains are wired for stories is key to how we communicate effectively—especially as leaders. We are constantly filtering information, deciding what's worth paying attention to and what's not. If I'm telling you something that doesn't engage you, your brain simply discards it. As a leader, if I want to get my point across, I can't just bombard you with data or technical jargon. I need to tell a compelling story that resonates emotionally.

For example, I could show you an architectural diagram and explain the importance of transparency and good communication in UX, using the most sophisticated technical language to build credibility and get my point across. But if it doesn't activate some key emotion, it likely won't stick. Instead, I could tell you a story about how a product we built, completely failed...*until* we realized we weren't communicating properly with our users and that's when everything transformed! Suddenly, with the storytelling-based delivery, you have a hero's journey, a narrative arc, and a true reason to care. That's what storytelling does—it brings the message to life and makes it memorable.

I was talking to a friend recently who was venting about an issue he was having with a product manager. He kept saying, "We're not getting along, and it's frustrating." I asked him, "Why do you care?" Eventually, he admitted that it was more about how the lack of cooperation was making him *feel*. That emotional impact is what makes the story stick. It's not just the technical details of the conflict that matters, it's how it affects you personally.

A lot of people say, "I'm not a good storyteller," just like they might say, "I'm not a good artist" or "I'm not a good musician." But I always tell them to stop right there. Everyone has the capacity to be a storyteller—it's a skill like any other. You might not be great right now, but if you want to get better, you can study, practice, and improve. There's a reason we all respond to certain kinds of stories, whether it's a medical drama like Grey's Anatomy or a period piece like Bridgerton. If you look closely, you'll see that they follow similar narrative patterns. Bridgerton, in many ways, is just Grey's Anatomy in a different time period with different costumes. Once you recognize these patterns, you can reverse-engineer creativity, just like we do with UX patterns.

People often think storytelling is this abstract, innate talent you either have or you don't. But really, it's a skill you can learn and refine. Take a TED Talk, for example. Most of us can describe the formula: 18 minutes long, a surprise twist, a personal story, and probably a dramatic pause around minute three. The presenter might adjust their glasses or walk to the side of the stage for effect. It's not magic—it's a practiced craft. And just like you can get better at public speaking or design, you can get better at storytelling.

Afshar: How do you maintain your creative spark?

Irizarry: I'm someone who finds joy in learning. That's why I make it a point to incorporate classes into my life to keep my creativity and curiosity alive. Over the years, I've taken flamenco classes, voice lessons, and even welding classes as part of my love for sculpture—just to get my hands back on those tools. My next adventure? Drumming! I can't wait to dive into that.

As a designer and a maker, I know that while my day-to-day job involves creating slides, presentations, and having strategic conversations, I'm not always the one physically crafting the UI. So, I seek out opportunities to get my hands dirty and stretch my brain.

One of the things that excites me most is the satisfaction of creating something tangible. There's nothing quite like having a finished product and being able to say, "I made this!" The act of creation is so fulfilling. When I take classes or explore something new, I find myself drawn to communities of people with similar interests, like when I tried glassblowing. I watch all those creative competition shows on Netflix too—they really keep me inspired.

But here's the truth: it's also the hardest thing I do. Trying something new means going back to being a beginner, and that's not always easy. There were times when I walked out of flamenco class on the verge of tears. Not because I'm totally ungraceful (though my typography is definitely better than my flamenco moves), but because it's challenging! In flamenco, I'd finally get the footwork down and feel like I was making progress. Then they'd say, "Now add the castanets," and I'd manage that. But then they'd throw in fans, and I'd be like, "Oh no, I just got the hang of this! Why are we having to add in fans now?"

What I love about it, though, is that it reminds me what it feels like to be a beginner. You see your improvement, and it reinforces the idea that mastery takes time. You start off not knowing, then you become aware of what you don't know, and eventually, with practice, you get better. I didn't choose to master flamenco, but that experience helped me appreciate the process of learning, the same process I apply to my work. Solving a UX problem might seem quick and easy to me now, but that's because of the years of practice I've put in. It's important to remember that when you're tackling something new, it's okay to be uncomfortable for a while because eventually, you will figure it out.

And I think this process of constantly trying new things is vital for sparking creativity. When you're at a certain level of mastery in your career, especially in something like design, the sense of accomplishment from learning new things might not come as frequently. You're often the one teaching or mentoring others. In design, especially UX, I've spent decades honing my skills, but one of the reasons I'm drawn to consulting is that every new project introduces me to aspects of the business I don't know much about—whether it's distribution, production, or even screenwriting. I may understand a sound stage, but I don't fully know how they mix stems or create soundscapes, and that excites me.

There's always a sense of awe and appreciation when you see someone who's mastered something you're just beginning to learn. For example, for anyone who's a musician, remember the moment when music finally clicked for you? Or for programmers, the moment when you first understood code? Before that moment, it was frustrating because your imagination far outpaced your skill set. That's the space where joy lives for me—the challenge of bridging that gap. Sure, sometimes I'll try and fail, hitting the wall and sliding back down, but that's part of the fun. I'll keep trying, because that's where the growth happens.

CHAPTER 6

Chooake Wongwattanasilpa
Bank of Singapore

Chooake Wongwattanasilpa is Chief Experience Officer at Bank of Singapore, the private banking arm of OCBC Bank, managing assets over $120bn.

Over the last several years, Chooake has led design at multiple financial institutions, responsible for institutional banking, consumer banking, wealth management, and internal enterprise applications. Prior to Bank of Singapore, Chooake served as the first Chief Design Officer for DBS and was Head of User Experience Design for PayPal's APAC division.

Jaleh Afshar: How did your interest in design begin?

Chooake Wongwattanasilpa: When I was eight years old, my dad had a garage shop where he fixed all sorts of cars. Directly next door to it, he had an empty space which he happened to rent out to two young architects. They had drafting tables, all the special pens, rulers, and blueprints. I was young with nothing to do, so I'd go around running inside their studio to see how they'd draw things and how they'd build the models. That's what got me interested in it; since then I was constantly drawing and drafting.

© Jaleh Afshar 2025
J. Afshar, *Chief Design Officers at Work*,
https://doi.org/10.1007/979-8-8688-1137-1_6

I finished high school in Thailand and was getting ready to take college entrance exams, wanting to attend architecture school, but they needed a high score in physics—which I failed! In light of that, I was recommended to try visual communication school instead, which I did. This was a mix of graphic design and commercial art.

In Thailand, advertising is one of the top dream jobs for fresh graduates. You may have seen Asian TV commercials and how high production they are. Advertising is huge there. So the jobs upon graduating were in art direction or creative direction for advertising agencies, which is where I began my career. I did a few radio spots, print ads, and TV commercials. Of course, sleeping under the desk in your sleeping bag is common in advertising agencies.

However, the dream of many Asian parents like mine was to help their kids study overseas. Many parents save for their whole life to help their kids have a chance to go abroad and further their education. My mom and dad never had a chance to go to university at all, so for them it was a huge accomplishment that they were able to send my brother and sister to Chicago to study. I followed in their footsteps and resigned from my advertising job of one year and went to pursue a master's at the School of the Art Institute of Chicago.

The dean at the School of the Art Institute of Chicago at that time was BJ Krivanek. He is a building architect who became a dean of Visual Communications at that time. When he first saw my work, he was very kind but said, I think you are not ready. A soft rejection, he was very kind! He suggested I enroll in typography and multimedia first to build a stronger design foundation. In addition, I also had to retake the TOEFL, a language exam. I took the TOEFL eight times before I passed. At that point, I was ready to embark on my MFA journey officially!

Afshar: In what ways did your fine arts background shape the way you approach design?

Wongwattanasilpa: I was fortunate to study under BJ Krivanek for a whole year after I began my enrollment. He taught me a lot about storytelling and how communication plays a lead role in design. He said, *design is not about you. It's about who sees your work and how they react to it.* I remember projects we did, like designing a monument for the city. Learning how to research a lot, to understand what would be meaningful for the city, for its citizens. Another helpful technique was learning how to storyboard, and blending it with audio and pacing to convey real emotion.

Learning unexpected things like neon bending, and the patience required to physically create an object like that. If you break a bend at the very last step of the process, the entire piece must be thrown away. It's interesting to be exposed to a wide variety of processes, and you learn that every discipline has a particular way to their craft, and that they all have important elements of skill and culture.

Afshar: You had an unexpected change of industries in your career, moving from creative agencies and fine arts to banking. How did that career evolution unfold?

Wongwattanasilpa: When I graduated with my MFA, I started working with Morningstar. Interestingly enough, Morningstar valued design in many ways. Their logo was designed by Paul Rand, and they had the renowned designer Phillip Burton, one of the professors at UIC School of Design, as a consultant.

Phillip taught me a lot about typography and how it is so important. Using an em dash properly, how to properly align, printers marks, really paying attention to the details. I also was exposed to new avenues like information design, visualizing graphs and data. I really learned a lot at Morningstar.

Another turning point was when I made the move to join PayPal. When I was there, I met an incredible leader named Soojin Jeong Lim, who is now a VP at Intuit. Soojin advocated for me to pursue management role opportunity at PayPal. I learned a lot from Soojin, especially how to be humble as a leader. She exemplified self-awareness and understood how to maintain balance and how to prioritize as a business leader and in life.

In 2000, PayPal expanded their business to Asia. My boss at the time, K.C. Teis, was working towards expanding the business to Asia. I took him on his first international business trip where we explored Singapore, Japan, and India to explore viability for the business, which led to me building our first design team in Asia-Pacific spanning Japan, Singapore, and Chennai.

Afshar: Did the APAC design team have a different focus than the Americas?

Wongwattanasilpa: Yes, we absolutely focused on localized products tailored to Asia Pacific. For example, at the time QR codes were already a huge thing in Asia, while now they have become more prevalent worldwide. We created experiences that would put those kinds of local-first, comfortable experiences in people's hands. We also needed to consider lower speed mobile networks and lower tiers of smartphones (various brands which are not as prominent in the United States, and also Android is a big market in Asia due to their price points) while we were developing the payment solutions. One important point was also building confidence for people to use their phone to scan QR code for making payments—reducing friction and providing a delightful first-time experience are the key to success.

Afshar: Having been in both the creative agency side, traditional tech like Motorola, and now banking, could you share any cultural challenges when it comes to design leadership across those business sectors?

Wongwattanasilpa: There are definitely some unexpected differences! For example, at DBS bank where I eventually became their first Chief Design Officer, they actually had their 3rd party external design agency interview me as they didn't have anyone in-house to vet a design candidate.

Another thing that's important for designers to know as they move through the career ladder is also how the job titles in the banking hierarchy are quite different from tech. In the tech world you may commonly see titles like junior, senior, then you become a lead, then you become manager and then become senior manager, then become a director, senior director, and VP. However, banking generally has titles which are quite different. You might hear the term "VP" at a bank and think, oh, that is a very high-level role, but in fact, in banking, it's more of a mid-level designation.

One cultural aspect which I worked to evolve was antiquated hiring practices. For example, at one of the companies I was at, a rule of hiring was that formal education was a requirement. We had incredibly skilled applicants who could not be hired because they were self-taught, without a certificate of education. This was an approach I worked with our HR partner to review the hiring policy so that we could consider the full breadth of experience a candidate had, instead of rejecting them due to not having a formal education. This also opens the door to more diverse talent from a broader range of backgrounds and locations.

Afshar: That's great to hear about your approach to shifting hiring practices to be more inclusive. Were there any other cultural shifts you made as a design leader?

Wongwattanasilpa: Another cultural shift I pushed for was for flexibility in how one can present oneself at work. When I was growing my team at DBS Bank, management was really pushing for formality in wardrobe.

Going against the norm though means enduring that people might look down at you for a while. I'll give an example. When I first started at DBS Bank about three months into the job, I started to "dress down" significantly. I told my manager that I could not hire anyone, because those talents are scared of what the culture is—and those creative leaders didn't want to lose their own identity. What I mean by that is wearing a regular shirt and sneakers, not the business formal attire that the banking industry generally had everyone wear. This prompted me to start a campaign to my boss that for the bank to succeed at the next level, you really need to embrace more than just bankers. Not everyone on the team needs to wear a suit and fit the visual mold of what a bank employee should look like. There are many qualified people who might not fit that archetype but would be excellent at the job.

When I joined DBS, it was only me and Ed Chu, our user researcher at that time. The two of us continued the design work after the agency left. We ended up hiring a small team together to start. So my first designer, from Indonesia, was named Bady Abbas. He was a very sensible designer with good taste in visual design, very talented, still in DBS today since ten years ago. The second designer HaoYuan Gu, a supersonic designer who can turn ideas to a full-blown prototype at speed, from Tencent, and Tao Bao, who works with me today at Bank of Singapore. The fourth hire was a Taiwanese designer who is great with design process and systems, Leo Lin, who is now still at DBS with Bady.

The five of us were really the ones responsible to build the culture of design there, and we all were responsible for growing the team and hiring designer number six, seven, eight, fifteen, up until we were 115 people by the time I left. We dressed the way that felt authentic to us, some of us had piercings, tattoos.

During the time we were growing, we often had people talk behind our backs a lot. Saying, look at how that team doesn't look professional, they don't dress up. I remember someone asking me or Ed if I was the food delivery person.

But over time, these people started to develop respect for us regardless of our appearance. We were delivering results that fundamentally changed the bank in a positive way. Now there was no problem with our look, and in fact, other teams started to "dress down" too.

So at the end of the day, whatever people want to say or think, it doesn't matter if you are transforming the product and the company in an undeniable way. I guided my team by saying hey, you need to believe in what you deliver. You don't need to impress people by dressing up. But you do need to impress people with your work. That's what's truly important to the company, product, and for our users.

Afshar: I noticed in our discussion that you named many people throughout your career story. It sounds like you collaborated with many great people and grew numerous designers into industry leaders, many of which have followed you from company to company. Any advice on how you fostered these lifelong relationships with people you have worked with?

Wongwattanasilpa: The most important thing is don't contact people only when you want something from them.

Between me and the first five designers I worked with, we still share articles, chat about all sorts of business and tech news regularly. Most importantly, even beyond having common ground through passion for design craft, the key thing is that we trust each other enough to be comfortable debating a lot of things. And, of course, for people further away from where I am physically, like in the United States, whenever I travel over there, I prioritize time to meet them.

Keeping in touch a lot of times it's a give and take. It means generously giving your advice to a child of an employee who is applying to colleges, and doing these things with sincerity. Spending good energy for the meaningful people in your life is important, whether they are people who report to you, people in the industry, or just people you may come across in your life. It might sound kind of silly or obvious to say, but I think for a lot of people, it's difficult for them to show up at work or with their team in a way that is authentic like that. But it really makes a difference, I believe, to how people respect you and how they look at you as a leader.

Afshar: If you were to kind of distill down your philosophy around leadership, what would it be?

Wongwattanasilpa: I have a bit of a funny quip about leadership, although I consider it to be rooted in truth. That is—leaders need to ship something impactful. Leader + ship = leadership. If you don't ship anything, your leadership will have limited meaning because you can't show the impact of your influence.

Another important concept is the "jar of life" metaphor, a classic story that I've read a few variations of. For those who may not have heard it, the concept is you have large rocks, pebbles, sand, and water, and one must fill their jar using all these elements. Of course the optimal way to fill the jar is to begin with the largest pieces first, then finally fill the gaps and cracks with the smaller or more fluid elements. A key learning here is the big rocks (representing the core foundational elements of your life) must be what fills the jar first. It's difficult to retroactively jam in the big rocks after the jar is filled with sand. The same is true of leadership. The key priorities for yourself, your team, your vision, needs to be established first. Through that solid base, the nice-to-haves like the pebbles, sand, and the water can follow to round out the whole.

Finally, I tell my mentees—the more you go up, the more optimistic you have to be. You cannot be unpredictable and moody because your energy will impact the team. If you're unpredictable, then the people on your team will become worried about why their boss is behaving that way. So no matter what in leadership, you truly need optimism.

CHAPTER 7

Chris No
Demand.io

As the Head of Design at Demand.io, Chris No leads a team of designers who are passionate about creating e-commerce solutions powered by AI and blockchain technology.

In past roles spanning over 18 years, Chris has led design for products spanning virtual reality, augmented reality, web3, and social media. Outside of work, he enjoys providing career mentorship. Chris resides in Los Angeles.

Jaleh Afshar: You are a self-taught designer—what inspired you to learn design?

Chris No: I was one of those kids that innately had a passion for something at a young age, and for me that passion was art. I was the art kid. I drew, I painted, I loved making art and any manifestations of art. I was a huge fan of animation and back when I was very young, I was obsessed with Studio Ghibli's work.

Hayao Miyazaki was my hero. He was my everything. In third grade, I had a dream that I still remember telling my parents about. In this dream, I became an animator, flew to Japan, and worked my butt off so that Hayao would hire me as one of his artists!

While I resonated with the art style of his films a lot, the other aspect I was a huge fan of is his ability to tell stories. Not a lot of animated movies, especially back at that time, could do the storytelling piece well. There's something about his character development, the environments, and the vision he crafts which was so different from everybody else. That stuck with me as a kid and made me feel I was meant to create.

I was also weirdly obsessed with understanding how things worked, from the technical and tactile angles. I was a huge fan of this show called BattleBots, which was a competition of fighting robots built by the participants. The part that interested me wasn't the carnage but really trying to figure out the mechanics of how they built the robots. I took circuit board classes in middle school because I wanted to get hands-on with electrical components and learn how to program things. I just wanted to understand how it all worked. Where to put the transistors, how to output a certain voltage of electricity… It was fascinating and I was obsessed with these things.

There's something about my brain that loves figuring those kind of things out, so, as I grew older, I realized I loved art in a more problem-solving oriented way. "Product design" as a discipline didn't exist back then, but there were manifestations of art and technology that fused together, which really hit home for me. For instance, as my career began, encountering web design was my first real pivot where I saw myself going, huh, this is visual art that is telling a story, and you're using code to put it together. It was the right recipe fused together in a way that honed in on my interests. This is what I was meant to do.

Afshar: What was the beginning of your career like?

No: In high school, I entered what was pitched as an internship-type program. Ironically enough, it turned out not to be a real internship. It was more like a part-time job which was actually a happy change, because I was able to get paid! I started out as a graphic designer for this book publishing company from Japan called Broccoli. My role consisted of formatting books, making sure they were properly translated, and ensuring the artwork was in the right place. I also needed to create websites—very basic HTML and CSS websites back then—that were used for promoting the books essentially. At this point, I picked up an HTML book and was figuring out the mechanics of how building a proper site works. This is when I first had that design spark truly ignited.

From there, as a freelance gig, I started getting web design clients. I delved deeper into learning CSS and the principles of what makes a good web page. I'd also go on Dribbble a lot back in the day. I would copy a lot of the other designers that I admired, and learn the techniques by sheer imitation. Reverse engineering these designs taught me a lot of fundamentals and structure. There's a lot of familiarity in terms of learning patterns, lots of commonalities in things such as a navigation menu or a hero image treatment. The first time

I attempted any of these re-creations, it took me a long time. The second time was much faster. Then you start getting used to patterns and hit your stride as you continue practicing.

From there, I was hired at the domain management company Thought Convergence. It was my first "real" web design job as a full-time employee.

Afshar: What were the most impactful moments that shaped your design career?

No: I have this nonsensical sort of career path; however, the biggest impactful moment was with this startup called Abacus. They are an insurance broker that provides a digital platform for big production films to get coverage for things like, if a stunt person is jumping out of a plane. I didn't even know this type of business existed before I applied at this company.

The truth is I was underprepared for this job and Kevin Lewin, who was the hiring manager, clearly knew that when we had our initial interview. It was very obvious I was nowhere near qualified for this job, but he saw how hungry I was for the job. I told him I would do anything it takes to work at Abacus and I was willing to learn anything that was needed. I don't know how but he saw something in me and he told me I could start on Monday. That was a pivotal moment in my life because it went from me struggling as a freelance designer with part-time jobs here and there, to having a stable, livable income. It was also a role where I was truly a "product designer" and my first real leap into building cohesive experiences. I loved it.

Finally figuring out my true calling was such a fundamental puzzle piece that I was previously missing. It completely changed the trajectory of my life. Becoming a product designer also helped me realize that problem solving was such an essential skill set I had, and I didn't even know it could be a job in my early career.

Afshar: How does the Head of Design role operate at a startup like Demand.io?

No: Head of Design at a startup is a unique position, where you balance the IC role with management. Normally, you'd fall into one bucket or the other but at a small company, you're doing both jobs at the exact same time. That's interesting because you are still very close to the experience and the product itself, while at the same time you are managing a team of designers who are also crafting the experience. It's important to be investing and growing them as well. For me that means I have to bring not only my hands-on experience but also the learnings from being a team leader and a pure manager and balancing the minutiae of all the responsibilities across those jobs.

Afshar: Who are some of your closest partners in your role today?

No: We're still a relatively small company, around 90 people. I collaborate in some way with many people across different roles.

I work very closely with the CEO, Michael Quoc. He's what you'd imagine a CEO would be—very charismatic, visionary, and always striving for the best. He's very opinionated, while also being very encouraging of people in his organization to take leadership in their roles and be open to trying new things. He's a very strong advocate of moving fast and taking action. I work with him almost daily.

Our VP of Product Management, Maria Ponomarchuk, is one of my other close collaborators. Before Demand.io, she was one of the first employees at TikTok. She's very familiar with fast growth companies, and she's helping me learn how to steer the ship, so to speak, for our company to grow.

Both of them are very design-focused people who are constantly invested in honing in on our long-term strategy, and how the direction of where we are going will impact the way we shape our product experience.

Another person who started recently but has a big impact on my work life has been Victoria Taylor. She's our Community Manager. She was part of the early team at Reddit. She's a crucial member of the team as the beacon of what our audience is saying. Our product is very social in many ways, so knowing what people are saying about it, and how they use it, and what they want is such a valuable asset for us.

Afshar: How do you set goals for your design team? Do you have design team goals which are separate from the overall business goals?

No: Ultimately, everything each employee focuses on should ladder up to the company mission and business goals. At the end of the day, everything that you're working on as a design team is based on the business, so having clear alignment on what the business goals are is super important. Of course it is also important to measure performance as a design team, for example, measuring if our designer's delivery turnaround time met deadlines.

Another important aspect for my team is how the rest of the org views the design team's role and contributions. If this isn't handled well, what tends to happen is the design team is treated almost like an agency, and is only a production power horse. Companies like that are very inefficient with their design strategy, and then becomes almost a reactionary discipline, where designers are simply executing on work versus shaping it. What's important to foster is a relationship where designers are included in the business conversations, and are part of the strategic discussions on if a project is worth doing in the first place. This means design must be oriented in the org where we have a strong voice in the direction of the company.

As a manager, there's also the importance of investing in and growing the individuals on my team. This is more around helping each person with their personal goal setting. For creatives, we want to do things that aren't just mundane grinds of work. We want to have inspiration and create inspiration. We want to grow our creative capacity, try new things. So as part of my role, it's also essential that everybody on my team has the environment and support they need to accomplish that sense of personal achievement.

I try to optimize project allocation so everybody has access to projects they care about. Of course, work is not always rainbows and sunshine, and sometimes there's just going to be grind work that comes with it. However, it's important that the workload is equitably balanced in a healthy way. That is my responsibility.

Afshar: You've had a career history of working at many companies at the cutting-edge of industry. For instance, you were one of the first designers at the virtual reality (VR) company Oculus, a year after the company was founded. You also worked on Web3 at Coinbase and are now Head of Design for an AI-powered organization. Is there a unique approach you take when leading design that is at the forefront of new technologies?

No: It's an interesting question because working in zero-to-one products has led me to something I now call a universal truth. I remember back in the day when VR was just in its most early infancy and organizations were frantically saying "where do we find good VR designers?" and the truth is, there were none. A good "VR" designer didn't exist. However, good designers can design anything, period.

When evaluating the skills of a design candidate, the specific medium they've had past experience in is very secondary. What is truly important is the candidate needs to inherently be a good problem solver. For example, when I interview, I don't ask web-specific or VR-specific questions. Instead, I focus on how someone thinks about deconstructing a problem, understanding what needs to be solved, and their process in coming up with a solution.

That being said, it is important to understand the technology one is creating for. That is an important building block for a designer, to truly understand how to apply their problem-solving skills in an optimal way.

For example, when I was working in VR, there were no guidelines on how to design for VR. It was so early, there was no playbook, no tutorials. There was not yet a community of "VR designers" established in the industry. All of us creating VR products just had to try a bazillion things to understand the basics that we now take for granted. For example, is it comfortable to reach out and grab something in VR past a certain distance? Is it hard to read text in VR if the UI is always slightly moving? There was a ton of testing we did and the conclusion was that designing for VR was almost more scientific than anything else. There's a physiological aspect of VR that I wasn't used to from my past experience. The experience isn't rectilinear like a traditional mobile device. Being in a fully immersive world means that all your human instincts kick in. If something's coming at you really fast in VR, you physically duck your head. If something jumpscares you, you back away. Those are all real things you have to design for and problem solve around.

It's no different than when I was designing for blockchain technology for the first time, and there were new assumptions that had to be taken into account like that every transaction was instantaneous, or everything is anonymous, and that meant there was a new layer of scams and abuse that had to be taken into account when solving any design problem.

The principles of good design are eternal and the challenge is how to apply them to any specific iteration of a completely new technology, but at the end of the day, a good designer is a good designer.

Afshar: Outside of work, you invest a lot of time into mentorship. What kind of advice do you often give to designers aspiring to grow in their careers?

No: A helpful foundational concept is learning the "three rule of thumb questions" that one should always ask when you're starting any design project.

The first question is asking what is the problem that you're trying to solve. Being able to articulate this clearly to yourself and your stakeholders is important. This should be a clear statement.

The second question is asking how do you know that this is an actual problem. This question can really trip people up. What is the evidence that supports the assumption that the problem is a meaningful one? For example, market research, user research, qualitative testing, whatever it may be, it's important to verify so the thing you are attempting is actually meaningful.

I'll give an example—I was coaching one of my mentees through a difficult project they were designing. They were designing a set of notification-related buttons, with icons, new text labels, et cetera. However, after analyzing the entire product flow, it became clear that it didn't even make sense to notify users in this part of the flow in the first place. My mentee came to the realization that they didn't even need to create all of these designs in the first place because this flow wasn't even a scenario an actual user would be faced with. This designer was so in the weeds looking at the nuances of what typography to use, what the icons should look like, and in fact, taking a step back allowed them to see they didn't even need to be designing this specific set of UI at all.

The third question is asking how do you know when the problem is solved. Designers, especially early in their career, can have a tendency to get overwhelmed with the sheer amount of responsibilities they feel are on their plate. Once there is a legitimate problem identified to solve, set a goal or milestone of what is the measurable next step of what you want to achieve. Maybe problems could be worked on and iterated on forever, so it's important to set boundaries on what the deliverable you want to land is. Time management is a common theme, so setting clear milestones where you are not trying to solve too many things at once is key.

Afshar: What are some hard truths about being a designer?

No: There's almost an expectation now for instant gratification, and it has manifested in the design industry in these extremely short boot camps where one can instantly "become a designer." Just like one can't be a pro chef in four weeks, even if one has used a stove for their entire adult life, it's also misleading to expect that someone can become a product designer in that same amount of time just because one has used apps before. It's honestly impossible for a short class to transform one into a pro unless you are some kind of unicorn prodigy. Developing your craft is a constant trial-and-error where it can take years of repeated practice before you start building the senses of being able to look at a design and have the intuition of what's not working well. It's almost like muscle memory.

Because of my background of being self-taught, sometimes I get asked how someone with no experience can very quickly learn how to be a designer. I tell the story I mentioned earlier in the interview, where I would spend two to four hours a day for years recreating design work from Dribbble and UI designs from apps to start building the design sense that was needed to work well as a professional designer. It would be misleading for me to claim that it is possible to learn in a month. It's just not real and the false expectations of what it really takes to be a good product designer can be damaging. Being a good product designer means an amalgamation of multiple skill sets—problem solving, product thinking, and visual craft.

CHAPTER

8

Christie Fremon
Asana

Christie Fremon is the Head of Content Design at Asana, an enterprise work management platform serving over 150,000 customers and millions of users in 200+ countries and territories. Prior to Asana, Fremon designed experiences used by millions worldwide at companies like Rivian, Google, and Apple with a focus on products that improve people's lives through privacy, accessibility, inclusion, and design systems thinking.

Fremon holds a bachelor's degree in English and Creative Writing from San Francisco State University.

Jaleh Afshar: For readers who may not be familiar with content design, could you share an overview of the discipline?

Christie Fremon: Like any type of design, we create experiences. Content Designers use words to do it.

For example, in a settings menu, a UX designer might use toggles to show whether something is on or off. As content designers, we also help the user understand the state of the setting—with words. A UI Designer might use color to help draw focus to the interaction. We also help draw focus—with words.

We help users get around an interface, make sense of things, and quickly get stuff done.

As a discipline, our expertise manifests in many ways; however, there are two elements I find particularly influential. First is *emotion in UX*. If Brand is the emotional memory of all our experiences with a company or product, then the emotions a product experience creates are really important. Content Designers control so much of the emotion of our experiences. We work to get the tone right.

For example, a group I led learned that including an exclamation mark in severe warning messages increased anxiety—and that the user would take the message just as seriously without the exclamation mark. That finding paved the way to change the written tone to confidence and calm, and inspired our visual and motion designers to match our intent.

If you want to ace your product's emotional feel, get a content designer involved.

Second is *tempo in UX*. I think an important role of content designers is being the keepers of tempo in UX. There are moments when we want to quickly move through flows—and other moments where it's so important to slow down and think carefully. Designers often don't realize how all the text on the page affects tempo. Or how something as small as a question mark can slow down a user at the right time. I'm personally really passionate about the idea of being the keepers of tempo and helping achieve a tempo that feels comfortable to the user.

When I think about interaction design, interaction happens over time. The question of: how long do we spend on something? Does it feel too slow? Does it feel rushed? Do we feel like we have the ability to take a breath at the right moment? These are all key parts of a healthy design and good tempo.

Afshar: Could you share an overview of how content design commonly works with cross-disciplinary teams?

Fremon: In my day-to-day work, it's common to run into people who either don't know what content design is, or who've only worked with one content designer before. In some cases, the content-adjacent folks they've worked with might have a completely different practice as well.

And so I think it's really common for people to think, what is this discipline? How can I work with it? How can I benefit from it?

I prioritize answering these questions with my stakeholders and those who my team collaborates with early on, because it really highlights how content design can drive value at every aspect of the design double diamond.

So, from the beginning of the product development cycle, whether that's participating in scoping discussions, getting into empathy, or journey mapping, finding out more about the legal requirements that you might be looking at—especially if you're writing about privacy or if you're writing about data that might be used for AI—these are all important for content design to contribute to.

And then after you get a sense for where you're headed with the project, content design might often create artifacts like early flows that you've co-written with UX design peers. Often one might find that there is a strategy document or a competitive analysis that takes place upon looking closer at the words that are being used in different products in the market or in the field that you're looking into.

Then from there, content design can lead efforts to look into the names or the words that you use as you take a look at a feature or how the feature integrates with other parts of the product. Working with localization, you might do some stress testing early on to make sure that that approach that you're trying out really fits across multiple markets.

When getting into that final copy deliverable, what words appear in the UI, what gets put into the code repository and then checked into your translation tool and sent out for review, these are all critical areas for content design to be present for.

Depending on the stakeholder, depending on who you're collaborating with, how this manifests is a little bit different. But at the end of the day, Content Design can be visible and influence a product during every step of this development journey

Afshar: How do you typically structure your workweek?

Fremon: Well, to start, I'm a single parent with a long commute. I used to be able to just work late, but now I have to be intentional about where I spend my time and energy.

I begin my week by getting a pulse check on my team and projects, understanding what needs my attention, and plan for the week. Asana has a hybrid work culture. We work in the office three days a week and remotely two days a week, including a no-meetings Wednesday. Almost everyone is on the same schedule, so it's easy to be in sync with others.

Connecting with people is a key aspect of my work. Most in-office days I spend with people. We often have team meetings that bring all of design together, as well as design crits, office hours, jams, project-based meetings, mentorships, cross-functional meetings, and leadership meetings. And I always make time for matcha, lunch, or a walk. Those moments are truly important—not just for relationship and influence building, but also for getting a chance to be human.

Heads-down time is also important to ensure deep work and creativity. Wednesdays are often the days I get the most focus time. Everyone else is heads-down too.

Fridays I focus on my own team, with one-on-one syncs and our weekly team meeting. I want that sense of community and camaraderie to carry my team into their weekend.

Afshar: What are the biggest challenges you face in your role?

Fremon: Collaboration is a critical factor. When your team is specialized, not everyone knows what type of work you do. And when your team is horizontal, working with several other teams, not everyone knows what to expect or how to collaborate. It can be tough honoring individual working styles while also setting expectations and making progress.

From a tactical lens, product and feature naming is another challenging aspect. Everyone expects one to three words to answer half a dozen questions—how to build a feature, how it'll perform in the market, whether it meets buyers' needs, and how to use the feature once it's built. And people often pick a favorite just on vibes. Getting everyone on the same page takes a thoughtful approach.

When it comes to specific examples of challenging situations, one of my favorite stories was from when I was pulled into a project where the entire user experience had already been created and baked in for a checkout flow.

Logistic decisions on the backend had already been made and the stakeholders were now looking for input on how to explain some of the choices that they've made.

Most of the flow was a typical checkout, with one major element that was unexpected. What wasn't standard is that the user could add multiple items to a cart and then be told at the very end, *oh, sorry, you can't check out because these items are in different warehouses.*

The stakeholders expected content design to fix that and to simply explain it in a way that would make the user happy. However, since we were brought in at the very tail end of the process, we weren't at a point where we could easily push a major change to the user experience.

It's moments like those where content design's value isn't in finding the right words, but in identifying that there's a deeper problem that needs to be investigated. How do we fix the logistics on the backend?

In that window between now and when we can actually fix the fundamental logistics issue, how do we talk about this to users and give them the best possible experience despite the odd circumstances? This might not just be changing some words at the point where they've already added items to their cart, but well before that, earlier in their experience with the product.

Another example comes from my experience running naming programs at a couple of different places. Naming programs really vary depending on the organizational needs. The organization that I'm with right now wants to get a great go-to-market name. There's a lot of emphasis on identifying that early on. Figuring out how do we pick something that allows us to transition that name to our product so that when we sit down to build what we've already marketed, how does it translate? How does it make sense to the user and provide a cohesive experience? How can we ensure we are not shipping an experience that reveals the seams of our org chart to the end user?

At other organizations, for instance at Rivian, naming was largely a challenge of coordinating a lot of different content creators. We had a service branch that was creating what was known as BOM (Bill of Materials), which are part lists for service providers. We had a technical writing branch that was creating manuals that would not only inform the people driving the vehicle, but also emergency responders. And we also had our content design team that I led there where we were trying to figure out how we talk about parts of the vehicle, these physical pieces, and also feature names on the screen. And then coordinating all of that with marketing, and our mobile team or our website team.

All of that alignment meant that we needed names and we needed words for features and parts that were crisp, that were easy to understand, that put safety first. Instead of it being more focused on marketing, it was really focused on how do we take a name and move that throughout all of these different content creation teams in a way that makes sense, in a way that's consistent, but that meets all of our different audience needs.

Sometimes you might have to retrofit things into a system that might not be fully sensical, but that's just simply what you have to work with. Because of that, I think that all design teams, but definitely content design, often have to make a choice: Are we trying to make something that's evergreen or are we trying to address a "now" problem?

Especially when we're looking at AI, the market, and the rapid speed of technological advancement, we often index for a solution that fits right now and maybe we reevaluate it later. But even for those evergreen moments, there are times where it doesn't make sense or isn't worth the effort to go back and retrofit everything to change everything in that moment.

That's the reason why having a content design team is so important is because those are strategic decisions.

Ensuring how the product is framed and described in a way that aligns with business goals and supports the business's success and the end user experience.

Afshar: How do you cultivate creativity and innovation when operating in a large-scale corporate environment?

Fremon: This can be really tough. It's a particularly important question during times when there's industry-wide financial uncertainty, budget cuts, or lay-offs—which is the current climate as we're having this chat.

Design teams everywhere are asked to get more stuff done, faster.

At work I am surrounded by incredibly deeply creative people. One of the pleasures that I have in my job is getting to chat with my peers, my fellow leaders, and the other designers that I work with. They have such diverse backgrounds and hobbies, some of them do digital art, some of them do textile creations, some of them are in industrial arts, some of them used to be architects, some do gaming, some do journaling. We have such a range of creativity in all of the companies that I work for, no matter how large.

The challenge comes with when you have such a tight schedule and when you're working in environments that really value getting stuff done, how do you build the practice of creativity into the work that you do? And how do you set goals that enable that creativity?

When managing a team, there are some important leadership aspects which help to facilitate a creatively healthy culture.

For example, reducing workload makes room for creativity. Of course, if you give time back and you're not setting a culture that challenges people or says, hey, we're making room for creativity, or we're creating a practice, you still might not see that creativity bubble up because there's already a culture established of the corporate day-to-day.

So how does one foster a team that is set up for creative habits? Set goals that leave room for creativity. Instead of asking for a better staircase, ask for a way to get to the second floor. Make play and experimentation built in. Use crazy 8s, mash-ups. Make it a part of the process to use time to expand and remix ideas before refining. Practice creativity and non-lateral thinking in social spaces and team meetings. Get creative with icebreakers. Play. It's a muscle. When you use it, you get in shape and gain confidence.

Afshar: Where do you see the role of a content designer heading in the coming years, especially considering advancements in AI?

Fremon: Are you sure you want to ask? I read so much sci-fi as a kid!

In five or ten years? Content designers are still there. And they know AI—how it works, how to design for products that use AI, and how to use AI themselves to be more effective and get more done.

Our focus is going to be different. We'll create a strategy and goals, and then ask an AI agent to follow that guidance to write many of our most common, easy strings. We'll step in where AI can't—in spaces that require new thinking and innovation and in design problems where a less standard and more nuanced approach is needed. We'll design new ways to interact with AI—like how we shifted from command-line to graphic interfaces—and we'll make it simple for our users to ask an AI for help, while maintaining informed control.

We humans are curious. We're always interacting with our world in new and unusual ways. As long as that's true, we'll always need designers. And content designers too.

I think the most important thing is to learn how AI works.

Go out there, read, be curious and find out more, because the way that you approach a problem will change depending on whether or not you understand what's happening on the backend. I've worked on a lot of different projects that use AI or machine learning to augment the consumer experience or to help the backend create a particular experience.

That ranges from music recommendations to vehicles with assisted driving to collaboration features where AI is really helping analyze data or identify action items.

And with all of these experiences, the thing that helps my team know where to put our effort is understanding what's actually happening under the hood.

So, for instance, if I have a forward-facing camera in a vehicle that's looking at a driver, and we're being told write a message that alerts drivers when they're drowsy, it helps to know what the camera is looking for and how that data is being analyzed and where some of the weak points in that system might be.

Knowing that lets us know, oh the AI it's looking for a certain number of blinks, or it's looking for your head nodding. Now the content designer will know what is being detected and be able to write something more effective. Otherwise we might write something that's just boilerplate and perhaps doesn't land with the user or doesn't truly address what's happening.

Knowing more about it allows us to think about that, create a good experience, and think through the whole flow. Demystifying the process an AI uses to analyze data also gives the team courage and the knowledge necessary to ask tougher questions.

Afshar: What unconventional piece of advice would you give to aspiring content designers?

Fremon: Take weird jobs. Many of the jobs I took in my career were unusual choices. I remember being asked how anyone could do UX writing for hardware, especially with devices getting smaller like watches or fitness devices. I got warned away from designing content for cars, and was told there weren't that many words in a car anyhow. Spoiler—there are so many words!

Because I took unusual jobs, I had experience that helped me stand out.

Before I got into content design, I was doing technical writing and one of the weirder jobs that I took was maintaining a knowledge base and learning how to maintain that.

This was an open source Wiki that could accept community contributions that were as short as a sentence. Sometimes we'd have users writing "this tool sucks" and that was their entire wiki article.

Other times we'd have really, really detailed articles that were so granular, but didn't match the scope of the other content. Learning about how flexibly a Wiki could be organized, learning about how to create better navigation, better information hierarchy, that has all been so instrumental in looking at UX design and saying, where does this information fit in a flow?

How is it discoverable? Can it be found via search? Can it be browsed? Can it be suggested content?

And all of that I learned through this very weird job of maintaining a side project that nobody loved and everybody was saying, let's give that to someone more junior.

Working on some weird and odd things teaches you a lot!

Afshar: What aspects of your identity have influenced your approach to management and design leadership?

Fremon: Gosh, I think all of them.

I think that if we shy away from the labels around identity and we just go back to the experience of having an identity that maybe doesn't meet the norm, it can all very much impact the experience of working on a team. Maybe your health is a little bit different and sickness hits you differently than other team members. Maybe the way that socially we interact with each other and we use gender roles, it doesn't hit quite the same. And maybe you want to forge a different path.

All of those are things that are on my mind when I'm working with members of my team in that I don't want an out-of-the-box solution.

I don't want to assume that the way that they show up at work, the way that they approach problems, the way that they balance their work life and their personal life are going to be the same cookie cutter approach.

Instead, I want to think about having empathy for the fact that it's gonna be different from person to person and that they want to be here as much as I want to be here and they want to succeed as much as I want to succeed. And now it's just up to us to figure out if the path needs to look a little different.

I've got fibromyalgia. It's an invisible disability, but most days I'm in pain—people just don't know it. It interferes with my ability to be consistent in my work—something that corporate America values. I work to build equity, by contributing more so that when I need to rest I can. Having a disability helps me advocate for accessibility.

I'm neurodivergent. I have ADHD and autism (lovingly called AuDHD), plus dyslexia, meaning I work almost exclusively with words that hop around the page. It's tough to excel when often you have to work harder or longer hours to keep up with peers. And when you don't have the sense of fitting in as easily. Of course—it's also a great source of energy, motivation, focus, and divergent thinking. It's so easy to forget the positives. However, there are certain things that I do a lot better if I have access to tools.

So, for example, yesterday I was in a meeting where somebody, in order to get the room to be more respectful of the person presenting, said laptops down and everybody closed their screens. But for me, that was a moment where I couldn't use the document that we were referencing to reinforce what I was hearing. It was significantly more challenging for me to be present in that conversation. That's obviously a challenge that's come up throughout my career and that I've spent a lot of time developing tactics for. But it does mean that after that meeting, I had to go back and I had to look at that document which means I had to do some extra work.

I have some colleagues on my larger team who have the same needs. Because of these experiences, I think about how we can provide more flexibility and more tools and more ability to allow people to choose the work style that works for them.

As a leader, I'm always thinking about the processes or the approaches or the attitudes that we try to bring forward for our teams. How are we building roads for success for them? Are we leaving a little bit of room for flexibility? Are we saying, hey, we trust you to come here and bring your best self and to pick the work style that is gonna lead you to success?

As design managers and leaders, we are here to augment that. We're here to provide scaffolding, but also that trust for you to pick an approach that helps.

Afshar: How have you experienced the intersection of gender expression and workplace culture in a predominantly binary corporate environment?

Fremon: I identify as a nonbinary woman. Some parts of me feel like a woman, but other parts of me don't feel like a woman or a man. I often don't easily fit in with other women. Sometimes more feminine approaches to work don't work for me—they either don't land or succeed or they leave me feeling disconnected and self-critical. I choose to use she/they pronouns at work, but often feel as though people still see me as a binary woman. I try to get that sense of belonging from my community. BRG (Business Resource Groups) and

Chapter 8 | Christie Fremon, Asana

ERG (Employee Resource Groups) social spaces are very important to me. But also, the personal connections I make with coworkers help me feel like I belong in a corporate culture that's almost exclusively binary, especially at the leadership level.

To back up a bit, I think about gender a lot like food in that it is cultural. So, for instance, the way that we think of pizza might be different if you were in Chicago, in New York, in Italy, in Japan, pizza's gonna look very different.

Gender, culturally, also looks different. It looks different across different intersections, different backgrounds.

The way that I was raised, I never really fit in as a girl. I never did the playing house or the sharing gossip or secrets approach to womanhood. Of course, there are so many different expressions of womanhood too, but I was never able to find one that felt like I fit.

In the workplace, it's the same way. There are ways that a lot of my colleagues approach work and it's tough being a woman in the workplace. It is really tough. For me, navigating that path and then realizing that even what my colleagues are finding brings them success can be a little bit more challenging for me to navigate is just a challenge.

I would love to see it shift because to be honest, there's a level of performance that's expected of us as designers.

I've been in groups where people shift what they wear to work so much that they show up and they're accidentally dressing like their coworkers. I've been in a meeting where everybody laughs about how they all have the same haircut and the same shirts on the day that they're meeting another team. That's us orienting around what we think we need to do to succeed and to fit in. That's us trying to find a place of safety so that we can come and do our best work.

And then to be expected to be the stylish one or the life of the party on top of all of that is another level of performance that can make it difficult, especially if you aren't the life of the party or if your style is a little bit different than what is currently trending.

For me, the way I navigate these expectations is that I invest more heavily in personal relationships. So, if I show up and I'm looking a little bit different than everyone else and nobody in the room knows me, that's a signal for people to wonder what's going on with her.

But if I've reached out and I've had those coffee talks, I've learned more about everyone, I know what's going on in their lives and I know what they're interested in and they see me as a person, they're not asking, why is Christie showing up not looking like everyone else? They're saying Christie looks like Christie.

CHAPTER 9

Courtney Allison Brown
CarMax

Courtney Allison Brown is a Senior Manager of Experience Design at CarMax, who leads Design Operations for the XD Organization, where she focuses on organization-wide culture, learning, upskilling, and professional growth programs, and operational excellence for a team of 60+ designers in collaboration with brand, design, and product leadership. Previously Courtney led operations at executive and senior producer roles at multiple companies including Capital One, 22squared, and Bionic. She resides in Richmond, Virginia.

Jaleh Afshar: What inspired you to pursue a career in design operations, and what motivates you to continue growing in this field?

Courtney Allison Brown: My career journey has taken some unexpected turns, leading me to where I am today. I began as a visual effects designer in post-production because I loved the hands-on process of creating content. However, over time, I found myself growing further from the routine elements of that role. My interest began to shift toward the logistics of projects, figuring out how to make things happen through cross-disciplinary leadership, and building strong relationships with clients.

© Jaleh Afshar 2025
J. Afshar, *Chief Design Officers at Work*,
https://doi.org/10.1007/979-8-8688-1137-1_9

This shift in focus naturally steered me toward advertising, where I worked as an integrated producer for a while. My career took a significant leap when I joined Capital One, marking my first experience with a large design organization. Although my background was primarily in branding from my time in advertising, Capital One was establishing its first design system, and I was brought in to help build and manage that team.

At Capital One, my role continued to evolve. I found great fulfillment in overseeing operations from different areas of the larger organization as a whole (the three groups I was focused on was Experience Strategy, Talent & Culture, and Practice Analytics over four of my five years there). What I enjoy most is ensuring that everyone on the team is well-supported, that designers have the resources and growth opportunities they need to thrive.

This experience has allowed me to combine my creative background with a more human-centered approach, blending creativity with the ability to influence and shape the overall design environment. It's been a rewarding journey, and I'm excited to continue bringing both my creative skills and my passion for people into everything I do.

Afshar: What does your workday routine look like?

Brown: When you're involved in design, it's common to wear many hats and take on various responsibilities, which adds a lot of variety to the work. For me, however, the most important aspect is the human connection. It's about having meaningful conversations with the people who support us in different capacities, ensuring they see the value in their contributions and that we're providing value in return.

My day-to-day responsibilities include administering our tools properly and managing the scheduling for key rituals, such as all-hands meetings and other critical activities that keep the team aligned. I also work closely with HR and recruiting, ensuring that we're well-supported from a people management perspective. Much of my role involves managing relationships and making sure we're steadily progressing, building, and scaling our efforts as we grow. It can be a slow process at times, but it's exciting to see the progress we're making when looking at the big picture.

In terms of collaboration, our design team is part of the larger product organization, so we're essentially an organization within an organization. I report directly to our Vice President of Experience Design, and I work closely with our Director of Experience Design. Together, we form a trifecta that manages the design organization. The three of us collaborate closely with senior managers who oversee their respective teams, creating a layered structure where we can influence both up and down the chain of command.

Afshar: How do you measure the effectiveness of Design Operations practitioners and their initiatives?

Brown: While at Capital One and in the larger design operations community, I've had the privilege of being part of initiatives honing in on upskilling and design quality improvement at an experience design org-wide level. I can't take full credit for its creation—since it originated within the broader design community—I have certainly been involved in the process of putting it into practice. One of the key tools developed was a set of skill assessments. These assessments are incredibly valuable because they allow us to track individual growth and ensure that the perceptions of both the practitioners and their managers are aligned. This alignment is crucial for making sure that everyone is investing in the right skills, whether those are directly tied to business objectives or broader organizational needs. By doing so, we ensure that we're well-prepared to tackle the diverse types of work we handle.

In addition to these functional assessments, myself and our Senior Design Managers place a strong emphasis on regular check-ins with team members. These conversations help us gauge how people are feeling and identify any underlying issues. These conversations help me gauge how people are feeling and identify any underlying issues. I like to take a broad view of what's happening across the organization, but I also focus on individual experiences to spot correlations. For instance, if a team is performing well overall but suddenly experiences a dip, I dig into what might have caused it. Was there an external event, a personal issue, or a team conflict? Understanding external influences—whether they're related to work, personal life, or broader world events—has been crucial in navigating these situations. This piecemeal approach, though more granular, allows me to understand specific needs and address potential problems before they escalate.

Afshar: Can you share an example of a time when you had to navigate a difficult team dynamic? How did you ensure a positive outcome?

Brown: I've been fortunate in my career to have rarely encountered intensely high friction situations, and for that, I'm grateful. However, when they do arise, most of the challenges I've faced have been handled in a more personal, one-on-one approach, which is my preferred method of addressing difficult situations in an empathetic way. I believe that addressing issues on a more personal, direct scale often prevents them from becoming bigger than necessary. For instance, when dealing with associates who might need a performance plan or are facing other career issues, I focus on understanding the root of the problem through direct, honest conversations. I might ask, "What's not fulfilling you right now?" or "Why do you feel unable to take action on this?" These discussions not only help in identifying the issues but also show the individual that I'm truly listening. As a leader, I aim to create a safe space where they feel supported, which is crucial for understanding what's really happening.

This approach also applies to resolving conflicts between teams or organizations. For example, I once worked on a design system where there was significant friction between the development and design teams, particularly during the handoff process. The tension stemmed from differences in how each team worked and communicated. To address this, we organized a series of workshops focused on working methods, which helped us identify that the core issue was a lack of effective communication. By aligning our language and expectations, we were able to bridge the gap, improve collaboration, and build trust between the teams. The developers could express their frustrations, the designers could share theirs, and both sides began to understand each other's perspectives. This process of open dialogue is my go-to technique when facing challenges—getting everyone to come together, respectfully yet openly laying out the issues, and figuring out a way forward together.

Afshar: In your current and past positions you've been positioned in roles with the responsibility of shaping the design operations discipline from the ground up. Can you share some reflections on the process of spearheading a nascent practice?

Brown: It's been fascinating to be the one initiating and shaping this new discipline at CarMax. Unlike previous roles where I stepped into established systems, here I had the chance to create something fully from scratch. Drawing on the best practices and insights I've gained from working with brilliant colleagues over the years, I was both excited and a little intimidated by the challenge. But it's been incredibly rewarding, especially with the support of my leadership, who have given me the freedom to experiment, make mistakes, and learn from them. This experience has not only allowed me to connect deeply with our designers but has also positioned me well for the next steps in my own personal development.

When I reflect on my past role at Capital One, service design was a significant aspect of our work there, and it was my first deep dive into that discipline as I transitioned from program management to design ops. Working closely with service designers, I absorbed a lot of their skills, which I now apply in my current role.

When I joined CarMax, design operations was a completely new discipline—they knew they needed support but had no firm framework in place. Over the past three years, I've been building this practice from the ground up, using service design principles to guide the process.

Another aspect of my role that has been unique for me to CarMax is I collaborate closely with our brand team. My background at Capital One, where I worked on bridging the gap between brand and design, has been invaluable here. There's often a natural friction between these two functions, as they operate differently due to the specific user and business goals they are solving. Between that tension, I see my role as translating and finding common ground. By integrating brand into our product work more effectively, we ensure that the brand is accurately reflected across all touchpoints that a customer and user sees and feels. This kind of collaboration is something I find both challenging and rewarding, and it's been a key part of my work in evolving our organization.

Afshar: How do you see Design Operations as a field evolving in the next five years?

Brown: I was browsing LinkedIn recently and came across a post from a fellow practitioner that really made me think. They mentioned that we're now entering the "2.0 age" of design operations, which is fascinating when you consider that design ops is still a relatively young discipline. While the underlying skills—like project management, program management, and portfolio management—have been around for ages, the formalization of design ops as a distinct field is only a few years old, maybe five to ten years at most. Yet, here we are, already talking about a new phase, a version 2.0.

One of the trends I see in the future is the expansion of tangential knowledge within our roles. In the past, people were often highly specialized, focusing deeply on their craft. But as the landscape evolves, we're seeing a growing need for generalists—professionals who have a broad range of skills and can cover multiple areas. This shift is partly due to the necessity of covering skill gaps, but also because companies increasingly value multidisciplinary talent. I foresee design ops professionals continuing to expand their expertise, adding more tools to their toolbox. It's not uncommon now to see a design ops person who also dabbles in visual design, product management, or technology. This multidisciplinary approach not only enriches our teams but also makes us more adaptable and capable of tackling complex challenges.

It's interesting to think about where this field is headed because we've already seen so many shifts in what our roles entail and how they're defined. This is especially true with the way hiring practices have evolved and how we've had to adapt our skills to fit into spaces that weren't as prominent a few years ago. Looking forward, I believe a big part of our future will involve engaging more with automation and AI—not to replace us, of course, but to enhance our capabilities. As designers increasingly lean into AI, we need to find ways to integrate it into our workflows effectively, ensuring that our discipline remains relevant and that we're not left behind. We're moving forward along the same path as the rest of the design industry, but we also have to remember our responsibility for legality, compliance, and ensuring we do things the right way. It's going to be an interesting journey, and who knows? Our title might not even be "design ops" in the future, but whatever it is, there are a lot of exciting unknowns ahead.

Afshar: What guiding principle do you apply to your work?

Brown: What continually resonates with me is the critical role of empathy in design operations. Rather than just advocating for another framework or method, my focus is on the emotional impact of our work—the way it affects the people we interact with, whether they're customers, colleagues, or partners.

In my view, design operations must emphasize caring—caring for the people involved, the work being done, and the company as a whole. It's not enough to concentrate solely on a product or a specific task. To be truly effective, one must adopt a holistic perspective, understanding how every piece connects and how our actions influence the entire system. This comprehensive approach allows us to identify and seize opportunities to make a meaningful impact.

This philosophy is at the heart of how I approach my work. It's about genuinely caring for all aspects of our operations, ensuring that we're not just addressing isolated problems but are always mindful of the bigger picture. This mindset is something I believe is essential in design operations and is a fundamental part of how I work.

CHAPTER

10

Daisuke Sakai
teamLab

Daisuke Sakai is the co-founder of teamLab, an international art collective exploring the convergence of art, science, and technology. Consisting of an interdisciplinary group of various specialists spanning artists, programmers, engineers, CG animators, mathematicians, and architects, teamLab's collaborative practice seeks to navigate the confluence of art, science, technology, and the natural world. With exhibitions in 27+ countries, teamLab pioneers global art and advances technology in system development and digital content creation.

Originally from Sapporo in Hokkaido, Japan, Sakai graduated from the University of Tokyo's Department of Mechanical and Information Engineering.

Jaleh Afshar: Could you share the story of how teamLab was first created?

Daisuke Sakai: In the late 1990s, I was studying humanoid robotics at the University of Tokyo. At the same time, I became the head of a social club dedicated to a traditional Japanese folk dance festival in Tokushima, a city on the island of Shikoku. The Tokushima Awaodori is a centuries-old festival that takes place every August, spanning four days of continuous celebration. Each year, we gathered students from the university—and sometimes recruited others from different universities—to form a team and dance for hours on end, experiencing pure happiness together.

© Jaleh Afshar 2025
J. Afshar, *Chief Design Officers at Work*,
https://doi.org/10.1007/979-8-8688-1137-1_10

In this club, I met another member, Inoko, who was studying engineering at the University of Tokyo. We attended the festival together every year. After we graduated from our respective faculties, we both pursued our master's degrees at the newly established University of Tokyo Graduate School of Interdisciplinary Information Studies. It was during a chance meeting in the school's cafeteria that Inoko mentioned he was planning to start a project and asked if I knew any engineers who might be interested in joining. I responded, "Tell me more—I might be interested myself." At that time, I was beginning to realize that academia might not be where I saw my future.

I soon visited a studio space Inoko had with another student, who later became one of the other co-founders of what would eventually become teamLab. The five co-founders all came from similar yet distinct backgrounds, but we all shared a deep passion for creation. This shared passion became the core value that initially brought us together.

Trusting my instincts, I decided to join them. Within a few months, we presented our first exhibition at the Shiseido Gallery in Tokyo. In many ways, the rest is history—but it's a history still very much in the making.

Afshar: Was there a specific moment in the early stages of your career that shaped your philosophy about the things you are creating?

Sakai: One of our key philosophies centers not so much on what we create but on how we create it. This approach is rooted in the backgrounds of my co-founders and me—we are all engineers. As engineers, we understood that success lies in the small, countless details. Paying close attention to every detail was the only way to achieve the level of excellence we aimed for. To do this, the entire team needed to share the same understanding and appreciation for each element and detail that composes a creation. In the early days, this was natural and easy. With a small team, we could all share this mindset and approach to our work.

Like any new operation, during our first three to four years, everyone was hands-on in whatever way was needed. Although we were all trained as engineers, we went far beyond our academic backgrounds. We took on tasks like project management, graphic design, finance, and anything else necessary to get our projects off the ground. This organic approach fostered a culture of meticulous attention to all aspects of our work. There was no clear division between roles—everyone was an engineer, and everyone did everything.

By around 2004, approximately three years in, teamLab had grown from five to nearly fifty members. This growth made us realize the need to restructure how we worked in order to maintain our original focus on details. By then, we had hired project managers, designers, and other specialists for specific roles. As our projects evolved, so did the flow of information among team members, and with that, the shared understanding of all the small details began to shift.

This was the moment we made a significant change in our working structure. We expanded role definitions within teamLab, creating a structure with a limited number of roles, yet one that still allowed teams to work in a fluid and dynamic way. This restructuring ensured that we retained our original commitment to meticulous attention to detail, even as we grew.

I believe this opportunity to redefine our working methods was crucial to our growth and development. It enabled us to create projects of varying scales, all of which we are very proud of, and all of which are rooted in an extreme level of attention to detail.

Afshar: You lead a highly multidisciplinary team, spanning mathematicians, architects, engineers, programmers, and more. What are some unexpected aspects of facilitating collaboration across these various disciplines?

Sakai: In many ways, there's still an element of the unexpected within the well-defined work stream of teamLab. This unpredictability is both exciting and energizing, and it's what fuels many of us to continue with such enthusiasm. A major contributing factor is the nature of our multidisciplinary team. Working on a project with team members who bring a wealth of diverse inputs, ideas, and solutions naturally pushes us beyond expectations. This can manifest in anything from small project details to significant shifts in a project's outcome. There are countless ways to navigate from the starting point of a project to its completion, especially when we have such a high level of diverse expertise around the table. The process and the final destination can change significantly depending on the contributions and perspectives of the team.

I strongly believe that there are no "big ideas," or rather, that big ideas hold little value until they can be executed and proven powerful in reality by being brought to life at the highest level. Over the years, we've adopted an approach of fine, step-by-step development, where each small idea contributes to the overall progress of a project. Every team member brings solutions to the table that move the project forward in different ways.

We've cultivated a method, or rhythm, of listening to one another. But this is only possible when every team member respects what others bring to the table and does so with humility. The focus is on imagining how we can incorporate these insights into our own roles and what we can contribute back to the team in the next phase.

We all share a common belief that our success isn't about our ability to create in isolation—we can't do it alone. We need the combined strengths of our multidisciplinary team, and we must also know how to harness that team's full potential. Fostering this atmosphere within the team and our workspace starts with the recruitment process, where we identify true team players—those who thrive in collaborative environments rather than as solo performers.

Reflecting on the way we've worked and the outcomes we've achieved over the past two decades, there are countless examples of unexpected twists and turns in the development of our projects. It's even surprising to see how individuals within our team have the power to generate and lead significant shifts that the entire team follows. This is once again rooted in the ability to bring proven insights to the table and the willingness of others to hear and develop them further.

Afshar: What do you find most challenging about your role?

Sakai: Maintaining simplicity within a growing organization is one of the greatest challenges. Rules and hierarchy are often the easiest, and sometimes the most logical, ways to manage a growing business, organization, or unique entity like ours. However, I am committed to preserving simplicity despite our growth and finding a way to sustain an organic evolution that embodies our core values.

At teamLab, I believe everyone shares a fundamental drive, a goal, and perhaps even something akin to a guiding principle: we strive for the highest quality. This commitment directs us at every juncture, and as one might imagine, our teams face countless decisions every day. In every situation or decision-making moment, one guiding principle should prevail: what will lead to the highest quality outcome?

In any creative endeavor, one of the most effective ways forward is by identifying the people around us who excel in the area we are working on—and once identified, seeking their advice. This approach is one of the best ways to elevate the quality of our work. However, as an organization grows and the number of members increases, the process becomes more complex. Those with the most experience, knowledge, and wisdom often become distanced from those who most need their guidance. This is what hierarchy tends to create: distance between people and barriers to communication, manifested in the layers one must navigate to reach those whose advice is most valuable.

Our goal is to maintain open access for everyone within the organization, allowing direct communication without the need to seek permission or navigate through intermediaries. This is the most efficient and effective way to operate. Traditional hierarchical systems often make this impossible. When communication passes through multiple layers, the information inevitably becomes diluted on both the way in and the way out. This is precisely what we want to avoid.

Over the years, as we have grown and evolved, we have developed our own methods for remaining free of rigid hierarchies. Everyone in teamLab is accessible to anyone else; none of us have secretaries or personal assistants who act as gatekeepers to arrange meetings. Furthermore, as we believe in and implement in our works and projects, space and digital technology have the power to influence the way people interact with one another. Therefore, we have designed our workspace to promote this mode of communication and collaboration.

It is always gratifying to see how over time new members adapt and integrate themselves into teamLab's unique flow of work and communication.

Afshar: One of teamLab's aims for digital art has been to explore relationships among people. Can you share more about how an immersive art experience can facilitate this concept?

Sakai: teamLab has been exploring new relationships with the world, particularly among people, through digital art. Our aim is to propose and create new values for humanity by expanding our understanding and perception of the world and those within it. While we might believe that we perceive everything around us, in reality, we are limited to seeing only what we are capable of perceiving. By expanding these perceptual boundaries, our visible world also grows, allowing us to see and interact with others in new ways.

Art and science have historically expanded our understanding of the world, and in the context of digital art, this expansion includes how we relate to one another. Humans understand the world through physical experiences, and immersive art provides a unique platform for such experiences. In traditional Japanese art, which is often spatial, viewers are invited to engage with the environment, as seen in different forms of art such as in fusuma paintings or Japanese traditional gardens. This influence is evident in teamLab's work, where we use a technique called "Ultra Subjective Space." This approach differs from Western perspective by immersing viewers in the artwork with their entire bodies, creating a shared experience that fosters a sense of connection among participants.

When experiencing teamLab's work, the boundaries between individuals and the artwork dissolve, allowing viewers to not only perceive the art but also to experience it alongside others. This shared immersion can create new relationships and values by bringing people together in a collective space where they interact with both the artwork and each other. With digital technology, this experience becomes even more profound, as it enables a level of interactivity and connection that transcends traditional boundaries. By including "others" within this immersive art world, we open up possibilities for discovering new relationships and deepening our understanding of how we relate to one another.

Afshar: What is your most memorable experience with teamLab?

Sakai: For me, it's not about one specific moment, but rather an accumulation of moments that share a strong, connecting narrative. These are a series of encounters where I witness the intersection between the general public and our work. Each instance is unique, shaped by the scale, location, and various other factors. Since so much of what we do revolves around how people interact with our creations, these moments hold significant meaning.

Certain milestones, where our work reaches new levels of public engagement, stand out as particularly memorable. In 2012, during our first major solo exhibition in Taiwan at the National Taiwan Museum of Fine Arts in Taichung, I vividly recall seeing a vast number of children and young people interacting with our work for the first time. Over the three-month duration of the exhibition, more than 500,000 visitors came to experience our art. This was likely our first encounter with such a large audience, and it was incredibly impactful and educational for us.

A couple of years later, in late 2014, we opened our first major solo exhibition in our hometown of Tokyo, at the Miraikan—The National Museum of Emerging Science and Innovation. This marked the first time hundreds of thousands of Japanese visitors engaged with our exhibition.

2018 was another landmark year, as we took a significant leap forward by opening two permanent museums in Tokyo: Borderless in Odaiba and Planets in Toyosu. I vividly remember the moment we recognized this as a major milestone. Since then, both before and after the challenges of COVID-19, we have been honored with the Guinness World Record for the most visited single-artist museum in the world.

These experiences are not only deeply rewarding, but they also serve as motivation to continue pushing the boundaries of our work. They remind us of the endless possibilities for creation and innovation, fueling our excitement for both the known and yet-to-be-discovered moments of future interaction.

CHAPTER 11

Geunbae "GB" Lee

Statsig

Geunbae Lee is the Head of Design at Statsig, a Bellevue-based feature flagging, experimentation, and analytics platform. Geunbae joined Statsig as the first hire after the founding members (employee #9) and became the first designer at the company. Now, Statsig is being used by many world-renowned companies and fast growing startups such as Figma, OpenAI, Microsoft, Notion, and more.

Prior to Statsig, Geunbae launched several products and features at Meta as a Senior Product Designer on the Ads and Gaming teams.

Jaleh Afshar: Let's learn a bit about your educational and professional journey. What were the milestones which influenced your trajectory?

Geunbae "GB" Lee: I started my college life at the University of Michigan. I got admitted as a Mechanical Engineering student, which is the degree that I applied for. Being Asian, being good at math and science—it was almost expected for me to go into engineering. I thought I would end up working at Ford or General Motors. But, as I made my way through school, I started to realize something. I didn't feel like I was in the right place. After two years of struggling through college, I had a GPA of 1.8. I didn't feel passionate about anything.

© Jaleh Afshar 2025
J. Afshar, *Chief Design Officers at Work*,
https://doi.org/10.1007/979-8-8688-1137-1_11

As a Korean, I had an obligation to go back to my country and serve in the army for two years. I left university to join the military, and during that time, I thought about my life and spent a lot of time discussing the meaning of life in general with many people older than me who were also in the military.

After my service period, I returned to college for my junior year. I had decided to switch my major to psychology. My mindset shifted to wanting to learn about human behavior, especially because I had personally gone through such a tough time.

My parents were worried about this change of major since their thought was, *what would someone with a psychology degree do after graduation?* Honestly, I was worried too, but I really wanted to try out something new. Because the first two years of my college studies as an engineering student didn't work out so well, I wanted to try out something that I'd be passionate about studying. I also thought that, naturally, if I regain my interest in learning, the GPA that I failed to maintain will slowly recover. I consequently did end up raising my GPA to a 3.2 at graduation.

However, my parents' fear came true when, sure enough, after graduation, I didn't immediately find work to do. I went back to Korea because I couldn't find a job, and was studying for an exam to go to law school.

Afshar: So during your early college years, you hadn't yet considered design as a career path.

Lee: That's right, but luck found a way! A professor I had from Michigan, Ram Mahalingam, coincidentally visited Korea to host a lecture, and he spoke about human computer interaction (HCI) and how his psychology students were getting into that field. We ended up catching up and going for Korean barbecue. He encouraged me to explore a user experience (UX) role. I still remember that night when I came home, for four or five hours, I was browsing on the web looking up what HCI really means. I found these job titles—UX researcher, UI designer... so I searched on LinkedIn the profiles of who were in these roles. I saw a lot of big tech names. And these people were getting these design roles from particular graduate programs at the time.

My mother was an artist, and I had some basic eye for design. However, the technical side—the coding, the design—was new to me. It intrigued me and I wanted to try it out. I wasn't immediately sure I would go into design, but I was very motivated to try my hand at learning these skills and tools. I was really hungry for it.

I was simultaneously studying for the Korean law school entrance exam, similar to the LSAT. It was a miserable experience, where the test was in Korean but I had spent much of my life abroad and the test prep was so hard for me. My heart wasn't in it. So I gave that up, and I had 3–4 months to prepare for applying to a design graduate program instead.

For those months, I slept at 4 a.m. every single night because I was up late trying to learn coding and teaching myself design. I was doing any and all design projects—designing icons, going to Dribbble, designing one-to-one something I saw as a technical challenge, and coming up with my own products. I coded my own website from scratch, built portfolio projects. This even landed me an internship at a small company prior to me getting into a degree program. They paid me probably $100 a month, basically working for free. I was hungry for the experience. Along with that, I would make random apps for my community and going to hackathons.

When it came time to submit graduate school applications, I applied to seven schools. I was accepted to all of them except Carnegie Mellon, and chose to enroll in Georgia Tech. In these applications, I wrote about my miserable failures in engineering and the self-taught momentum I had in design. I included my portfolio and was open about the fact that it was designed over just the last few months. These programs definitely look for established, proven candidates. But they also look for potential. That was my angle, someone who isn't polished yet but who would succeed with the right support. I showed them that I was ready to learn.

Afshar: You briefly mentioned an internship you were able to secure, even before your graduate schooling began. What skills did you learn from this internship?

Lee: The internship was interesting in that it was quite different from the type of career I ended up pursuing. It was a small startup and for my role, I was to create things such as table cards for restaurants, signage, and banners. However I ended up learning a lot of design basics, like typography, and terminology, like padding, margins, essentially visual design 101.

It was helpful to learn these skills in a graphic design environment. For example, I was given a physical menu design project. You get the text and logo, and from that you have to come up with a solid design by using the right fonts, visual elements, spacing, hierarchy and shadows, colors, et cetera. These foundational principles helped me grow my digital design skills as well.

I had a mentor there, Hyeun Ju Park, who coached me in these skills. She even gave me homework every day since she knew I wanted to learn more. For instance, she'd clip a newspaper page for me and say, hey, take the information from these columns and turn it into an improved layout. I'm grateful to say we are still friends!

Afshar: While in the midst of lots of skill building, you relocated quite a bit during your university and internship days. How was balancing your life across continents?

Lee: Yes, there was a lot of back and forth between Korea and the United States. The funny thing is my wife was studying law because her dad is a lawyer and her parents wanted her to follow the path. We got married right before I arrived in the United States for my graduate program. She sacrificed a lot to come with me to the States, and came on an F-2 visa. I didn't have a job, and she was pregnant a week into my first semester. I was so motivated to upgrade my skills and get a job as I had a growing family to support. I would listen to talks while also coding, trying my best to balance my time and go all in to finding work.

Around that time is when I applied to Facebook, and I was almost *immediately* rejected. I remember when I heard the news. I was crying…washing the dishes and crying. I promised my wife's parents that I would get into Facebook or Google to take care of the family. Those were the only tech companies her parents really knew in the States. I felt so bad about the rejection, like I was letting all of them down. My wife was so supportive and guess what, in the end, I was hired to work at Facebook eventually.

Afshar: Hearing these stories about your early years, "perseverance" seems to be a recurring theme.

Lee: Yes, and it still comes into play in my approach. Along with that, responsibility and accountability is also so important. Now, my wife and I have two kids, and that continues to motivate me to strive to be better every day.

Afshar: Could you share a bit about that Facebook role you landed?

Lee: When I was working at Facebook, I had a stint for two years on an ads measurement team working on split testing tools, essentially A/B testing tools for marketers. Now, while that is a bit different from what I do today, it did set me up with a strong design foundation and understanding of building technical tooling and business oriented tools.

When COVID hit, some of the colleagues who were most influential to me moved over to work in the gaming space. These online tournaments were getting even more attention, as people were staying home and playing games. I had the opportunity to work on these consumer products, and I was excited to try it out as my product design background had been mostly focused on B2B previously. This new role gave me the chance to also learn how to build a product from scratch. A true zero to one. It was a cool experience and the product launched globally. It was the first time I saw a design mockup I made in the press.

Afshar: Now you're heading up the design org at Statsig. You started as their first external, non-founder hire. What were the early days like at Statsig?

Lee: It was during my time in gaming where I met a leader named Vijaye Raji, who was the VP of Entertainment at the company. He was also the Seattle site lead which is the office I worked out of. I'd describe him as a leader with an excellent track record, who was extremely well respected and a kind leader.

Later on, Vijaye left to start Statsig. He was very successful with raising money with quality investors like Sequoia Capital, and he had a fleet of other established engineers and leaders who had already joined him as founding members. So, when I had the opportunity to join Statsig, I made the decision quickly, and in two weeks I was there.

For the first year, I was the lone designer. I was doing product design, the website, coming up with branding, anything that was needed. I love all that stuff.

The company's growth was solid and we started hiring more and more. We needed the expertise of more people on the team, so we began the search for product designers. I was looking for very senior designers who already had experience building tools for experimentation. Not only that, but people who would not just say yes to everything but are comfortable to debate, voice their own opinion, and would rapidly grow the design to the next level. The truth is that combination of skills are incredibly difficult to find! I've also found that many people with that kind of experience were already in excellent, high visibility roles in large companies.

Honestly this first recruiting search was a bit of a failure. We even had situations where offer letters were signed but the candidate withdrew at the last minute. It was also a tough time for many startups in general, economic-wise, as valuations were dropping across the board in the industry. I had to shift my strategy and instead I looked at how we could recruit people who would want to grow together with me. Candidates who were aligned on our approach but maybe didn't have the extensive experience in the exact sector yet, and who wanted to grow into confident designers in a fast-paced environment. That led to us hiring brand design support and new graduates for product design, who we were invested in coaching and growing.

Personally, even though technically I'm not one of the founders, just being such an early stage employee instilled a deep level of accountability. There is a real feeling that everything I do, everything I can learn, is directly contributing to the company's success. I am proud to say I took some good steps, but I also made mistakes and learned from them.

One aspect that's been an especially cool experience is seeing how company-wide affecting decisions are made, and being like a part of the decision-making process. I report directly to the CEO and I learn so much from him.

Afshar: How do you collaborate with the other C-level leaders at the company?

Lee: When I was first in this position, your question was one I posed to myself! How can I best work with the other leaders, how should my team and function be represented, and what's the approach my team and I should take in partnering with other executives? Because frankly, I didn't have the experience from my past jobs. I was really wondering what a good process was.

One ritual that our CEO initiated and has been going for over eight months is a weekly Wednesday dinner. All of us who report to the CEO, including our Heads of Sales, Marketing, Product Management, Engineering, Enterprise Engineering join this gathering. When we get together our talks are generally about the future of the company, product direction, how people are feeling, and also getting deep into business details like financials.

Those weekly dinners and the openness of the leadership team really influenced me. Some other rituals are Monday weekly goal setting, where we all get together and discuss how we are trending towards project milestones and quarterly goals.

I have particularly close partnerships with my fellow leads in Engineering and Product Management. Our dynamic is very close knit where we all have a team-playing role. We aim to operate as a unified trio when it comes to aligning on the product's vision and our respective teams' responsibilities. At an overarching business level, we are lucky in that we have a very clear target in mind for our product, so much of what we need to do is executing at a high quality. We have a clear roadmap established and we balance that with the existing customers' new feature requests and ad hoc tactical tasks coming in.

Afshar: What is design's role in the product development process?

Lee: We are fortunate to be known as a product that has polished UI as a market differentiator. It was important for our CEO to hire designers so early in a B2B SaaS company, which can be unconventional for typical businesses in our sector. User-facing quality was key to our early success.

Very early on, in beta mode, companies that were exploring our tool would frequently comment that, wow, the UI is really nice. And even investors were like, you guys have a really good looking and easy to use product. When you hear that from prospective customers and VCs, especially as a small company, leaders internally clearly see the value of design and appreciate the investment in it. This also inspired our early decision to build a design system to accelerate product development, allowing us to move much faster towards a cohesive user experience.

Afshar: When you have a creative block, how do you get inspired?

Lee: My work at Statsig has been extremely motivating. The product feels like my baby and I truly feel like part of the company. I owe a big chunk of that to the company culture. My motivation expands with how the company grows and seeing the ways customers end up using our products. Learning more about the other sides of a company too, like sales, partnerships, marketing, that's all so inspiring.

Of course, there are a lot of cool things happening in the tech world especially the new companies in B2B, B2C, all sorts of sectors. I like to go to TechCrunch or other outlets to see what other people are doing, what trends they are witnessing, and I try to stay updated. Even if those companies are not in the space that my company is in, I find it fascinating. I like to check in on my former colleagues from past roles and see what they're up to and the new companies they are joining. This way I discover products that maybe I wouldn't otherwise come across. And, of course, playing with AI tools like MidJourney and ChatGPT has been fun in my free time at home.

Afshar: As we wrap up, could you share the critical leadership skills a Head of Design must possess?

Lee: For a startup company in its earlier stages, a lot of respect for leadership really comes down to what results you directly influence. I mentioned earlier that I still stay close to the IC work, and this ensures I know our product in and out. Coaching other designers well really comes from that first-hand knowledge. Ability to unblock and give helpful feedback builds credibility and earns trust with your team, and naturally they will come to you not just for approval, but to ask for my early opinion and be part of the earliest discussion process when they have ideas.

Modeling this behavior also fosters a sense of ownership in the work for each individual designer, where they also feel pride in their responsibilities for their workstream pods. This is essential for a Head of Design, as there is so much work that needs to be overseen and much of that has to be delegated. Giving true responsibility and autonomy to people as a part of that delegation is effective. This can be achieved by openly talking to each person on the team about their passion areas and their personal goals for the future.

CHAPTER

12

Gianluca Brugnoli
TomTom

Gianluca Brugnoli is the Vice President of User Experience at TomTom, leading a team of over 60 designers and researchers. His past roles include Chief Digital Design Officer at Huawei Milan Aesthetic Research Center (MARC), Expert Associate Partner at McKinsey Digital, and Executive Director of User Experience at frog. Gianluca holds a PhD in Industrial Design from the Politecnico di Milano, where he additionally holds a Professor of User Experience and Research Associate role with areas of expertise spanning interaction design, service design, strategic design, and design thinking.

Jaleh Afshar: What were the significant career turning points that led you to your current role?

Gianluca Brugnoli: There have been many turning points in my career over the years, most of them tied to the people I have met and worked with. Two stand out as the most significant.

The first was when, as a young design student, I began using the Internet and web browsers. This was at the dawn of the World Wide Web revolution, and I learned to build my first websites by writing HTML with Notepad. So far nothing special; this is how many designers of my generation started their career. However, my first professional digital design jobs as a young freelancer were in the corporate sector, where I had to work on complex enterprise software applications. It was a very strong engineering environment, where every solution was driven by technology and nobody knew what user-centered design was. So, I had to quickly develop hard skills in UX, interaction design, interface design, and user research for business applications. At the same time, I learned how to navigate the complexities of working with business and technology stakeholders to get my solutions implemented. While many designers entered the digital field through creative multimedia, my entry point was through business software.

The second major turning point in my career was joining frog in Milan. frog really changed my life, not only on a professional level but also on a personal level. It's been a real privilege and a pleasure for me to meet and work with so many brilliant, creative, and driven people. Creativity flourishes when multidisciplinary teams come together blending diverse talents, perspectives, and backgrounds to tackle complex challenges. This highly collaborative and expert environment allowed us to deliver innovative and high-quality solutions across many different industries, while creating an open and empowering culture that has fostered personal growth for many of us. One of the most valuable lessons I've learned as a designer is to always surround yourself with bright minds and never stop learning from them.

There have been other important moments with clients and companies who have trusted me as a designer and manager, But these two experiences stand out as having had a profound impact on my professional journey.

Jaleh Afshar: You earned a PhD in Industrial Design from the Politecnico di Milano in Italy. How did your formal education prepare you for your career?

Brugnoli: My PhD years at Politecnico have been very important for me. During that time, I collaborated with a research team focused on service and strategic design. It was the early 1990s, and design was still largely centered around industrial design. However, our group was pioneering a new approach, integrating design with systemic thinking. We explored the concept of the "product as a system" which combines multiple tangible and intangible components, and outlined innovative design processes to address this complexity.

This point of view gave me a completely different and new perspective on the role of design, which shaped my mindset as a designer. I started to see design not just as a way to create objects but as a tool to tackle bigger and more complex business, technological, and social challenges. Even today, I still think of myself as a design strategist, a systemic thinker who bridges design and business. My approach to design has always centered on investigating and understanding the underlying business complexity of every design problem and exploring how design can create systemic impact on both businesses and people.

Afshar: You've had an impressive history in the design field, spanning over 30 years across notable companies and significant projects. How has your creative philosophy changed over the years?

Brugnoli: Design as a discipline and profession has come a long way in the last 30 years. I think what's fascinating is how design and business have really co-evolved. There's been a continuous transformation in business needs and strategies which required designers to step up and address these challenges in new and innovative ways. Thirty years ago, design was often seen as more of a support role, focusing mainly on aesthetics or usability. Certainly, we have seen design more and more becoming a strategic asset for many companies, helping to shape decisions and drive innovation far beyond what was its traditional scope back then.

Perhaps I am too optimistic, but over the years the most important changes I have seen are in the increasing scale and complexity of the impact of design. When companies shift their focus from competing with individual products to competing with integrated experiences, everything changes and design has to do a different job too. With the mobile revolution, digital has truly become a consumer experience for the masses, and digital technologies can become a consumer experience only through design. So, design has grown everywhere, is much more integrated into business processes and many companies now have in-house design teams. At last, design got a "seat at the table" (with all its pros and cons that are causing so much discussion in the design community). In general, some fundamental principles, such as user-centered design and service design, are now widely accepted and the idea that design has an impact on business success seems well established.

My work has definitely evolved with these shifts. Early in my career, I was more focused on individual products, but as things progressed, I found myself dealing with much more complex digital ecosystems. I went from traditional product design to using design as a tool to shape entire business processes and tackle complex problems. I've moved from execution to research, and that's allowed me to develop innovative concepts and visions for new consumer experiences.

In general, however, at the core, my design philosophy has not changed much. My primary focus has always been on how to keep my team and myself relevant to the company and the teams we work with, making a positive impact and creating customer experiences we can be proud of. Keeping the design team engaged, in charge, and successful. Understanding and influencing business priorities and product roadmaps with design insights and visions. What has evolved significantly is the business context and how these outcomes are achieved. The approach varies constantly from project to project and product to product.

There are always many external factors at play that you can't control, so you have to stay adaptable. This is a critical point for me: you must continuously learn and adjust, keeping up with the major trends and directions of the industry while navigating the evolving business needs and strategies of the organization you work for.

Currently, we're in a difficult phase for design. The business environment is harder than it was just a few years ago. UX is getting commoditized and with the increasing overlap with product management, many in-house design teams are struggling to demonstrate their business value within their organizations. Staying relevant and optimistic isn't easy right now, but I believe this is just one of the many phases in our industry, and it will pass soon.

Afshar: You have worked for clients and companies spanning vastly different geographic locations throughout your career. Can you describe any significant cultural or regional differences you've encountered in your design work?

Brugnoli: China is definitely one of the most interesting digital markets today. It's very dynamic, fast, and highly receptive to innovation.

From the consumer experience point of view, Chinese consumers see technology as part of a premium and luxury experience, and value high quality design and well-crafted digital experiences that offer convenience, personalization, and exclusivity. Brands are not just individual products or services: they are often seen as integrated ecosystems that seamlessly combine multiple products, features, and needs into a single platform. The Chinese super apps are a very good example.

Looking at the automotive industry, for example, Chinese brands are setting new standards for the in-car user experience. Rather than relying on numerous suppliers to deliver separate software components that are then assembled in the dashboard, Chinese automakers are approaching the car experience as a fully integrated system.

This reminds me of the period before the iPhone launch, when many mobile phone brands were struggling to develop their own operating systems for their smartphones. The result was a fragmented landscape of incompatible and proprietary platforms with poor user experiences. Then Apple introduced a fully integrated system, where hardware and software were designed to work together seamlessly, and ended up dominating the market and setting new standards for consumers. I feel like we're going through a similar phase in the automotive industry today, and it's fascinating.

I don't think it's a coincidence that many Chinese car brands are building their intelligent cockpit experience starting with smartphone operating systems, ensuring that many native smartphone features work seamlessly in the car. The success of the Xiaomi car, for example, highlights this approach of treating the technology as a cohesive system, where everything—digital and physical—is seamlessly connected. This integration is driving innovation and shaping the future of the in-car user experience of the automotive industry.

From a business perspective, the Chinese market is very competitive, characterized by rapid development cycles and continuous product iteration. Companies rely on real-time user feedback to refine and improve their offerings quickly. This approach enables businesses to stay ahead in an environment where consumer expectations are constantly evolving. In industries such as automotive, China is not just participating in the competition, it's setting new standards and leading the way globally.

Afshar: What creative accomplishments are you most proud of?

Brugnoli: There are many projects and products that I am proud of. In general, I like those where we were able to redefine business priorities and strategies using research insights and a design vision based on customer journeys.

Probably the most important and impactful accomplishment of my career was the digital transformation of the Italian national postal service. It was a large-scale program with multiple projects and tracks aimed at modernizing a set of public services used every day by millions of people across the country. We are talking about ordinary people with very practical needs, far away from the typical early adopter tech savvy consumer profile with the latest smartphone in their pocket. It was a big responsibility, but also an incredibly rewarding professional experience, because it was an innovation program in which design played a strategic role in creating new and simpler digital touchpoints for everyone to interact with such a large and complex public service platform.

Another accomplishment I often mention, also in my lessons, is a project for a leading consumer electronics retailer. Our task was to design the user experience for in-store digital kiosks. The goal was to make it possible for customers to get product details independently, taking some of the pressure off the shop assistants. So, the company already had a solution in mind, and if you are a designer, you know this happens regularly. But after a thorough analysis based on in-depth user research into how people actually shop in the physical stores, we realized that the best solution wasn't a digital interface. We found that the primary touchpoints for customers seeking information were actually the paper price labels displayed on the shelves and products. So, instead of focusing on a digital kiosk, we completely redesigned the paper price labels, making them much clearer to read and more informative. It was a bit unexpected; we were supposed to design a digital interface, and instead, we developed a pretty complex graphic design system to generate millions of paper price labels. I love this story because it shows just how powerful design can be when you question assumptions and really listen to the needs of your users. That's one of the real superpowers of design.

Every project has its own lessons. I recall many challenges, not just for the outcome, but for what we learned along the way. Sometimes we tackled a new set of problems, or experimented with a new technique, tool, or process. Or we simply remember the positive energy of the team or the engaging collaboration with business stakeholders. Of course, I also have a long list of failed projects and activities that were never implemented, from which we learned a lot.

Afshar: What are examples of timeless design principles?

Brugnoli: The most important design principle comes from user-centered design: understanding who the people you are designing for are and what their experience is like. Without these insights, it's hard to make a positive and meaningful impact with design. As designers, we solve problems by understanding the human experience and how to improve it. This is the fundamental core expertise of a designer; it's how we create value and achieve strategic impact. And it's what makes a designer different from other roles and functions in the team and in the organization. Without user-centricity there is no design.

Another principle is simplicity. It's such a universal problem for designers: it's the first business requirement of any project and the most common feedback from users. For me, it goes beyond the idea of "less is more." I believe that true simplicity is about "clarity": making interactions and tasks easy to identify, understand, and access with confidence. Our guiding design principle shouldn't just be "make it simple." It should be "make it clear." Achieving clarity is challenging because it requires reducing complexity while preserving meaning. It is not just about minimizing visual elements (which can lead to hiding content) but about designing interactions that users can easily understand and use effectively. This is why true simplicity is so hard to achieve.

A third principle is that design creates value to organizations when it cooperates with other functions and disciplines. The value of design is not created by design alone. As designers, we aim to go beyond the surface, creating solutions and experiences that influence user behavior and drive business success. And in doing so, we aim not just to execute someone else's decisions but to be involved in and influence the processes that lead to those decisions. The good news is that design can create value in many ways: by fostering a user-centered culture within the organization, providing strategic insights into users and their experiences, improving both the product experience and the processes for developing it, supporting delivery and product roadmaps, and collecting continuous user feedback to improve the product. In any case, the value is created through cross-functional collaboration, when designers work closely with product managers and engineers, stepping outside the comfort of the "design zone," to align on priorities and goals, and breaking down communication barriers. Otherwise, our contribution gets watered down or relegated to aesthetics or decoration. This cross-disciplinary cooperation can be challenging for many designers, but it's definitely a necessary skill for design leaders.

CHAPTER 13

Helena Seo
DoorDash

Helena Seo is the Head of Design at DoorDash, a publicly traded company that operates the largest food delivery platform in the United States. Helena's design organization oversees multiple UX functions, including Product Design, Design Systems, Research, Content Strategy, and Operations. Headquartered in the Bay Area, DoorDash's design team spans offices in San Francisco, Seattle, and New York.

Previously, Helena has worked in design roles across eBay, Citrix, Groupon, and more.

Afshar: It seems like you've had a longstanding interest in design, even starting academically from your very first degree in fashion design and merchandising. How did you go about formalizing your interest in design through education?

Helena Seo: My mom was an artist and my dad was an engineer. Growing up in a household where creativity and precision coexisted, I was that kid constantly sketching and building things. I can't recall a day without some form of drawing and making happening in my life. My parents instilled in me a deep appreciation for craftsmanship and skill. When asked about my dream job, my answers always revolved around art and design in my childhood: a painter, an architect, a greeting card or packaging designer, and more. So, when it came to considering college, the world of design was a natural choice.

For my first bachelor's degree, I studied Fashion Design in South Korea, where I discovered the joy of creating for people, using textiles and clothing as a medium. Design not only fueled my creativity but also held the potential to impact lives on a grand scale. However, the deeper I delved into the fashion industry, the more I realized that it might not offer me sustainability as a career. That led me to pursue Graphic Design at the California College of the Arts in San Francisco, formerly the California College of Arts and Crafts. In the realm of Graphic Design, it felt like finding my element. Everything about it resonated with me—extreme attention to detail, the artistic sensibility, the pursuit of aesthetics, and, most importantly, the thrill of solving design problems. Whether it involved a client's business objectives, communication strategies, or enhancing usability, Graphic Design felt like diving into a world of endless possibilities that could truly leverage my strengths and interests.

Afshar: Reminiscing back to the early days of your career—what were the initial steps you took after completing your education to land your first design job?

Seo: Around the time I was finishing up my second degree in Graphic Design at CCA, I attended Portfolio Day in school and had the chance to meet several future hiring managers and portfolio reviewers from different companies. I still remember how I prepared for the review that day—my school projects were carefully mounted on black artboards with meticulous spray-gluing, and I used to carry a large and heavy black portfolio bag. Not many designers carried a laptop or had an online portfolio website then. It's pretty mind-boggling to think about how much more analog design used to be back then—both what we designed and how the design was presented.

Each reviewer at the Portfolio Day offered priceless feedback and advice on my portfolio, and I was scheduled with multiple different reviewers throughout the day. One of them was Gordon Mortensen, who not only provided guidance but also eventually invited me for an interview at his studio. That meeting turned into my first full-time job at Mortensen Design, a small boutique brand design studio. During my time there, I got to collaborate with a small group of talented designers and practice graphic design in all ranges of projects, from logos and print collaterals to large-scale signages. I'll never forget the adrenaline rush of the early morning press checks, surrounded by the scent of ink and paper, as well as the loud noise from the large industrial press machines. Being a part of a small brand studio, I also learned to wear many different hats and be scrappy and resourceful.

Afshar: Pursuing a creative career can sometimes require balancing passion and practicality. How did you navigate this balance in the start of your professional journey?

Seo: I've always been an extremely pragmatic person, so balancing passion and practicality has never been much of a real challenge for me. In fact, what I loved about product design was that it always had to solve human problems with some constraints vs. being pure creative expression. There's always a customer problem that gives you a good starting point, and there are always methodical ways to validate the design decisions.

There were some other areas that I needed to learn to balance, and some of them happened during some pivotal moments in my career:

First, transitioning from a graphic designer to a product designer. Graphic design and product design both tackle human issues, yet their methodologies for addressing problems and validating solutions diverge.

While graphic design primarily focuses on establishing an intuitive information hierarchy and aesthetic taste within a confined page/surface, product design operates within a more expansive, multi-dimensional, and experiential realm. In product design, emphasis is placed on conceptualizing designs within a flow and contextual framework, considering various situations.

Furthermore, unlike graphic design, where design becomes permanent once the ink settles on paper, product design is an iterative process that dynamically integrates user feedback and evolves over time. Data emerges as a crucial indicator for your product's success, particularly in marketplace product designs. Having the graphic design background tremendously helped me apply the best visual design practice and general design sensibility on digital product.

Second, transitioning from agency to in-house. Following graduation with a BFA in Graphic Design, I dedicated my first ten years to the dynamic realm of design agencies, from working at smaller boutique agencies to establishing my own studio.

Transitioning into the tech industry marked a pivotal shift when I joined eBay's in-house team after a decade of client-service endeavors. Adapting wasn't seamless to say the least. I faced a learning curve in discerning the balance between incorporating others' feedback and asserting my convictions while aligning goals with cross-functional teams.

It wasn't merely about presenting multiple options for cross-functional leaders to pick from; I had to explore all alternatives while maintaining a clear perspective on the recommended direction. It took time to develop my distinct viewpoint and build the confidence to lead decisively. It required a major pivot from a people-pleaser mindset.

Next, transitioning from an IC to a manager. As a first-time people manager, my initial error was micromanaging. Believing that achieving a finely crafted product meant overseeing every pixel my team produced, I inadvertently led them to focus solely on details, neglecting the broader perspective.

Realizing this shortfall, in the next manager role, I swung too far in the opposite direction, distancing myself to avoid micromanagement. However, this left me without a deep understanding of my team's work, hindering my ability to effectively represent or defend their efforts.

Over time, I've learned to strike a balance: zooming in enough to contribute to product innovation while also zooming out to grant creative autonomy to the team. Mastering this balance remains an ongoing and lifelong journey for me.

Finally, transitioning from a Design Director to a Head of Design. As a design director focusing on a specific product charter, my priorities used to organically align well with my cross-functional counterparts, and I had a very clear "first team" with my cross-functional partners. However, stepping into the role of Head of Design brought a new level of latitude and autonomy. The breadth of responsibilities widely ranges from overseeing team operations, recruitment, and stakeholder relationships to engaging in design thinking and driving product strategy/development.

My intuition and principles play a big role in determining my priorities, and my success hinges on adaptability to evolving business needs. I tend to adhere to a 30/30/40 rule: allocating a minimum of 30% of my time to people management and team operations, another 30% to product development and design strategy at any given time—both aspects are critical and non-neglectable. The remaining 40% remains flexible, tailored to address evolving business demands. For example, during performance review season, my focus shifts toward team calibrations and fostering the team's career development. In critical product phases, I immerse myself in design sprints, user testing, and product reviews. Toward year-end, I collaborate extensively with our Finance partners to align headcount and departmental budget strategy with the company's forthcoming goals. Being a functional leader comes with its own unique challenges, which I elaborated in other sections below.

Afshar: Reflecting on the early stages of your management career, how did you cultivate and refine your leadership skills? Were there specific experiences or resources that proved especially beneficial?

Seo: Stepping into management, I sought wisdom from external sources like books, articles, and conferences, which provided a solid theoretical framework. However, the most impactful lessons for me came from lived experiences—both by my own experience of managing teams and observing how my managers manage. Learning from mistakes and successes was invaluable, and it helped me form guiding principles as follows:

- **Managers need to create an environment where everyone can be authentically themselves.** Encouraging authenticity allows individuals to express their true selves without the pressure to conform to a specific "culture fit," which often steers energy in unproductive directions. I firmly believe that when people feel accepted for who they are, rather than being compelled to act in a certain way, their performance excels. In DoorDash Design, we've deliberately phased out the term "culture fit" from our interview evaluation criteria for this very reason. Instead, our focus is on discovering the distinctive value and perspective that each candidate can contribute to our culture. One of the highlights at our monthly all-hands meetings in the Design team is featuring a speaker within the team sharing their unique skills, experience or background. This emphasis on individuality fosters a culture of vulnerability and open-mindedness, allowing everyone to shine in their own unique way.

- **Managers must constantly seek opportunities that will challenge and excite the team.** Good managers ensure efficient execution today, but great ones unlock larger possibilities for tomorrow. I've been fortunate to have managers who understood my strengths and growth areas better than I did myself. Their guidance propelled me in the right direction and catalyzed leaps in my career. It's important to train managers to stretch the team's thinking and grow their potential 1% better every day.

- **Setting the right tone means leading by example—reflecting the team's ethos through actions.** Transparency, maintaining positivity in tough times, offering constructive feedback, and fostering inclusive meetings are foundational. I can't expect my team to do things I wouldn't stand for myself. This is actually one of the most critical responsibilities as a Head of Design. I can't direct every single decision on the product, but it's my role to set the right tone and principles that the cross-functional team can rally behind.

- **Taking ownership of the team's outcomes, both positive and negative, defines genuine leadership.** It's easy to praise the team when things go well, but it takes courage for leaders to admit faults and mistakes. Fostering trust within the team involves acknowledging failures without placing blame. These actions constitute the most significant distinctions between a healthy culture and a toxic one.

- **Leaders must make the right hires despite pressure to fill roles swiftly.** Resisting the urge to compromise on quality for speed is pivotal in hiring; one wrong hire can disrupt an otherwise exceptional team. Hiring demands a significant portion of my time and effort because a stellar team forms the backbone of a thriving ecosystem. A great team elevates individual capabilities, leading to superior work, ultimately driving user satisfaction and company success.

Afshar: How do you navigate the tensions which may arise between different departments, disciplines, or business units?

Seo: Navigating various problem-solving methods involves collaborating with individuals of various personalities and interests. To maintain a consistent and disciplined approach amid this diversity, I consistently rely on the first-principles approach. This method centers decision-making on what serves customers' long-term needs rather than short-term gains and thinks through what works best for the company as a whole rather than specific individuals. Prioritizing the company's interests ensures a decision-making process that's hard to challenge.

Another effective tactic involves proactively aligning collective goals with stakeholder interests. Conflict often arises due to misalignment within the team regarding the mission and objectives rather than malicious intent. Continuously realigning goals reinforces the understanding that everyone shares a common purpose, fostering unity across various departments and partnerships. As a Head of Design, although my reports own the direct relationship with their respective counterparts in PM and Engineering, I still hold regular one-on-ones with those counterparts for the pulse checks on health of the collaboration and recalibrate on the overarching goals.

Furthermore, when disagreements persist regarding product solutions, showcasing potential alternatives through design can swiftly resolve the issue. Sometimes seeing is believing, and that's where Design can leverage our superpower. Design exploration allows for testing with users, either through user testing for qualitative feedback or AB testing for quantitative data. Ultimately, the customer's voice remains the most influential factor in guiding decisions.

Afshar: You recently published an essay, entitled *Untold Narrative as a Head of Design*, where you addressed how executive roles can be isolating, and struggles of openly discussing those feelings of loneliness in a leadership role. Can you share with our readers your philosophies on how one can embrace their imperfections and build connections?

Seo: Acknowledging your imperfections begins with recognizing your humanity. It's important to begin with humility, honesty, and self-empathy, understanding that no leader can achieve perfection, possess all the right solutions, or garner universal approval. Similar to how we encourage our team members, embracing your own vulnerability by seeking assistance and guidance when necessary is not only acceptable but also commendable. As someone trained to be a perfectionist in many years of design education, it took me some time to grasp this concept. From my journey, I've learned that teams relate better with me as a leader when I occasionally reveal vulnerability, and in return, we can nurture deeper connections and rapport in the teamwork. Establishing connections can unfold across various dimensions: downward, upward, sideways, and outward.

- **Downward:** As you climb the professional ladder, the idea is that your "first team" should become more cross-functional. However, it gets tricky when you're leading different functions, each with its own unique problems and goals that don't always overlap. In such scenarios, seeking guidance within your team becomes crucial. Luckily, I've built a strong design leadership team that I work closely with to handle challenges and come up with solutions in DoorDash. Having a trusted group that speaks the same language is like having a dependable sounding board.

- **Upward:** We might forget that even our leaders go through their career journeys feeling alone at times. I regularly make an effort to connect with my manager, aiming for a partnership where we have common priorities and principles. Understanding their basic human need for support, recognition, and someone to bounce ideas off of strengthens our relationship. Building this partnership is incredibly helpful in dealing with professional isolation and presenting a united front.

- **Sideways:** Talking to other exec leaders or cross-functional leads in various roles, I've noticed a common theme: the feeling of being alone is not unique to design leaders. It comes up in conversations, no matter the size or how long a team has been around. Many leaders share that they get limited guidance from higher-ups because they are seen as the top experts in their areas.

- **Outward:** Talking to other Heads of Design from different companies, I discovered a common feeling: although many companies acknowledge the importance of design, not many have fully unlocked its transformative power. Many design leaders are still struggling to find their way and are working toward establishing a meaningful presence within their organizations. Knowing we were

> on a similar journey eased the feeling of being alone. Sharing insights, experiences, and tips, and expanding my network turned out to be really helpful.

Addressing the isolation that often accompanies leadership involves several strategies. Starting with self-empathy and seeking support internally and externally, forging connections with other leaders, embracing a mindset of ownership, viewing failure as a growth opportunity, and nurturing authenticity can significantly mitigate these challenges. By adopting these approaches, we can overcome isolation and flourish as impactful leaders.

Afshar: If I may get a bit personal here, I'd love to learn about your experience as an immigrant who is now working as an executive in Silicon Valley. A few years ago, you had written an essay on *Becoming a Leader as a First-Generation Immigrant*, where you touched upon how this shaped your professional life. Could you share some of those challenges and takeaways with our readers?

Seo: Leadership as a first-generation immigrant resonates deeply with me, having navigated this journey over the past two decades in the United States. Despite the corporate emphasis on diversity and inclusion, being the lone female exec in many tech industry rooms remains a common occurrence. Additionally, I often find myself as the sole first-generation immigrant who learned English as a second language. Reflecting on my experiences, I hope my story inspires future leaders.

In 1999, I arrived in San Francisco from Korea with just one piece of luggage when I was admitted to the California College of the Arts (CCA). While this may sound like the quintessential American dream, my journey wasn't all smooth sailing. Overcoming the language barrier proved far more challenging than anticipated. Grammar differences and learning unfamiliar idioms and expressions from scratch made me constantly self-conscious about my communication ability.

The cultural adjustment posed an even greater hurdle. In Korea, I was taught to read between the lines, to listen more than express. Showing opinions or emotions outwardly was often frowned upon because that was considered as rebellious, impatient, obnoxious, or standoffish. When I pursued Design at CCA, my innate obedience clashed with the expectation of active participation in class, preventing me from getting an A grade despite the superior design output. Feeling guilty for my silence, I struggled to adapt.

Numerous moments tempted me to return to Korea, where blending in with similar backgrounds and language would have made my life so much more comfortable and easier. However, I chose to persist in the United States, determined not to give in. Twenty-five years later, I'm grateful to myself for persevering through those unique challenges that shaped who I am today. These experiences also significantly influenced my leadership style that is distinguished from other native leaders.

My persistent worry about being misunderstood and the recognition that relying on subtle cues or assumptions wasn't viable turned me into an over-communicator and a candid individual. I strive to be an open and transparent leader rather than a mysterious enigma. I firmly believe that proactive communication and straightforwardness expedite alignment among people and reduce unnecessary speculation. Ensuring my team stays informed is crucial to facilitate their decision-making, preventing any bottleneck in access to critical information.

As English is my second language, I've come to accept that I would never be as eloquent or inspiring in my words as native speakers. Embracing this reality has shaped me into someone inclined toward action—a doer. I find myself less engaged in meetings centered on endless philosophical discussions that lack tangible progress. My satisfaction thrives in actively tackling problems and propelling forward momentum. I have a strong affinity for collaborating with the individuals who share this proactive mindset, capable of achieving remarkable outcomes swiftly and efficiently. This inclination toward execution makes me feel most impactful in situations where tangible action and implementation are paramount.

The poignant memory of feeling misunderstood emphasized the significance of fostering an authentic environment where everyone feels valued for who they truly are. This encompasses honoring diverse backgrounds, traits, perspectives, strengths, and weaknesses. True excellence and productivity emerge when individuals can embrace their genuine selves. A culture steeped in pretense and insincerity breeds toxicity, diverting focus from the quality of work. I always want to cultivate an open, truthful, and transparent culture where individuals feel secure to make mistakes, openly share experiences, and engage in mutual learning.

Having once been the quiet individual observing from the sidelines, it's become a personal mission for me to ensure inclusivity in every room. I thrive on leading discussions where every voice, whether introverted or extroverted, feels heard and contributes meaningfully to our shared goals. The goal isn't about including everyone in every meeting or soliciting opinions from all, but rather about thoughtful and intentional meeting "design"—considering factors like location, timing, duration, agenda, and attendees. Even small gestures such as sharing the agenda beforehand and summarizing meeting outcomes afterward contribute to a more inclusive and engaging atmosphere. Before scheduling any meeting, I envision its dynamics and potential outcomes.

I also consider the tone of the discussion, anticipate who might dominate the conversation, and identify those who might feel less engaged. Some might view this as overly calculated, but I view it as a fundamental level of preparation essential for empathetic leadership.

Based on what I've learned, I want readers to understand that what might appear as a weakness can become your remarkable strength. Your individuality holds incredible power—uniqueness is your magic.

Afshar: You wrote about the Korean concept of "noon-chi," and the skill of reading between the lines and acting accordingly. How did this virtue shape the way you approach management, and your value for emotional intelligence?

Seo: In Korean, there exists a concept known as "noon-chi." Finding an exact English equivalent is nearly impossible, but the closest translation is likely "tact." It embodies the skill of deciphering implicit messages and sensibly navigating situations based on a perceptive understanding. It's a virtue deeply ingrained in me from my upbringing in Korea—a sixth sense that allows one to grasp emotional cues and connect with others. When combined with empathy, authenticity, and self-awareness, it fosters high emotional intelligence, enabling effective team leadership.

Emotional intelligence isn't an elusive quality reserved for select leaders and managers; it's a trait we should seek in every potential hire, who will eventually become our future leaders. During interviews, I keenly observe various aspects of each candidate: How do they respectfully engage with team members? Are they self-aware? Do their aspirations align with our objectives? Can they empathize and understand others' perspectives? Even seemingly small gestures, such as adjusting their laptop screen for others to view their presentations, speak volumes about their consideration and adaptability.

Afshar: There were moments when you considered returning to your birth country of Korea, but you chose to stay in the United States. What motivated you to persist despite the trials, and what advice would you give to others facing similar dilemmas?

Seo: Simply put, I refused to succumb to disappointment, both for myself and those around me. I was resolute in sharpening my ability to conquer challenges, ensuring no lingering regrets. Reflecting two decades later, I deeply appreciate persevering through those demanding yet priceless moments that sculpted who I am today. Living abroad opened my eyes to cherish aspects of life I wouldn't have otherwise embraced, and I aspire to inspire those navigating a similar journey.

Firstly, be compassionate with yourself and embrace forgiveness. Dwelling excessively on mistakes serves little purpose. Instead, focus on learning from them and evolving for the future. People usually don't fixate on your missteps as much as you might believe—it often looms larger in your mind than theirs.

Secondly, shape your career path with purpose. What propelled my journey might not mirror yours; everyone's path is distinct. Success doesn't have a universal definition; it's rather personal. Prioritize your contentment over conforming to industry norms. Tailor your career trajectory to align with your unique strengths and aspirations. Self-awareness and tenacity will illuminate this path.

Lastly, once you've set your sights on a goal, give it your all. There's no substitute for dedicated effort. I resonate with Conan O'Brien's mantra: "Work hard, be kind, and amazing things will happen."

Afshar: Over the years you've been at DoorDash, you've grown to now be at the very top of the design executive structure. How do you continue to actively seek feedback on your own leadership approach and performance?

Seo: Given the breadth of my responsibilities reaches as broadly as the entire product suite, I proactively set my goals and success criteria at the outset of each quarter so my quarterly focus is clear. This approach, known as iOKR (Individual Objectives and Key Results), offers a concise way to assess achievements and areas for improvement regularly. Sharing my iOKR with my org and leadership has been a great way to align our priorities and visibly communicate my focus within the organization. At the end of the quarter, I also take some time to reflect and self-assess my performance based on the iOKR.

My personal success aligns closely with the happiness and satisfaction of my team. At DoorDash, we conduct an employee engagement survey quarterly, gauging the team's sentiments about their career growth, cross-functional collaboration, work efficiency, sustainability, and their intent to stay. I invest significant time in analyzing the results, extracting actionable insights, and communicating our plan to the team. Demonstrating that leadership takes feedback seriously and is committed to enhancing culture, and well-being is vital for employee morale.

In terms of how I solicit feedback on my leadership approach and performance, I maintain an open-door policy, encouraging real-time, unfiltered input from everyone around me. One should never wait until the performance review season to provide feedback; instead, I try to foster a psychologically safe space where honest feedback is valued as a gift. I believe feedback can come from any direction—superiors, peers, and subordinates—accelerating personal growth when embraced with an open mind and a willingness to learn. I'd expect a similar mindset from my team, peers, and leadership.

Afshar: How did the IPO impact the company's design culture? Were there steps you had to take to preserve or evolve the aspects that contributed to the company's success?

Seo: I recall the exhilarating morning of our IPO day in December 2020 vividly. Rising at 5 a.m. for the IPO bell ceremony at the NYSE, the celebration took place virtually due to the COVID-19 spike at that time. I could feel the true sense of big accomplishment, and the team enjoyed the festive moment.

By that same afternoon though, we swiftly resumed our regular business operations. Our leadership consistently emphasizes that an IPO signifies the start of our long journey rather than the culmination. They stress the importance of remaining humble and sustaining our hunger for progress.

I believe DoorDash's success recipe comprises four crucial elements: (1) unwavering dedication to customers; (2) swift action and decisiveness; (3) ambition and taking ownership; and (4) upholding optimism and resilience. Having been part of the company for over five years, these principles have remained constant, if not strengthened, as the company expanded further. I consider myself incredibly fortunate to be a part of this inspiring journey, especially having the privilege of experiencing milestones as honorable as the IPO.

Afshar: DoorDash has many types of users—Dashers who deliver the food, the merchants making up the restaurant partnerships, customers placing orders, and more. How do you balance evolving the design and adding new features to stay competitive in the industry, while ensuring stability and reliability for your users?

Seo: The ever-evolving landscape of DoorDash's three-sided marketplace presents an ideal playing field for user experience designers. It's a realm teeming with intricate human challenges—complex and often ambiguous. Frequently, these issues interconnect across diverse user groups, creating a web of complexities. Take, for instance, the seemingly simple task of ensuring one flawless food delivery; it demands impeccable coordination from all sides of the audience. Consumers must provide accurate delivery information, restaurants need to prepare and package orders efficiently, Dashers (drivers) must ensure timely pickups and drop-offs, and DoorDash orchestrates seamless logistics behind the scenes. Amid this multifaceted process, the probability of human errors looms large. Yet, despite these odds, DoorDash has sustained remarkable growth, cementing its position as an industry leader for many years.

What is our competitive edge and secret for the success of the product? It's deceptively simple yet exceptionally challenging to achieve—the unwavering commitment to our customers. At DoorDash, one of our core values is being "Customer-obsessed, not competitor focused." We firmly believe that by addressing our customers' needs, long-term business success naturally follows. We eschew chasing fleeting trends solely because competitors do so. Every new product introduction undergoes rigorous operational vetting, extensive gathering of insights, and A/B testing to bolster our confidence in its direction. Moreover, we meticulously ensure that each new feature seamlessly integrates into the overall product experience, contributing gracefully to our platform's cohesion. Emphasizing scalability allows us to embed predictability into our user experience over time, steering clear of makeshift and arbitrary solutions.

Afshar: Something else I'd like to touch upon is that, at DoorDash, you didn't come in initially as Head of Design—you built a team. Building a team is not just about hiring; it's also about developing talent. How did you approach mentorship and skill development to facilitate successful team growth?

Seo: You're absolutely right; team building isn't simply about expanding with more people and hoping for magic to happen. It requires intentional, strategic growth of the team as a whole.

When I joined the DoorDash design team in January 2019, we were a mere nine-person crew, myself included. The team was small and family-like, and there was a lot of trust and support in the culture, which I was determined to preserve no matter how big the team would become in the future. One of the perks of being among the founding members was the boundless autonomy to shape everything from scratch—from org structure, recruiting bar and process, team's culture principles, review processes, collaboration models, and product quality/craft bar.

A big part of my job was to establish the explicit structure to align everyone's expectation about what growth means in DoorDash Design, and empower them to grow in the most tailored way. One of the first tasks at hand was to define the career ladder and compensation band for the Design team, which gave us a good foundation for hiring candidates, performance reviews, and career growth conversations with the team. As our team evolved, we also focused on nurturing talent from within. We introduced initiatives like internal mobility within DoorDash Design and guidelines for transitioning from individual contributor roles to managerial positions. Our aim was to create the best possible career opportunities within DoorDash, ensuring growth possibilities across all dimensions. We also created multiple venues to learn from each other via org-wide mentorship programs as well as skill-sharing sessions. The company also invests in top talent with a Learning and Development budget for external conferences, classes, and various coaching programs.

I strongly advocate for the development of leaders who can foster greatness in others. Currently, I serve as the executive sponsor for DoorDash's Product-org-wide mentorship program. In this capacity, I oversee the program alongside the committee, providing guidance on best practices to mentors and mentees. My responsibilities also include matching mentees with mentors whose skills and interests align. This initiative has proven to be highly effective in facilitating mutual learning within the team and fostering strong connections. Especially when pairs are formed across different functions, it opens up avenues for developing empathy across various disciplines.

Another part of the team's development was through leading by example. I believe observing how other leaders solve problems is the most effective way to learn. I had to be the role model for setting a high bar in everything we do, from hiring, evaluating talents, carrying culture to quality of every product we ship. It was important to set the tone with the right principles in place, especially as we scaled fast.

Afshar: How do you approach developing a strong leadership bench and succession planning? What key qualities do you seek in potential leaders rising within your organization?

Seo: Developing a robust leadership bench is one of the priorities that consumes much of my focus and time. I often emphasize that we must hire leaders that we will all report to someday. These individuals should bring unique strengths to the table, something they excel in compared to our current team, allowing us to learn from their expertise and elevate the organizational standards.

While every company values distinct skills and attributes, certain qualities stand out for success within DoorDash. Firstly, the ability to delve into intricate details is crucial. We don't view a manager's role merely as overseeing people; they need to have a strong point of view in product strategy and lead with a clear vision. When a leader operates with only a 10,000-foot view and is not able to get to the lowest level of detail and innovation, they will more likely not succeed in DoorDash.

Moreover, we seek pragmatic, action-oriented leaders who tackle problems efficiently and lead with optimism. Many of our customers truly rely on the DoorDash platform—whether it's a sick parent who needs to feed their family at home, a restaurant owner who needs to stay in business, or a gig worker who leverages our app to make some extra money. Addressing these critical mission-driven human problems demands a sense of urgency, unwavering resilience, and strong commitment from the team.

Lastly, our culture strongly emphasizes a "company-first" mindset—embracing the ethos of "one team, one fight." Effective leaders represent not just their immediate teams but also the entire organization, and it's especially true at the exec level. Selflessness is a celebrated trait within our ranks.

Afshar: How do you strike the balance of giving your direct reports creative freedom while still providing guidance and direction?

Seo: My fundamental principle is to recruit self-sufficient individuals and empower them with the autonomy they deserve. My job should focus on developing high-level strategic direction and growing the leadership bench by helping them continue to expand their horizons. It serves no purpose to enlist seasoned and capable talent only to dictate their every move, as exceptional individuals are averse to micromanagement.

However, effective leaders should possess the agility to delve into intricate details when the situation demands. Immersing oneself at the most minute level is often imperative for achieving product excellence and understanding one's team thoroughly. The finesse of seamlessly transitioning between macro and micro perspectives daily necessitates a distinctive skill set—managing frequent context switches, discerning overarching patterns, employing a first-principles approach, and adept problem-solving at all scales.

Moreover, each quarter, I immerse myself in pivotal product domains that hold top priority for the company, assuming the role of executive sponsor. This involves direct collaboration with individual contributors—be it designers, researchers, product managers, or engineering counterparts—to shape product strategy and actualize visions in these projects. These endeavors not only deepen my connection to the product but also enable me to cultivate direct relationships with the teams involved in the actual work.

Afshar: In one of your Medium articles, you write about the principles of "managing up," and how one can be most effective in proactively communicating with and influencing one's own manager. You posed the question of whether there is a "secret art to managing up." It would be great to hear your perspective on this. Are there specific tactics you've found universally effective across leaders, or do you recommend a more nuanced approach?

Seo: Throughout my 25-year career, I've reported to approximately 20 managers, each distinct in their approach and personality. Managing up isn't a one-size-fits-all strategy, because each manager prefers a unique style, much like their diverse personalities. However, a universal truth underlies them all: they are human. It's innate for humans to seek understanding and acknowledgment, just like all of us do.

After numerous trials and experiences, a foundational realization dawned on me: managing up should mirror how you wish to be managed.

This involves comprehending and accepting your managers for who they are. Teamwork is a very human affair, and it all begins with getting to know each other. Just like your manager tunes into your needs, it's equally important for you to adjust your approach to connect with them. Each manager has their own unique style, priorities, and daily challenges, not to mention their personality quirks and preferred way of communication. What keeps them awake at night? What gets them excited about work each morning? Understanding the dynamics they navigate within the organization is key. Try stepping into their shoes, see things from their point of view, and amplify their position. Once you get a better feel for your manager, it opens the door to more meaningful, empathetic, and genuine conversations with them. It's all about creating a connection that goes beyond the professional surface.

Approachability and attentive listening are crucial. Just as you appreciate being heard, remember that managers also value having a sounding board, not encountering a brick wall. Practice active listening and create an environment where they feel at ease reaching out to you in the future. If your interactions are solely centered around your own concerns, there's a risk of steering the relationship into a one-way street. Some mistakes I made in the past were when I went to the managers only to ask what I need when I need it. It turned every conversation transactional and we barely had a chance to build a relationship. In an optimal employee/manager partnership, there's a robust mutual trust. Both parties should feel free to discuss challenges without the fear of judgment, fostering a shared commitment to collaboratively solve problems.

Regardless of titles or hierarchy, we're all individuals seeking insights into how others perceive us. Therefore, offering feedback to your leadership in real-time is valuable. This way, your manager stays informed about areas for improvement throughout the year, avoiding the need to wait for annual reviews or employee surveys. The feedback can be either positive or constructive. When you find inspiration in your manager's actions, share your positive feedback—it holds significant value. Similarly, if you notice areas where there could be improvement, providing that feedback is equally important. Any well-intentioned manager will appreciate your honesty and constructive input. And hopefully you've cultivated your relationship to be open and honest.

Furthermore, it's imperative to not just report problems but also present solutions. While your manager plays a crucial role in providing guidance, it's important to recognize that they may not have all the answers to your challenges. The reality is, they have numerous other responsibilities on their plate, and it's not reasonable to assume they possess a solution for every problem you present. At times, it's necessary to break down your issues for them at the appropriate level of detail and guide them through the complexities. In many cases, you likely have better context and knowledge about the specific project and team you're working with. This positions you well not only to articulate the problem but also to lead the optimal path to a solution. Before presenting a problem to your manager, consider brainstorming potential solutions. This not only sets the stage for a more constructive conversation but also portrays you as a proactive problem solver and collaborative thought partner, rather than someone who merely complains. This skill becomes increasingly valuable as you take on more senior roles.

Building trust and loyalty is key in any long-lasting partnership with your manager. When you both share goals, expectations, and motivations, amazing things can happen, opening up more opportunities. In most cases, when you help your manager succeed, it's a win-win. It's about creating a vibe of "we" instead of just "you." Think of it as being part of the same team, fighting for the same goals. Invite them into your thought process, welcome their input when it makes sense, and take joint ownership. We're all here to grow together and build on each other's successes.

I've made many mistakes and incorrect assumptions about managing up, and mastering the skill will be a life-long journey for anyone. By applying the first-principles approach, I hope your journey of managing up will be as inspiring and rewarding.

CHAPTER 14

Joann Wu
Uber

Joann Wu is the VP and Global Head of Product Design at Uber, where she leads a diverse, global team of product designers, user researchers, content designers, and design operation managers. Spanning the United States, Canada, India, Europe, and Latin America, her team is responsible for the design and user experience of Uber's entire product suite, including Uber Mobility, Delivery, and Core Services.

Originally from China, Joann moved to the United States, where she earned a master's Degree in Design from the Academy of Art University in San Francisco. Earlier in her career, she held designer and design leadership roles at agencies such as USWeb/CKS, SapientRazorfish, OgilvyOne, and Silverlign Group, working on brands and digital experiences for Fortune 500 clients. Before joining Uber, Joann served as VP of Product Design at LinkedIn, shaping the user experience for nearly 900 million members worldwide. She currently resides in San Francisco, California.

Jaleh Afshar: You've had a broad range of professional experience across numerous prolific companies. How did you begin your career?

Joann Wu: Aspects of my career path have been quite unconventional. I grew up in China and earned a college degree in Russian language and literature. However, when I moved to the United States to join my husband, I had to start from scratch—Russian language as a career wasn't exactly in high demand in the States!

Fortunately, I had a background in art, having studied drawing and painting when I was younger under the guidance of my father. This artistic foundation made pursuing a new career in design feel natural to me. So, I enrolled in the Academy of Art to study graphic design, eventually earning a master's degree.

After graduation, I landed a job at the interactive design agency USWeb/CKS, right in the midst of the dot-com boom. While my formal training was in traditional graphic design—covering everything from design principles to typography, brand identity, package, and publication design—working at USWeb/CKS gave me hands-on experience in digital interactive design. The focus at that time was all about websites, particularly e-commerce sites for clients like Levi's, Dockers, Mattel, and Williams Sonoma to create their first ever digital brand and e-commerce platforms. This experience allowed me to dive into interaction design and information architecture, areas that weren't covered in my academic studies. The combination of my graphic design education and real-world technical experience provided a solid foundation for my career.

For the first 10+ years of my career, I worked primarily in agencies, serving a diverse range of clients. This agency experience was hugely valuable in helping me hone my design skills and develop a deep understanding of target audiences, marketing positioning, and more. However, I noticed a significant shift in the industry around 2010 when many agency designers were moving to high-tech companies, or what was referred to at that time as "in-house" positions.

This shift got me thinking about the differences between agency work and in-house roles. In an agency, you're often distanced from the end user, receiving briefs from client services and crafting designs that, while beautiful, might not always be user-centric because you simply were completely distanced from the actual end user of the product. You also hand off your work without fully knowing its impact. I realized that I wanted to be closer to the user and to have a more direct long-term influence on the products and services I was designing.

At the same time, I saw an opportunity in the tech industry. Companies like Google, Facebook, LinkedIn, and Microsoft were starting to emerge and pick up steam, but many of their websites and apps lacked compelling design. I thought, what if agency designers could bring our skills in-house and really make a difference?

Motivated by this idea, I joined LinkedIn in 2011. Since then, I've had the opportunity to make a tangible impact on both the business and the design itself, fulfilling my goal of creating meaningful, user-centered designs in the tech industry.

Afshar: In particular, you've had significant leadership experience across major agencies as well as large product companies. What are the major differences you've observed within the design organizations across these two sectors?

Wu: There were absolutely differences I observed, although it's important to acknowledge that agencies have likely evolved over the last 10–15 years since I was in that sector. Reflecting on my own experience, working in an agency setting was instrumental in developing my craftsmanship. I still hold a deep respect for the teams and experiences I had at that time because it played a significant role in shaping the designer I am today.

However, one of the limitations of agency work, as I experienced it, is the lack of direct access to data and technology. In my earlier career, I was so focused on honing my craft that I didn't fully understand this limitation. But as I grew in my career, my curiosity naturally expanded. I started asking myself, "What else can I do?" This question led me to realize that my growth was being constrained by the agency environment, which wasn't providing the same level of access to the data, insights, and tools I needed to evolve further.

The operational model of an agency is also different. You're surrounded by design peers—art directors, creative directors, and a high concentration of design talent. But this environment often lacks the direct interaction with other disciplines, like engineering, data science, or business, that you find in a tech company. When I transitioned to the tech industry, I quickly realized the importance of understanding the multidisciplinary side of things.

For me, this shift was eye-opening. In design school, we are trained to perfect our craft, which sometimes makes us less open to exploring the business and technology sides of things. I've noticed that even today, many designers entering high-tech roles can inadvertently limit their own growth by staying within the confines of their design expertise. They might wonder how to make a bigger impact, but without a curiosity to broaden their horizons, their influence remains confined.

Ultimately, embracing curiosity and being willing to step outside of your comfort zone—into business, technology, and beyond—is what allows you to expand your impact and truly grow as a designer.

Afshar: For our readers who are looking to move into management roles, what skills are essential for success?

Wu: Along the lines of multidisciplinary curiosity, the thing I wish I had understood earlier in my career is the importance of paying attention to the business side of things. I believe this is a crucial aspect that early career designers should start focusing on while developing their careers. Even if you're working at an agency and primarily reading pre-written briefs that you're assigned to execute on, it's vital to understand the "why" behind them—what are the business goals driving these projects?

As you advance in your career, especially if you're considering a move into management, it's crucial to understand the business. The further you grow the scope, the more essential it becomes to speak the language of your stakeholders and to add value beyond just design. If you only focus on pixels and aesthetics, your influence may be limited. But when you grasp the business context, you can help your team align with business priorities, and better connect the design work with the bigger picture. For example, how your design solutions can drive acquisition, retention, or engagement—that's when you truly start connecting the dots and to make a significant impact.

In the tech sector, product managers are leading with a business impact perspective, but as designers, we also need to cultivate this awareness. While our primary role is to represent the user and solve user's pain points through design, we also have a responsibility to understand and contribute to the broader business objectives. Whether you aspire to be a confident designer or a design leader, having a strong business sense is, in my opinion, essential.

I wish more designers would cultivate at least a curiosity about the business side, if not actively pursue business education. In fact, some of us who are now design leaders are working with design schools to encourage them to integrate business courses into their curricula. I highly recommend that designers consider taking a business course as part of their education—it's an investment that can significantly enhance your impact and career growth.

Afshar: Can you describe your approach to research and how it informs the work of the broader design team?

Wu: Research plays a crucial role in the product design process, as it provides the insights and learnings that inform our solutions and help decision-making. I firmly believe that research should be closely integrated with the product team, creating a seamless collaboration that ensures our designs are both data-informed and insight-driven. This approach not only benefits the users but also aligns with the business goals.

To keep our teams and stakeholders aligned, we share research findings through multiple channels, including targeted share-outs with cross-functional stakeholders and monthly newsletters that reach a broader audience. These efforts ensure that everyone is informed and that the insights gained are effectively integrated into our design process.

We also have a user empathy-building practice as "fieldwork." We drive, pick and pack, deliver, and visit merchants. Our user researchers help facilitate conversations, and we often bring cross-functional teams along on these field trips to observe and participate. This hands-on experience not only strengthens our understanding of the customers but also fosters team bonding and builds empathy across all functions. It's part of being "Trip obsessed" as one of Uber's cultural values.

I also believe that designers need to develop their own research skills. You don't have to be a professional researcher, but simply having a mindset rooted in empathy and a willingness to engage in research activities is crucial. By participating in fieldwork and collaborating closely with researchers, designers can better understand the user experience and create more impactful solutions.

It's interesting to note that while integrating research with design seems like an obvious and efficient approach, it's not always the standard practice. In my career, I've seen this integration vary, but I believe it's a model that will continue to evolve. Some organizations are even experimenting with merging data science, marketing research and user research, creating what's sometimes referred to as an "insights group."

Afshar: Uber has a vast global user base. Can you share an example of a design solution that had to be adapted for different regions?

Wu: In the early days of Uber, our strategy was to launch features on a local level first, proving our model in one city before expanding globally. This approach allowed us to tailor our services to each market's unique needs and conditions. However, as we've grown and scaled, we've shifted toward a more global-first strategy. That said, we still place a strong emphasis on learning from unique local market strategies and scaling them when appropriate.

Take Uber Moto, for example. This service, which allows users to hail motorbikes, has become incredibly popular in Latin America, especially in places like Brazil. In cities like São Paulo, where traffic congestion is a significant issue, motorbikes offer a quick and efficient way to navigate through the city. People use them not just for rapid transportation but also to carry items like groceries. While this might seem a bit too adventurous for the US market, it's a completely normal and widely accepted mode of transportation in Brazil.

Designing an experience like Uber Moto requires a deep understanding of the local context, particularly from a safety perspective. For instance, the driver needs to keep both hands on the handlebars while sometimes interacting with the app. This poses unique design challenges, as we must ensure that interactions are both safe and intuitive. Despite these local adaptations, we still operate within a broader global framework to maintain consistency and scalability across markets. We can't design every feature as a one-off; instead, we balance the need for a cohesive global design framework with the flexibility to address local use cases.

This balancing act between a global framework and local customization is a fascinating challenge. It's reminiscent of how broad platforms like LinkedIn operate, where everything is globally aligned, but with adaptations for different market dynamics, regulations, and user behaviors. As we expand and scale, it's crucial to think in terms of playbooks, frameworks, and system thinking, rather than focusing solely on individual use cases.

Of course, this approach can lead to conflicts and trade-offs. Deciding how to balance global consistency with local relevance is not always straightforward, and there are trade-offs associated with these decisions. But it's a critical part of our work, and it's something I've found to be both a great learning experience and an essential aspect of leading a design team. The tension between system-wide thinking and addressing specific local needs is challenging, but it's also what makes our work so compelling and impactful.

Afshar: Can you share an example of when design influenced a major business decision at Uber?

Wu: There are several examples that highlight how design influenced the Uber business at large, so I'll focus on one that particularly resonates with me: safety features.

From the very beginning, the idea of getting into a stranger's car was unusual, even unsettling for many people. Safety has always been a top priority at Uber, especially considering how essential it is for users to feel secure during their rides. As a woman, safety is constantly on my mind, particularly when taking a ride late at night or traveling in areas I'm not very familiar with. This concern is not unique to me; it's something that many women share, and it's an area where research has played a critical role in shaping Uber's design and product features.

One of the most impactful safety features is what we call the "safety check." Once you're in the car, if the vehicle stops unexpectedly for a long period, the app will send you a message asking, "Need help? Your vehicle's been stationary for a while. Please let us know if everything is OK." This feature is so simple yet profoundly human. Even though it's driven by technology, it creates a sense that someone is looking out for you, offering peace of mind when you're in a potentially vulnerable situation.

Another feature that stands out is the ability to set personal safety preferences. For instance, you can enable a PIN code that you share with your driver before the ride begins to ensure you're getting into the correct car. This might seem like a small step, but it can make a huge difference in how safe one feels. Additionally, there's the option to have your ride safety check on periodically, or at specific times and locations, based on your preferences. This feature is customizable, allowing you to decide how much or how little monitoring you want, making it both flexible and reassuring.

The integration of technology and human-centered design doesn't stop there. Uber also offers features like the ability for your friend or loved one to track you during the ride. Furthermore, there's an option to record audio or video during the ride, which is stored securely and only accessed by Uber if there's a safety concern or complaint. This respects privacy while providing an additional layer of security.

These safety features, driven by both user research and technological advancements, demonstrate how Uber has become more sensitive and smarter over time, always keeping the user's experience in mind. The design function, in particular, plays a crucial role in bridging the gap between digital and physical experiences. As designers, it's our responsibility to think from the user's perspective, to consider what we would need in those situations, and to leverage technology to make these interactions feel more human and caring.

This example of safety features not only highlights Uber's commitment to user well-being but also serves as a reminder of the importance of integrating user research into the design process. By continuously learning from users and adapting to their needs, we can create solutions that resonate deeply and make a real difference in people's lives.

Afshar: What role does design at Uber play in addressing societal challenges?

Wu: That's a very insightful question, and I've been thinking deeply about particularly significant challenges our society faces today in terms of transportation and environmental sustainability. Some of these challenges can feel overwhelming, almost hopeless to change, as they are deeply rooted in complex systems. However, there are also areas where we can make meaningful changes, and Uber, is uniquely positioned to contribute.

One area where Uber can make a significant impact is in addressing the accessibility of transportation. In many regions, especially those lacking robust public transportation, Uber can serve as a vital link, providing people with reliable mobility options. While Uber is often perceived as a luxury service, it's important to remember that the platform also offers more affordable options, such as two or three-wheelers, Group Ride or Uber Share. These options can be crucial for individuals who otherwise might not have any other transportation choices, enabling them to reach essential destinations like offices, doctor's appointments, or the grocery stores.

Uber also has the potential to improve accessibility for those who rely on others for transportation, such as the elderly or individuals with disabilities. By providing a dependable way for these people to get around. Uber can help them stay connected to their communities and maintain their independence—"Go anywhere and get anything."

On the environmental front, transportation is a major contributor to greenhouse gas emissions, and Uber is actively working to address this issue. The company has been focusing on promoting the use of electric vehicles (EVs) among its drivers, recognizing that the cost of purchasing an EV can be prohibitive for many. By creating a platform where drivers can rent EVs at an affordable rate, Uber is making it easier for them to transition to greener options. This not only reduces the carbon footprint of each ride but also contributes to broader efforts to make cities more sustainable.

For riders, Uber has made it easier to choose environmentally friendly options. When selecting a vehicle, the app clearly indicates which options are green, offering a subtle nudge to make a more eco-conscious choice. Additionally, there's a feature for users to track and view how many carbon emissions you've saved by choosing greener ride options. This feature can be a great motivator, as it provides tangible evidence of your contributions to environmental sustainability. Personally, I've found it inspiring to see how much of a difference my choices can make, and it encourages me to opt for green rides whenever possible.

Afshar: What are the most significant challenges facing designers in the next five years?

Wu: Design and the role of designers is constantly evolving, and every few years, we witness shifts that reshape the industry. As we look forward, one of the most significant forces likely to influence design is the rise of generative AI. However, the challenge isn't about AI replacing designers; it's about how AI might change the way we approach design thinking.

When I reflect on the essence of design, I'm reminded of the Saul Bass quote, "Design is thinking made visual." This phrase captures the heart of what we do: the process of thoughtful problem-solving that results in visual and functional outcomes. Yet, with the advent of powerful tools and AI, there's a growing risk that we might lose sight of this process. Today, tools enable even someone who's new to design to produce visually stunning work with remarkable speed. But often, these designs can feel somewhat shallow, lacking the depth and considerations that come from a well-considered thought process.

Back when I started in design, we would spend days purely thinking about concepts and ideating before putting pen to paper or mouse to screen. There was a focus on the end-to-end journey, from the initial wireframe to the final outputs, ensuring that every design choice was intentional and grounded in a deep understanding of the user and the problem at hand. Now, I sometimes see designers jumping straight into high-fidelity work using tools and design system components without first mapping out the foundational thinking. While these tools are incredibly useful for efficiency, they can sometimes short-circuit the deeper exploration and critical thinking that are vital to great design solutions.

Looking forward, I worry that this trend might intensify, especially as AI continues to advance. If we're not careful, we might find ourselves relying on AI to do more of the thinking for us, producing work that's technically proficient but lacking in true insight or innovation. The danger isn't that AI will replace human designers, but that it could lead us to overlook the importance of thoughtful and tasteful decision-making.

Ultimately, the core of design isn't just about creating something beautiful or functional—it's about making informed, responsible decisions. This is where human designers will always have an edge over machines. Machines can process data and generate designs quickly, but they don't possess the empathy, intuition, and ethical judgment that are crucial to making decisions that truly resonate with users and meet their needs.

As we move forward, I believe the real challenge will be to keep ourselves accountable for the decisions we make as designers. We need to stay focused on the thinking behind our designs, ensuring that we're not just creating for efficiency's sake but are also considering the broader implications of our work.

So, instead of worrying about AI replacing us, I believe we should focus on honing our ability to think deeply and make thoughtful decisions. We need to put ourselves in the shoes of our users and be intentional about the choices we make in our designs. This is where the real value of human designers lies, and it's what will continue to set us apart in an increasingly automated world.

Afshar: Can you share a personal passion that influences your mindset?

Wu: Outside of work, my two teenage daughters are both my inspiration and my biggest challenge, as you can imagine! I genuinely enjoy being challenged by them. It can be refreshing when they push back or question things, as it often leads to some of the most thought-provoking conversations.

For example, during COVID, my younger daughter asked me a question that really made me pause: "Mom, why do I need to go to school when I can just ask Google for all the answers?" And now, of course, they can ask AI tools like ChatGPT as well. This question sparked a lot of reflection for me about the true purpose of education. What are we really teaching our kids? Beyond just information, what does it mean to be educated in today's world? How do we instill the ability to make thoughtful, informed decisions?

These are the kinds of questions that keep me on my toes, thanks to my daughters. They remind me that the challenges facing the next generation are evolving rapidly. While we talk a lot about the design challenges of our time, the bigger picture is about the human challenges our kids will face as they grow up. With so much information at their fingertips, it's crucial that they learn how to ask the right questions and think critically about the answers they find.

I'm often amazed at how much information they already have access to—when I was growing up, this kind of access was unimaginable. But with this abundance of information comes the need for deeper guidance. It's no longer just about finding answers but about understanding what those answers mean and how to apply them wisely in life.

What I love about these interactions with my daughters is that they force me to think in ways that my usual circles—whether at work or with friends—might not. Teenagers have a way of cutting straight to the point, often asking the blunt questions that make you stop and think. Sometimes, when I share my struggles with them, they'll just cut through all my overthinking and say, "Mom, it's really simple. Why make it so complicated?" It's humbling, and frankly, kids are fascinating in that way.

Their perspectives are a constant reminder to stay curious, to keep questioning, and to never lose sight of the fundamental human elements in everything we do. Let's stay simple, stay true.

CHAPTER

15

Josh Mahoney
Breadfast

Josh Mahoney is the VP of Design for Breadfast, one of Egypt's leading online grocery brands and the first company in the MENA region to be recognized as Y Combinator Top Company. Josh leads the product design and research teams and is responsible for championing customers and using design thinking to accelerate growth. Prior to Breadfast, Josh was Head of Consumer Design at Yelp and a Product Manager at Google. He holds a Bachelor of Computer Science from the Royal Melbourne Institute of Technology.

Jaleh Afshar: Breadfast was founded in 2017, and is now a regional leader in the grocery delivery space in Egypt. What drew you to the startup world, and what was it about this particular company that resonated with you?

Josh Mahoney: To answer that, let me share a bit of history. My most recent stint prior to Breadfast was at Yelp, which is a place I owe a lot to for significantly shaping my design career. After leaving Yelp, however, I found myself disillusioned with the tech industry and uncertain about my next move. Did I want to return to a big tech company? I knew what those roles entailed and, frankly, I wasn't excited about it.

© Jaleh Afshar 2025
J. Afshar, *Chief Design Officers at Work*,
https://doi.org/10.1007/979-8-8688-1137-1_15

I experimented with returning to agency work, where I had started my career, looking for more dynamic projects without the constant pressure of metrics and growth. However, having worked at a number of agencies, and having experienced a range of company sizes throughout my career, I felt a pull toward a smaller more focused company. This sentiment was shared by many in my position: we'd done the big company thing and now craved a place where we could have more impact, be closer to the work, and avoid the bureaucratic layers.

At Yelp, my team was about 40 people, and my role had become increasingly about managing politics, people, and processes. Ironically, despite being a design leader, I felt like I only got involved in design work when there was an escalation or issue. This was far from the reason I transitioned from product to product design at Yelp; I wanted to stay close to the creative process.

Egypt was not part of my plan. I was late-stage interviewing with a major tech company in San Francisco when I happened to attend a dinner party. There, I met the CFO who told me about this grocery startup in Egypt. Intrigued, I learned more, and one thing led to another. The role offered everything I missed about tech a decade ago: rapid growth, excitement, and a bit of chaos that made it fun. It felt like a grand adventure.

On the business front, the product itself is a marketplace delivering groceries, with a focus on baked goods. This was reminiscent of my early days at Yelp when I worked on Eat24, a similar marketplace product. While the core product issues are comparable, the logistical and cultural differences in Egypt are significant, and this has also been a wonderful journey in broadening my understanding of the world and of commerce.

Working in an emerging market has been incredibly eye-opening from a managerial lens as well, especially coming from my past experience. The challenges are not just about the product and users but also about hiring, retaining, and training people from non-traditional backgrounds. In many regions, you might have the expectation that most people on design teams have experience from famous schools or intensive bootcamps. In Egypt, many of my team members are self-trained and from various non-design and non-tech backgrounds. This diversity has been both challenging to navigate and fascinating and inspiring to learn from.

Overall, this journey has taught me that working in a growing economy comes with unique challenges and rewards. It's been a humbling and enriching experience, providing a fresh perspective on design and leadership.

Afshar: Let's delve a bit more into those unique team aspects that you mentioned. What's the design culture like at your company?

Mahoney: Going into this role from a background of working in the tech hub of the world, I expected things to be wildly different and possibly a step down in various ways. However, what I found within the design community was surprising and fascinating. The designers I inherited were far stronger than I anticipated. It turns out, you don't need to go to Stanford's d.school or attend the top bootcamps to be successful as a designer. Many of these talented individuals on my team at Breadfast were self-taught, maybe had some startup experience, or completed a few online courses here and there. When it comes to their hands-on work, in actuality, the difference between them and those with elite education was not as significant as expected. Passion and drive can be just as powerful as formal education and prestigious internships.

This realization was humbling. It challenged the Silicon Valley bias, reminding me that talent exists everywhere. I have to say though that on the flip side, recruiting senior managerial talent proved difficult. The exposure to industry best practices and challenging scenarios that comes from many years of working at large companies is what often makes managers and directors incredibly strong. In emerging markets, this experience is often missing as experienced leaders often leave the market.

Because of this, my focus rapidly shifted to developing in-house senior leader talent. How can we accelerate someone from senior to lead to manager? This meant investing more in defining the core responsibilities of a lead and creating safety nets to support rapid growth.

Another noticeable difference was working with cross-functional stakeholders. In big tech hubs, product managers generally understand design processes and value the collaborative approach. In emerging markets, the perception of design can be more traditional, with business leaders directing designers and engineers in a very top-down way. My role as a head of design often involved educating product partners on how to integrate design and technology teams into business decisions, emphasizing that we're all in the same boat.

This experience has made me reflect on advice for newcomers in the industry. Should they join a big company or a small startup? The best approach is to try both. Startups teach you ownership and the ability to hustle and compromise. Big companies teach you about structured design critiques, cross-functional collaboration, and stakeholder management. Ultimately, the choice should be influenced by the manager you'll be working under. A great manager can provide opportunities and mentorship that accelerate your growth.

In Egypt, I've seen the importance of exposing team members to strong processes, practices, and peers. Finding a top-notch individual contributor, like a principal designer, would be invaluable for their craft learning. At Yelp, I had an amazing principal designer who was an incredible mentor. Having someone of that caliber is crucial for a team's development.

Geographic trends also play a significant role. For instance, the lower cost of labor in Egypt allows us to solve problems differently. Instead of building complex technical solutions for every single problem, we can hire more people to handle tasks, enhancing the overall service design which can also significantly improve the product for our users just as well as a software solution. This flexibility extends to the design team as well. For example, we can hire illustrators to create custom work rather than purchasing pre-made assets.

Overall, working in an emerging market like Egypt has been eye-opening. Understanding and adapting to these cultural and economic differences has been a valuable lesson in how to approach design and management.

Afshar: From a product perspective, are there differences in what your users expect in Egypt vs. other markets?

Mahoney: One particularly unexpected and fascinating aspect of our work has been conducting user research with our customers in this unique environment. The audience here is so unfamiliar with the culture of giving feedback that recruiting for user interviews has been extremely challenging. Unlike other parts of the world, where established tools and panels make it easy to find users, we find ourselves coordinating over WhatsApp, conversing with people who are uncomfortable or unwilling to discuss certain topics.

Connecting with users here is a different ballgame. They are not used to being asked for their opinions, and they often feel embarrassed or hesitant to say things like, "This looks bad" or "It feels slow." It's a classic user research challenge in many ways—getting them out of the mindset that we want feedback on the app and instead guiding them through the process. But their initial reaction is often one of confusion: "Why would you want to do this?" There is limited understanding of why a perspective of a user or customer would be valuable to a company.

Additionally, cultural factors play a significant role. Our product has aspects in the financial tech space. For many users, discussing anything too personal, particularly financial matters, brings a lot of discomfort. There's also a deep-seated distrust of the government, which adds another layer of hesitation and suspicion.

While these challenges do exist everywhere, the cultural nuances here are profound. Even basic practices, like framing questions correctly, require a deep understanding of these cultural differences. This experience has underscored how cultural norms vary not just from country to country but also within different workplaces.

Having worked in Australia, the United States, and London, I've noticed subtle differences in each place. Egypt is now yet another case, with specific cultural expectations affecting every part of the job—from the user's perception of the product to how we collaborate with our team. The most valuable lesson I've learned here is the importance of being self-aware of your own cultural norms and understanding those of others. This skill is crucial when working with international teams and can greatly enhance collaboration and communication.

Afshar: You've shared recent discourse on the concept of "late-stage UX" a term that encompasses issues such as an unbalanced focus on financialization and commodification of design, that ultimately puts user needs at risk. What's your assessment of this potentially emerging landscape?

Mahoney: I try not to be too cynical, but there's a growing sentiment in the design industry that's hard to ignore. Recently, at a panel with several design leaders, the topic came up, and there was a palpable vibe in the room. Someone aptly framed it by saying, "The promise of design thinking was a lie."

There was a time, a generation ago, when we believed that design thinking and design practices would change the world. We thought that by applying these principles to product development, we'd create a user-focused utopia where we'd build perfect products and profit handsomely. Unfortunately, reality has been more complex.

Design thinking does help—I'm a huge proponent of it, and it has profoundly changed how I approach my work. But we live in a capitalist society driven by profit. When financial pressures mount, corporations make hard compromises. You can have the deepest empathy for your users, but if your company isn't making money, it will fail. Recent economic shifts have made this abundantly clear; everyone is now focused on growth and profitability.

Design often bears the brunt of this reality. Throughout my career, I've noticed that while both designers and product managers care about the user and the business, product managers have always leaned more toward business metrics and profitability. Designers, on the other hand, focus more on user experience and delight. In challenging times, this difference becomes more pronounced, and design can feel sidelined.

This isn't just a complaint; it's a symptom of a maturing industry. Our roles as design leaders have evolved. It's not just about championing the user anymore but also balancing business needs and accepting necessary compromises. This is the nature of having a job where you get a paycheck.

I've noticed this shift as a consumer, too. Products I once loved seem to be getting worse as companies prioritize margins and make tougher feature trade-offs. The joy of discovering genuinely new features and products, like those iconic Apple presentations, feels increasingly rare. Now, the focus is often on meeting quarterly targets.

This maturity in the industry has its benefits. We have sophisticated logging and metrics now, eliminating the guesswork of earlier days. While this data-driven approach removes some of the art and intuition from design, it also provides clear insights into what works and why. However, it can feel like we've become more scientists than artists, and I can't help but miss the days when creativity and gut instinct played a bigger role.

Many in the product design field are questioning their career choices, especially with the rise of AI and its impact on various industries. AI highlights a broader trend: the tools and technologies we once saw as revolutionary now come with a price tag and a business model. If Gmail had been invented today, it wouldn't be free; it would come with a trial period and a subscription fee. This shift reflects a broader change in how we think about product development.

There was a time when building products felt like a craft, full of passion and innovation, much like the early days of car manufacturing. Today, it's more about efficiency and profitability. We've become incredibly good at selling products, creating value, but we've lost some of that early magic and creativity.

In the end, while I acknowledge the benefits of a mature, data-driven industry, I still yearn for those days when innovation felt pure and more inspired.

Afshar: When exploring a new product or design direction, what is the most unusual source of inspiration you've drawn from?

Mahoney: My creative inspiration has always been complex. Starting as a self-taught designer, moving through startups, becoming a product manager, and returning to design has left me feeling insecure about my visual design and creative abilities. I never went to art school or formally learned to appreciate art, though I love it. I haven't integrated it into my process as much as I'd like, unlike the great creative directors I admire. Developing this creative side, alongside my problem-solving skills, is something I aspire to.

Traveling and meeting other designers across the world, working closely with product people in different countries, has also been incredibly inspiring. It's given me a sense of gratitude and excitement. While "excited" might not be the exact word, it has certainly helped me appreciate my opportunities and feel reinvigorated.

One of the most powerful things I've gained from this experience of worldwide exposure, is also an immense gratitude for the privileges I've had. Working in areas like the Bay Area, and learning from incredible people working at the largest most influential companies making global products has been a unique blessing. Anyone in San Francisco, especially in design, is incredibly lucky on a global scale.

I've also always been driven by seeing the impact my work has on end users. When you work on a product that's new to the market and solves fresh problems, it's thrilling to hear a user say, "I love your product because it does

X," or "It really helped me make this decision." At Yelp, hearing a business owner say, "You helped my business stay afloat by bringing in customers," was incredibly rewarding. Solving problems for users has always been a huge source of inspiration—even if it's just one person, making their life better, piece by piece, excites me the most.

The pursuit of learning and solving problems for people drove me into product design and continues to drive me as a manager. Solving my team's problems, like fixing a broken process or helping someone make a good career decision, is incredibly satisfying. Treating team members and colleagues as users, applying the same principles of empathy and problem-solving, is crucial. Good managers, especially in product design, build empathy, focus on the problem, and apply these techniques to their teams.

I tell many designers when dealing with a difficult partner, like an engineer or PM, is to think of them as users. Understand their goals and motivations. Apply the same techniques used in design: empathize, understand the problem, brainstorm solutions, and converge on a specific solution. Whether choosing a career path, deciding what to watch on Netflix, or building an app, the process is the same. This design thinking approach has been powerful in my life, and I truly believe in its universal application.

Afshar: During your professional career, you've shifted from design to product management, and then back to design. How did you know it was time for a change?

Mahoney: I've always been driven by the desire to solve problems for people. That passion led me to stumble into the world of design. I found myself in the right place at the right time, initially working in TV, video, and film, which gradually transitioned into web design as technology evolved. Eventually, this journey brought me to what we now call product design.

Back in those days, I was living in Australia. At the time, it was a place where design was still emerging compared to the fast-paced environment of Silicon Valley. I didn't even fully understand what excelling at a design job entailed to be honest, but I just kept doing it and trying my hand at approaching problem solving. However, at that time, I felt my ability to create what I considered "good" design work was often hindered by upstream decisions that misunderstood or misdefined the problems we were tackling. I wanted to have a more significant impact, to approach projects differently, and to solve problems in innovative ways. However, what I had felt at the time was that it wasn't typically the designer's role to make that call.

At the time, I wasn't working with product managers per se, but with business development, sales, and other departments. I noticed that the people in these roles made decisions impacting my design work. This realization pushed me toward product management, thinking that by stepping into that role, I could make better decisions and ultimately create better designs.

My big break came with a call from Google. I was a huge fan, so the opportunity to work at Google was irresistible, and I eagerly applied to a product management position without fully understanding the role. I quickly read *Cracking the PM Interview* by Gayle Laakmann McDowell and Jackie Bavaro to prepare and unexpectedly and fortunately succeeded in the interview. However, I soon realized that being a product manager didn't mean making all the decisions. Instead, it involved facilitating team decision-making, which could be done from any role in a good company, including design!

Through my experiences, I learned that titles alone don't grant the impact I sought. I also found that I enjoyed activities overlapping with design and disliked those that didn't. Reading *Designing Your Life* by Bill Burnett and Dave Evans was transformative for me. It helped me understand which daily activities brought me joy and engagement and which didn't. I realized that I wasn't happy as a product manager and at my heart, I was a designer.

Switching to a PM role at Yelp confirmed this. Yelp was excellent at fitting people into roles that suited them, and it soon became clear that I needed to return to design. Despite concerns about lower pay and less decision-making power, the move to design felt right almost immediately. I never looked back.

One crucial lesson I learned is the importance of having a good PM partner as a design leader. Misalignment with one's PM partner can greatly affect workplace happiness and success. This consideration now plays a significant role in my decision-making about future roles. At Yelp, building empathy and collaboration between design and product management was key to overcoming friction and working together effectively.

This journey taught me that solving problems creatively and collaboratively is at the heart of what I love about design.

CHAPTER

16

Linda Sum
Samsung Electronics America

Linda Sum is the Head of Design for Visual Display UX at Samsung Electronics America. Prior to Samsung, Linda held a senior management role at Meta, building innovative mobile calling and messaging bets for Instagram and Messenger such as expressive avatars, augmented reality effects, and virtual entertainment. Sum has previously held leadership roles at Hulu and American Express. She holds a BFA in Graphic Design from Otis College of Art and Design.

Jaleh Afshar: How did you discover your love for the design field?

Linda Sum: I grew up in Hong Kong, and living in a big city exposed me to packaging design and advertisements from a young age. I also had a love for comics, so as a kid, I was always drawing, mostly creating my own comics and zines. At the time, I didn't even realize what I was doing was design—I just thought it was fun and a way to express myself visually. Growing up, art was the one thing that kept me going, and I think that's where it all started for me.

Around that same time, I got into video games as well. One of my all-time favorites was *SimCity 2000*. That game was my first real interaction with something that was a vast experience and fully digital. Although I didn't know it at the time, I was fascinated by the user interface (UI) design—the icons, the way you could edit your city—it was all quite complex when I look back now, but at the time it simply felt natural and fun to engage with. Even though I didn't speak much English then, I somehow figured out how to interact with the game. Honestly as a kid, I didn't even fully understand what I was doing from a gameplay perspective, but I loved it!

As I got older, I began attending design exhibitions and started noticing how different things like furniture and architecture were also forms of design. I learned that design wasn't just one thing—it could encompass so much more.

When it came time to go to college, I initially thought I would study fine art, but I realized I wasn't skilled enough to make a career out of it. So, I took some art and design classes, like 2D and 3D design, calligraphy, and life drawing. Through that experience I found myself drawn to graphic design in particular. That's how I officially began formally learning design skills and thus kicked off my official career journey.

My academic background is in graphic and print design, but what I've always had a particular passion for is environmental graphics, like metro maps and station signage. Since I was a child, I've collected metro maps from every city I've visited because I find it fascinating how they manage to convey so much information in a clear, seamless way. Through colors, typography, and the angles of the lines, they can guide millions of people through a city, and I thought that was incredibly cool.

That early love of visual communication prepared me for the world of design, where I've learned to use design to express not just information but emotions as well. Now, with user research, I understand the motivations of end users and how to use art and design to bridge the gap between technology and the user. That process has always fascinated me.

Afshar: What are some of the most significant projects you've led during your career? What made them so meaningful for you?

Sum: One of the projects that made me feel truly accomplished, not just because of its scale but also because of its mission, was a project I worked on at American Express. We developed a financial product aimed at people who may not have a sufficient credit score to open a bank account.

In the United States, many people accumulate significant credit card debt, and some find themselves unable to even open a basic account to deposit checks or manage their finances. This product was designed to help those underserved individuals by offering a prepaid option where they wouldn't need a traditional bank account. Instead, they could go to a CVS or Walmart, purchase a prepaid card, load money onto it, and then use tools we provided—either online or through a mobile app—to deposit funds, track their spending, or send money to others.

This project really resonated with me because it was about creating something for people who are often overlooked, like immigrant families who may not have the resources to open a traditional bank account, or those who need to send money back to their families in other countries. It was eye-opening to learn about these needs, as I recognized my own privilege and the challenges I might not have personally faced which were a daily reality for our user group.

One of the most impactful parts of this experience was when our team actually went out into the field to better understand our users. We visited payday loan locations to see firsthand how people handle their finances. We learned that many would cash their paychecks immediately and head straight to payday loan centers, unaware of the high fees they were being charged just to access their money. Conducting interviews on the street and listening to these people's pain points really struck me. As a design manager at the time, I realized the importance of translating those experiences into designs that not only met usability and aesthetic standards but also genuinely addressed the personal needs of these users.

A particular challenge was ensuring that the design was intuitive and accessible. Many of our users might not be fluent in English or highly educated in financial terminology, so we had to carefully consider how to convey information through iconography, clear messaging, and even communication points like email confirmations. The goal was to facilitate understanding in the most effective way possible, without overwhelming them.

Another unforgettable part of the process was when we worked on designing a remittance product for transferring money across US states and internationally. We visited a MoneyGram location to observe the experience. People had to fill out long forms and then wait in line for 30 minutes to an hour just to send money, often while being late for their next job or picking up their child. This experience gave us valuable insights into how to improve that process digitally, making it more seamless and accessible for users. The entire journey was eye-opening and deeply fulfilling. It reinforced the importance of truly understanding the user's experience and translating that into meaningful design solutions.

The most rewarding moments came at the end of each month when we received customer feedback from users who expressed how much our product had helped them. It was amazing to realize that we weren't simply building something functional; we were truly making a difference in people's daily lives.

Afshar: What were some key experiences that prepared you for your leadership roles?

Sum: The first major milestone in my career happened rather unexpectedly. I kind of stumbled into UX design organically, without really knowing what it was. I come from a print design background, and after graduating, I had no clear path in front of me of how to break into UX design and the tech space. Luckily, I had a mentor at my first job who really guided me. He introduced me to the idea of working with cross-functional teams, which was new to me at the time. I remember thinking, "Wait, I'm a designer, what do you mean by working across teams?" I didn't even know what roles like product managers or researchers did! Having that guidance and someone to open doors for me was incredibly meaningful.

As I moved into working at a startup, I faced new challenges. I was one of three women in the entire startup. I remember receiving feedback from the executive team that I needed to be "edgier" to lead the team. I had no idea what that meant! English isn't my first language, so I literally Googled the definition of "edgy" in a professional context. That feedback threw me off and shook my confidence a bit. I was open to improving, but I didn't know how to act on feedback so vague. It made me reflect on what kind of leader I wanted to be, someone who inspires their team to do their best work and helps them to grow by providing clear guidance and actionable feedback.

Being a woman in tech also shaped my journey. Even today, the ratio of men to women in tech leadership roles is far from equitable, and I've seen firsthand how that imbalance plays out, both in startups and in corporate environments. I've always been mindful of that, and it fuels my desire to help change the system. Since I don't come from a tech background, I feel lucky to have had the opportunity to break into the space, and I want to help provide that same opportunity to others.

At places like Hulu, Meta, and Samsung, I've made it a priority to be available for mentorship, especially when people reach out to me. I've also been involved in diversity, equity, and inclusion (DEI) initiatives and various women's leadership communities, because giving back is important to me. I'm also passionate about bringing design education to high school students. There's still a stigma around studying art and design—many people, especially parents, think it won't lead to a successful career. I often hear that same mindset when I talk to parents today, and I want to change that.

In my day-to-day work, I try to strike a balance between the company's bottom line—yes, we're here to make a profit—and the responsibility I have as a leader to take care of my team. It's not just about promoting work–life balance in theory, but actually creating the conditions that allow for it. Another priority for me is helping women and underrepresented groups move up in their careers. Hiring more women is only part of the solution. Once you've landed great people on your team, the journey doesn't end there. The evergreen coaching, training, and consistency in creating clear pathways for growth is what ensures people have the opportunities to excel and be seen over the course of their career. Giving them the visibility they need to continue advancing in their careers is something I'm deeply committed to.

Afshar: That's very inspiring! Could you share some steps that managers can actively take to support the professional development of underrepresented people on their teams?

Sum: I've coached many people as they've been reaching these pivotal moments. I spend a lot of time with them, helping them stretch their vision of what's possible. Many express broad concerns like, "I don't feel like I have the management or leadership skills." My approach is to break that down with them to truly understand what they perceive as the necessary skill set. I ask them to reflect on what they believe makes a good leader and to visualize it as a set of technical skills—skills that can be learned and developed. Being an excellent manager is not about suddenly becoming more extroverted. These are misconceptions about what actual high quality leadership should entail. The job shouldn't require someone to change who they are at their core.

I've always coached my team with this philosophy: if a job requires you to fundamentally change who you are, then it's not the right job for you—run in the opposite direction. I want them to know that leadership and management are skills they can continue to grow, and they have every right to explore these roles if they're interested. I've also had women come to me with concerns like, "I'm thinking of starting a family; is now the right time for this?" And my response is, "What *is* the right time?" It's about walking through these questions with them so they don't feel alone, trapped by their thoughts without a safe space to voice them or explore the answers.

Another key area where I advocate is during promotion time and performance reviews. I've noticed that even though some companies have strong, unbiased calibration processes with many checks and reviews, many others do not have a system like that in place. As a woman leader, I believe it's crucial to show up in those moments and do the homework. If I'm confident that someone deserves a promotion or recognition, I make sure to start advocating for them early on. I connect with cross-functional teams, gather feedback, and provide it to the individual so they can continue growing. By the end of the year, when it's time to make the case for promotion, I've already laid the groundwork, and it's not just a last-minute effort.

Too often, I see managers who sit quietly in these employee evaluation meetings without actively engaging or without the necessary information to advocate for their team members. This kind of passive management can hold people back, especially those who are already underrepresented. I want to see more managers take the time to truly understand their team's work so they can confidently present it when those individuals aren't in the room. True advocacy means being prepared and proactive, not waiting until the opportunity has passed.

Equally important is creating a space where people feel safe to share their thoughts and concerns. Many hesitate to vocalize their ambitions or personal goals, like wanting to start a family or pursue further education, because they fear it might be seen as a lack of focus on the job. So, building that trust is essential. It requires leaders to be vulnerable and self-aware themselves, creating an environment where everyone feels supported to share their true selves.

It's all about striking the right balance, fostering an environment of trust, and being the kind of leader who's willing to put in the work to truly advocate for their team.

Afshar: Can you share some of the partnerships you've developed with institutions supporting students pursuing careers in Design?

Sum: It can be challenging for young students to have a conversation with their parents about art or something aesthetically-related as a viable profession. Many parents hesitate at the idea, thinking, "Why should I spend thousands of dollars for my child to pursue this?" I believe it's crucial for these parents to understand the actual job opportunities in the creative market.

In the past, I've partnered with the LA Chamber of Commerce, my alma mater Otis College of Art and Design, and Santa Monica College. The reason I collaborate with these institutions is because I believe students face key decision points throughout their lives. Those moments are when they are high school seniors choosing a college, when they declare a major in college, and when they graduate and decide what to do with their degree. My passion is helping to facilitate that process and give students and parents more insight into making informed decisions.

For example, I've been invited to give talks and participate in meetings with high school students and their parents. Many parents have questions like, "If my child chooses animation or costume design, won't they face long hours and low pay compared to other fields?" My response is always that a career is about longevity—it's something that spans decades. Sure, if you're only looking at the return on investment (ROI) right after graduation, finance might seem like a better option. But if you want to help your child build a fulfilling career, one they enjoy and that offers a healthy balance, a creative career can also be a good solution.

I emphasize that it's not just about the salary directly after graduation, but about enabling their children to develop critical thinking skills, pursue something they love, and find long-term satisfaction. When I break it down that way, many parents begin to see that a creative career offers more than just financial rewards—it's about personal fulfillment and long-term success.

There's also a growing body of research that shows the job market for those with proven creative skillsets is expanding year by year, with increasing demand for talent. This helps parents understand that there is demand for creative professionals, not only in the United States but also globally. If their children want to explore opportunities abroad, the skills they develop in creative fields can help them find meaningful employment worldwide.

Helping parents and students visualize the benefits and long-term returns of a creative career together is key. I find these programs and partnerships so valuable for the next generation. They help young people and their parents think beyond the immediate future and consider the broader, lifelong journey of finding purpose and fulfillment in their careers.

Afshar: Can you discuss any unexpected design challenges that come with creating experiences for TV and large screen devices?

Sum: Designing for what's called *10-foot UX* means creating experiences that are viewed and interacted with from a distance, like a TV. This presents unique challenges compared to designing for mobile or personal computers, which are private and personal devices. TVs are shared devices, so the design considerations are entirely different.

One of the main challenges is ensuring usability from a distance. We have to think about the visual hierarchy and how to simplify information, knowing that users are interacting with the UI in a different way. Although users can control the TV with their phones or game consoles, the primary input method is still the remote control, which usually has a four-directional D-pad and a select button. This simplicity introduces complexity in terms of designing intuitive navigation. We need to make sure users can easily orient themselves and understand what action to take next, without confusion.

At the end of the day, it's important to remember that TV is primarily about entertainment. It's not supposed to be an experience that requires deep thinking or effort from the user. So, when designing messaging, confirmations, and other communications, we aim to keep everything as simple and streamlined as possible.

I've encountered product challenges in the past where there was a perception that the role of TV was to compete with mobile devices for screen time. But that's not where the focus should be. Instead, we should be thinking about how TV can complement people's lives, enhancing their overall experience. TV shouldn't just be competing for attention; it should provide a destination for entertainment, organization, and relaxation.

This shift in perspective opened the door to some interesting ideas. Rather than just replicating what's been done before, we started thinking about why people want to own a TV and what role the device plays in their daily lives. For instance, we know people don't keep their TVs on 24/7, so when the TV is off, can it serve another purpose? Could it act as a decorative element in the living room, or provide useful information, like a digital bulletin board?

These considerations are very different from my past experiences designing for financial products or web and mobile platforms. Designing for TV requires a deep understanding not only of user intent but also of the broader role the device plays in people's homes and lifestyles. It's about making the TV more than just an entertainment platform—it's about thinking creatively about how it can enhance everyday life.

Afshar: What user research methods does your team leverage to inform product decisions?

Sum: I'm grateful to have worked with companies that have the budget for research, which is a luxury that many organizations don't have. It's fascinating because there's often a preconceived notion of how a product should function or how users will interact with it, and research can very much help quickly demystify that. For example, on past teams, some leadership stakeholders initially believed that most households had multiple TVs, with each person having their own dedicated screen. However, through research, we discovered that this wasn't the case at all. Many households actually share devices, and people are often multitasking—watching TV while also using their phones—so they don't dedicate their full attention to a single interface.

Research allowed us to uncover these behaviors, especially through ethnographic studies and in-home observations. We found that, on average, people spent about three hours a day watching TV, but they often weren't focused on just one screen. Additionally, we saw that different age groups had distinct viewing habits, and the number of hours they spent watching varied widely across demographics. This helped us realize that while we needed to design for shared audiences across various demographics, there were certain design principles that had to be tailored to specific user groups.

For instance, we worked on a project involving gaming on TVs. We discovered that a significant portion of gamers were 50 years old and older. While they might not consider themselves "gamers," they still played casual games and other types of games. This raised important questions about the role of gaming experiences on TV and how we could design for this specific audience.

Through our research, which included ethnographic studies as well as both qualitative and quantitative surveys, we were able to formulate design hypotheses and either prove or disprove them. Usability studies were also key, though we couldn't always conduct in-house A/B testing due to technical limitations. Instead, we relied on prototyped pseudo-A/B testing within usability studies, which, while not ideal, still gave us valuable quantitative data. We also conducted focus groups to gather open-ended feedback and gained deeper insights from our audience.

The value of research cannot be overstated—it has been incredibly important to our design process. However, one challenge we face is getting executives to avoid cherry-picking data that fits their own personal beliefs or assumptions. This is always a tricky part of working in consumer products. Executives can easily derail the research by saying, "Well, I feel a different way than all this research," and that can sometimes overshadow the broader insights we've gathered from the studies. Regardless, having a robust research program with multiple inputs has been crucial, and it's something I deeply appreciate.

Afshar: What are some of the biggest challenges you've faced as a design leader, and how have you overcome them?

Sum: The most difficult challenge I faced was leading a team during the pandemic, especially after the lockdown. As a leader, I constantly grappled with how to keep the team motivated while also being empathetic. During that time, I often questioned my role. Am I still just the person focused on meeting goals and driving the bottom line, knowing that the world was going through so much—whether it was the pandemic, the Black Lives Matter movement, or the social unrest? It was such a stressful period for many people, and I realized that our team, like any team, is a reflection of society. Trying to operate as though everything was normal simply wouldn't work.

At that point, I realized that no one had all the answers on how to lead during such unprecedented times. So, I decided that the best thing I could do was to show up as my authentic self. There was no other way to move forward. At the same time, we were in the process of launching a major redesign across the TV, mobile, and web platforms with only six months to go. Balancing the project deadline while keeping the team motivated and focused was a challenge.

For some team members, work became an anchor, providing a much-needed distraction. I made it clear to them: "Keep working if it helps, but if you need a break or have personal matters to sort out, I'm here for you." For others, who were struggling both personally and mentally, I focused on showing up and supporting them however I could. I leaned on the trusting relationships I had built with the team to help guide and uplift them, which was both challenging and incredibly rewarding.

Another significant challenge during this time was navigating the company's response to the Black Lives Matter movement. There was a push for DEI initiatives and all-hands meetings about what the company planned to do. However, when I spoke to my team, particularly those who were from underrepresented groups themselves, they felt an immense burden. They were being asked to work extra hours, without being compensated, to help solve problems that the company itself should have been addressing.

I advocated for two of my team members and took the issue to HR. I made it clear that it wasn't fair to place all this pressure on our team members when the company needed to step up to provide support and ensure the team can be compensated accordingly. I might have ruffled some feathers, but I'm proud of standing up for them. As a leader, I felt it was my responsibility. If I didn't advocate for them, who would?

Looking back, I learned a lot from the experience. It was a challenging period of my career, but in the end, I'm so thankful to see that my team came through it okay and successfully launched a major product redesign that we are all very proud of.

CHAPTER

17

Lissette Sotelo Parr
Personio

Lissette Sotelo Parr has witnessed the evolution of design operations over the years. Since her early years at design consultancies, to experiencing rapid growth in tech, Lissette has led design ops at companies both large and small. Lissette is currently the Head of Design Operations at Personio, leading a team focused on developing an all-in-one HR software solution that, valued at $8.5bn, is one of Europe's most valuable software startups.

Before Personio, Lissette held executive roles across multiple organizations, including serving as Head of Design Operations for Meta's Facebook Connections teams, Director of Design Operations at Faire, and Head of Design Operations at Lyft. She resides in the United Kingdom.

Jaleh Afshar: How do you define "Design Ops"?

Lissette Sotelo Parr: Design Ops is all about making the design organization work more effectively and efficiently. Now, I know that might not sound particularly exciting or glamorous, but the truth is, like any good operations team, it all boils down to making it easy to do high quality work.

When I think about Design Ops, I see designers as our users. Just as designers focus on the people using their products, the operations team focuses on the designers themselves. They're the ones we are solving problems for. So, I like to approach Design Ops by thinking about the designer's user journey, just as a designer would consider their end user's journey.

For me, that journey begins even before a designer joins a company. What is their perception of the brand? What do they know about the design culture at the company? Then, as they go through the interview and recruitment process, what touchpoints do they encounter? Once they join the team and go through onboarding, what is that experience like? As they ramp up, how do they find the information they need? What tools are they using? How are they learning and growing? And as they work with their team and cross-functional partners, what systems and tools are in place to support them?

When I map out this user journey, I see Design Ops as having three core components: People Operations, Business Operations, and Processes or Programs. These three areas form the foundation of how I envision Design Ops coverage at a company.

People Operations is all about the people within the organization—recruiting, hiring, onboarding, learning and development, and evaluation. It's about how we support the people on the team.

Business Operations focuses on the nuts and bolts of a company—budgets, headcount, the rhythm of business, tools, and knowledge management systems. It's about establishing the business needs of the design team.

Processes or Programs are about the day-to-day rituals and systems that help the team work together more effectively. What templates or systems do we have in place? How are we collaborating? What are our team rituals?

When I approach Design Ops, I use these three areas to assess how effectively and efficiently the team is operating. I even have a template that serves as an audit tool to evaluate these areas, although I often do this assessment more subtly, depending on the company. It's really about understanding where the biggest needs are and where to focus my time and energy.

In a nutshell, that's what Design Ops is all about—helping a design team operate more effectively and efficiently across people operations, business operations, and processes and tools.

Afshar: What's the story of how you got into the field of design ops?

Parr: I started out studying psychology, and my first job was in HR as a project manager for a global team at Landor, a design branding agency. That's where I first got exposed to the world of design, and I was instantly hooked. From there, I naturally found myself moving into roles that focused on project and program management, as well as client management, especially within design consultancies and agencies.

While working at places like IDEO and Smart Design, I had the opportunity to collaborate closely with engineers, designers, and researchers. My role was often in operational project management, which I loved. I spent a significant amount of time in this space, and it was incredibly rewarding.

Over time, I transitioned into the tech industry. My first tech role was at a small startup in New York, where I served as the Chief of Staff, handling all things operational. This shift was eye-opening for me. Coming from an agency background, where you're often applying a set method to various industries and clients, I found myself wanting to see the fruits of our labor. I wanted to see how the work we did actually launched or evolved within a company, and working on the client side allowed me to do just that.

This transition happened around 2014, just as Design Ops was starting to take shape as a distinct field. This was a pivotal time for me because when I began working in Design Operations more officially, Design Ops as a field was also becoming more formally defined and developed. My background in consulting and working in design agencies translated seamlessly to the needs of tech companies, especially startups.

One of my first significant roles in this space was at Meta, during a time of rapid growth and scaling. The skills I developed in consulting, such as being resourceful, maintaining operational rigor, and having a bias towards action, were invaluable. I also carried with me the ethos of prototyping and iterating, which was something I learned at IDEO. This mindset—putting something out there, seeing how it works, and then iterating—was a perfect fit for the world of Design Ops. I've been working in this field ever since, and it's been a fulfilling journey.

Afshar: It sounds like design ops teams are often responsible for maintaining the delicate balance of managing resources efficiently while undertaking ambitious project work. What's your approach in optimizing resources?

Parr: One of the key lessons I've learned in my career is the importance of planning for scale, even if it doesn't seem like the design organization will grow significantly in the next year or so. It's crucial to set up systems and processes that are as lightweight and low-maintenance as possible, so they can run autonomously without requiring constant oversight.

I'm always emphasizing the need to think ahead with my team. For example, when it comes to something like our internal wiki, I'm constantly advocating for making it as evergreen as possible by linking to the company-wide resources, like the budget guidelines, rather than duplicating information. If we were to input the current budget details ourselves, we'd be stuck constantly updating and maintaining that information as the company's needs change. By planning for long-term, lightweight management, we avoid the trap of having to manage and own a sprawling array of tasks and resources.

For smaller teams, where resource allocation is tight, I usually adopt a consultative or triage approach. We start by mapping out the team's needs and identifying the biggest challenges. Then, we come in, help set things on the right track, establish the necessary systems, create documents, set up templates, and facilitate key conversations. Once everything is moving in the right direction, we step back. This approach allows us to function like a specialized team—swiftly addressing issues and then moving on, rather than becoming permanently embedded in the ongoing management of a project.

One challenge in operations is avoiding the trap of continually accumulating responsibilities. I often use the analogy of spinning plates: you start with one plate spinning smoothly, but then you add another, and another, until you're overwhelmed trying to keep all of them going. To break this cycle, I focus on solving problems by setting up a self-service infrastructure and then moving on, rather than getting stuck in long-term involvement.

When it comes to more ambitious or complex projects, I evaluate them carefully. I consider how complicated the project is, whether it spans multiple teams or organizations, and if it's something that only Design Ops can effectively manage. If there's another person or role that could handle it just as well with the right support, I prefer to set them up for success and step back, rather than taking on the project ourselves. This ensures that we allocate our resources wisely and focus on the projects where we can make the most significant impact.

Afshar: I imagine your role often involves collaboration across multiple functions at the company. How do you foster effective collaboration between not only design but engineering, product management, and other departments?

Parr: Operations often plays the role of a facilitator and, when necessary, a mediator. In Design Operations, this role is critical in fostering collaboration within the design team and across different functions. By understanding the unique needs of each function and what's driving those needs, as well as aligning with design's goals, we can take a solutions-oriented approach to bridge gaps and build stronger partnerships.

It's not uncommon, whether in tech or consulting companies, to see different roles focused solely on their own priorities, which can sometimes lead to silos. That's why it's so important to foster open conversations about everyone's needs, goals, and desired outcomes. By bringing these diverse perspectives together, we can collaboratively identify a path forward that works for everyone.

For example, a classic scenario is one where designers want to create something innovative, but the technical constraints seem too significant, leading to collaboration challenges. In such situations, it's crucial to dig deeper. Why does the design team want to build this? What problem are they trying to solve? Understanding the "why" behind these desires can help in communicating these motivations to other teams, like engineering, and can also help in understanding the technical constraints they face.

From an operations standpoint, it's about facilitating these discussions and finding a staged approach that works. Maybe the full vision can't be realized immediately, but by agreeing on a phased plan—where initial steps are taken and fast follows are planned—we can move towards an outcome that satisfies everyone. This way, we build consensus and ensure that all teams are aligned and happy with the progress.

Design Operations isn't just about managing processes; it's about creating an environment where collaboration thrives, where different functions understand each other, and where solutions are built together, step by step.

Afshar: How do you measure the success of design operations? What measurement criteria do you find most valuable in assessing the impact of operational work?

Parr: Measuring the success of Design Operations is both an art and a science, involving a mix of qualitative and quantitative metrics. First and foremost, it's crucial for the Design Ops team—whether it's an entire department, a small team, or even just one individual—to have a clear roadmap with well-defined goals. Just like any product team, having a structured roadmap allows us to align our efforts and adapt our goals as needed over time.

For example, in the first year of a Design Ops team forming at a company, they might focus on building foundational infrastructure to support growth. In the following year, the goal might shift to scaling that infrastructure, and then perhaps to fostering team cohesion and culture. These goals aren't mutually exclusive, but having a focused approach helps in managing resources effectively, especially in resource-constrained environments. With a clear roadmap in place, it's easier to define what success looks like for each objective, leading to the identification of both qualitative and quantitative success metrics.

When it comes to these metrics, some areas are easier to quantify than others. For instance, measuring improvements in team culture or cohesion can be challenging. However, tools like engagement surveys, which many companies already have in place, can be invaluable. These surveys often measure the same factors over time, providing a consistent way to track progress. For instance, if we're trying to gauge whether team cohesion is improving, we might look at trends in engagement survey results over several quarters.

Beyond culture, other key areas of Design Ops that require measurement include ensuring that people have the information they need to do their jobs and that they feel connected to the larger design organization. These aspects can be measured in various ways, some lightweight and informal, such as tracking how frequently team members reference the wiki, monitoring questions asked in Slack channels, or conducting quick polls during meetings to assess whether people feel they're spending too much time searching for information.

However, it's important to recognize that the responsibility for these outcomes doesn't rest solely on the shoulders of the Design Ops team. For example, improving engagement survey scores isn't just an ops challenge; it's also a leadership challenge. Success in these areas often requires close collaboration between Design Ops and design leadership. Together, they can address gaps and challenges to ensure the design organization operates as efficiently and effectively as possible.

Afshar: Can you share an example of how the intersection of product design and design operations played a crucial role in the success of the business?

Parr: One of the most pervasive challenges I've seen across nearly every company is the issue of design capacity and allocation. It's often underestimated at tech corporations, even though it's historically always been a critical component of success in the agency and consultancy world. In the latter environments, there's a strong emphasis on capacity and allocation—knowing exactly who is working on what, how much time they're dedicating to each project, billing based on the exact employee assigned, and maintaining rigorous oversight. This focus is essential to that business model and is key to delivering high-quality work.

However, in tech companies, allocation tends to be much looser. I've observed this in both large corporations and small startups. A common scenario is when product managers are requesting too much from designers, leading to an overload of work. The designer may struggle to keep up, and this often happens because there hasn't been a clear conversation about what's realistic in terms of their workload.

One of the fundamental issues is that conversations about "where the waterline is"—essentially, understanding what the designer can reasonably handle—aren't happening as often as they should. For example, there might be a situation where a designer is working with multiple PMs, each of whom is unaware of the other's demands. I remember one instance where we brought all the PMs into a room and revealed that their shared designer was juggling work from three different teams. The PMs had no idea this was the case, and once they understood, they immediately reprioritized their requests. They realized that their specific tasks weren't as critical compared to other projects, and this new awareness led to a more manageable workload for the designer.

This highlights the importance of having more rigor around how we allocate resources within a design team. Open and honest conversations about allocation are crucial because they directly impact the quality of work and, ultimately, the business's success. When designers are spread too thin, working on too many things at once without enough time to engage in deep thinking and problem-solving, it negatively affects the quality of the design. This, in turn, impacts the customer experience, which can have a significant ripple effect on the business's overall success.

Ensuring that designers have the space to focus on their work allows them to contribute meaningfully to the product, leading to better outcomes for both the users and the business. So, while it might seem like a small operational detail, proper design allocation is actually a critical factor in driving business impact.

Afshar: What leadership qualities contribute most to building a high-performing and cohesive Design Ops team?

Parr: When it comes to hiring, I focus heavily on mindset—particularly for roles in operations. In operations, it's essential to have a mindset that is geared towards identifying gaps and knowing how to address them effectively. Not everyone has this perspective, and it's crucial for success in this field.

One of the key qualities I look for is resourcefulness. In most companies, especially those that are resource-constrained, there's often not a large team to help out with every task. The best operations professionals are those who don't need to ask for permission every step of the way. They're the ones who, when they don't know how to do something, figure it out. They ask around, dig deep to find the root of a problem, and drive toward a solution. This resourcefulness is closely tied to having a bias toward action—taking the initiative to move things forward independently.

Another critical quality for operations roles is the ability to drive clarity. In today's remote or hybrid work environments, there's an overwhelming amount of noise—constant communication, updates, and information coming from all directions. Operations professionals are uniquely suited to cut through this noise and bring clarity to their teams and processes. They're able to take complex, cluttered situations and distill them into clear, actionable steps.

Problem-solving is another essential trait. Those who enjoy tackling challenges head-on tend to be the ones who are naturally resourceful, action-oriented, and clarity-driven. In operations, the most successful individuals are those who can spot gaps and challenges without being explicitly told what they are. They take the initiative to find solutions, taking ownership and accountability for the outcomes.

This mindset is important for any role in tech companies, where sometimes there's less rigor compared to an agency environment. In tech, there can be a tendency to become a bit complacent and siloed because the level of tracking and oversight isn't as intense. This can lead to a lack of resourcefulness, where people might not push themselves as hard to be proactive or innovative.

That's why it's crucial to hire people who naturally exhibit these qualities—they won't rely solely on ops to drive things forward, but instead, will actively contribute to the organization's success.

Afshar: What books, podcasts, or other sources of inspiration do you turn to for personal and professional development?

Parr: Interestingly, as a parent of two young children, I find that the skills I'm developing at home—like fostering empathy, listening, and helping people feel heard—are incredibly relevant to my professional life as well. For example, when I talk to my kids, I often approach it by acknowledging their feelings, understanding why they're upset, and then working with them to figure out a solution. This approach translates well to leadership, where creating a space where people feel understood and supported is crucial.

I also enjoy participating in the *DesignOps Assembly*, which was started by Meredith Black, a Director at Figma who I worked with at IDEO. It's a fantastic community, especially for those new to Design Ops, and it provides great resources and a supportive network.

Recently, I started reading *Stolen Focus: Why You Can't Pay Attention* by Johann Hari, which has been really eye-opening. I've learned that it takes about 20 minutes to get back into a flow state after being interrupted, which is incredibly relevant from an operations perspective. My goal is to help design teams have more uninterrupted "makers' time," and this book reinforces the importance of minimizing distractions to improve both the quality of work and overall productivity.

In the future, I'd love to explore creating open-access tools that anyone can use, tailored to the specific needs of design teams. It's exciting to think about where technology can take us in operations, and I'm looking forward to diving deeper into more technical aspects. I'm always thinking about how to apply new ideas and tools to improve how we work—and I'm looking forward to contributing back to the community and sharing more of what I've learned and created.

CHAPTER

18

Michael Nitsopoulos
Thentia

Michael 'NITSØ' Nitsopoulos is the Chief Design Officer at Thentia, a venture-backed GovTech company focused on SaaS regulatory products. Leading their experience design (XD) revolution, his role centers on infusing XD strategies with design direction. His team's commitment to the innovation of the platform has elevated the brand, positioning their product as a market leader in the Regulatory and Government Tech space.

Across his career history, Michael is a proven builder, a zero-to-one agency founder, and seed-to-series design executive. His experience as an entrepreneur and business operator sets the precedent of his philosophy that design is more than aesthetics.

In addition to his corporate roles and consulting, Michael is a Designer in Residence and part-time faculty member at the School of Design (SOD) at George Brown College. He resides in Toronto, Canada.

© Jaleh Afshar 2025
J. Afshar, *Chief Design Officers at Work*,
https://doi.org/10.1007/979-8-8688-1137-1_18

Jaleh Afshar: In your role at Thentia, your team works on developing technology for government entities. What are the unique challenges you've encountered when creating products for this clientele vs. other industries you've led design for?

Michael Nitsopoulos: The unique challenges are a part of why I decided to work at Thentia after a long career at agencies. I'll share a bit of background context to delve into that.

I graduated from the University of Toronto with a degree in biology, initially planning to become a dentist. However, through some twists and turns, my passion eventually led me to design school. I've always been performance-oriented, striving to win design awards in school, work for award-winning studios, and eventually open my own award-winning studio.

I started out honing my skills in design throughout various studios in Toronto. Eventually, I co-founded my own agency, CINDERBLOC, with a business partner in 2008, right in the midst of an economic downturn. This challenging environment taught me to approach projects differently. While creative work is fulfilling, it doesn't always pay the bills. Some of our most rewarding projects were for clients you'd never expect, like law firms. Convincing traditionally conservative industries to embrace innovative solutions was incredibly satisfying.

I continued with CINDERBLOC until 2014, when I decided to divest my shares and go all-in on a digital-first approach. Balancing professional decisions with personal relationships was tough—my business partner was even my best man at my wedding! However, I knew it was time to move on and refocus on family (my son had recently been diagnosed with ASD).

I still loved designing, but I wanted to dive deeper into the digital space. After some contracting work, including a stint as head of design at a traditional brand studio, I joined RBC, one of Canada's largest banks, as part of their digital arm. This role exposed me to the stark differences in design maturity between institutional businesses and more agile environments.

One day, a former client—who had founded a gov-tech company—reached out. He was surprised to find me at a bank and invited me to join the founding executive team. I thought this would be a pure tech company experience, but it was another eye-opener. The design and product maturity were very low, and their delivery was more consultative than agile.

Working in gov-tech presented unique challenges. Our clients were often stuck in the past, using outdated legacy systems and processes. Imagine inspectors literally jotting notes on paper, stuffing them into manila envelopes, and delivering them to their agency for processing. Ultimately, the goal was to modernize these processes without overwhelming the users.

Interestingly enough, in the design and tech industry, there's often a preference for working with B2C companies on "cool" projects. But taking the easy path isn't always the most rewarding. It's like designing a brand for a hipster coffee shop—creative, but not necessarily challenging. I found fulfillment in tackling projects for less glamorous sectors, like law firms, where innovative problem-solving truly stands out.

Our database software solution is akin to a CRM, designed to operationalize agencies and professional licensing boards. Initially, we focused on Canada, but soon realized the market was more receptive in the United States. There was a turning point after landing a major statewide client during COVID and we began gaining momentum.

Selling to institutionalized businesses involves longer sales cycles and a lot of relationship-building. It's crucial to make clients feel comfortable transitioning from their familiar ways to our more efficient digital solutions. The challenge of adapting to different environments and continuously pushing the boundaries of design and technology has been immensely rewarding, and it's been great to work with clients and partners through that journey together.

Afshar: You've resided in Toronto for many years; however, throughout your career, you've had significant experience working with clients worldwide. What are the unique aspects of Canada's approach to innovation and product development?

Nitsopoulos: In Canada, there's a stereotype that we're nice but not particularly innovative. Many businesses here talk about making purchases but rarely follow through, leading to a lot of tire-kicking. This happens across industries, including professional colleges and physical product sales. Our professional colleges are publicly funded, and their spending can be quite odd, often focused on job safety creation rather than pragmatic investments. In contrast, American businesses can be more ruthless in a sense, however, that can also foster an environment that builds amazing talent and forward-thinking products.

Selling design services in Canada often involves long sales cycles. For instance, a typical sales cycle in the United States might be 12 months, but in Canada, it could be 18 months or longer. This slow pace is similarly mirrored in the governmental systems. For example, our court systems remained paper-based until COVID-19, unlike the digitized systems in the United States, where many states accommodated remote court hearings much earlier. I've found that even less well-known states in the United States can be ahead of Canada in certain aspects of digitization. This might be due to less bureaucratic alignment needed behind the scenes. States like California and Texas, with their immense GDPs, operate almost like countries and drive significant innovation.

Working across borders has been eye-opening. The differences in business cultures and processes have provided valuable insights. However, I see there is a lot of potential for innovation in Canada, and many sectors are hungry for modernization.

Afshar: I'm curious how your background as an entrepreneur has shaped how you approach executive leadership.

Nitsopoulos: I hesitate to distill it down to simply the term "empathy," but that was definitely a key piece to how I understood the challenges of leadership. Many assume startups are purely tech companies, but a startup can be any small business. When people are hard on the CEO, they often overlook how difficult it is to start/build a business. Especially one that becomes venture-backed is under the pressure of scaling, and has to answer to a board of directors and investors. To understand this requires a broad understanding of entrepreneurship's mechanisms.

In a startup with fewer than 20 people, it's easy to criticize someone without recognizing the complexities they face. The journey of entrepreneurship is not a straight path but rather a series of highs and lows. It's like a graph with erratic movements before it stabilizes, unlike the steady progression seen in traditional career paths.

During hardships, you gain invaluable lessons. The recent salary spikes and job security for some tech workers during COVID-19 led many to think everything was fine, only for a significant number of people to get laid off, causing widespread dissatisfaction. This situation highlighted the lack of resilience among many who hadn't experienced such unpredictability before.

Ultimately, having a realistic outlook is essential. Even top performers can be let go due to various business mechanisms, be it financial constraints or other factors. This reality is part of the entrepreneurial journey. Betting on yourself means you bear the responsibility for your success or failure. While entrepreneurship offers the potential to create lifelong work, it's far from easy. There is no such thing as an 'overnight success' and what most people don't see is the 10–20 years of hard work, commitment, and dedication leading up to it.

Accountability through constant change is crucial. Many people struggle with uncertainty, but those who have navigated the zero-to-one phase of starting a business know what it's like to have everything on the line. When I started my business, I had been married for only a couple of years. There were moments when the uncertainty threatened my marriage, my ability to pay the mortgage, and more. Experiencing these challenges firsthand gives you a deep appreciation for the difficulties involved in entrepreneurship, and shapes how I lead today.

Afshar: Have you encountered challenging collaborations? How did you work through those situations?

Nitsopoulos: One type of resistance I've encountered stems from operational culture at the highest levels of an organization. For example, the C-suite's decisions heavily influence the processes throughout an organization. If that executive already has preconceived notions of design as a siloed discipline, this makes it challenging to propose evolved ways of working.

As an example, when I started in my current role, our team was small and engineering-dominated. The design process was very prescriptive, with clear requirements and expectations that had to be met—leaving little room for creative freedom. It took years to transition toward a more productized and compartmentalized offering. Even though our CEO is a strong advocate for design, the reality is that design isn't the sole driver of the final product we ship; it's part of a larger process. Many products were originally designed with an engineering focus. This made it challenging to rewire the mindset without stepping on toes. Terms and content design were often rooted in engineering jargon, which needed to be translated into more user-friendly language.

I believe design, at its core, is about problem-solving, not just aesthetics. However, convincing others of this can be difficult because many still see design as merely visual artifact and pretty images. Effective communication becomes crucial here. Sometimes, that means choosing words that resonate better with your audience internally. For instance, we branded our design system as a "DDS," standing for a Dev Design System. Putting "dev" first means we are clearly including and prioritizing the voice and needs of developers. Such subtle word choices can significantly impact perception, making things more inclusive/collaborative.

At times, I've even had to remove the word "design" altogether from discussions to avoid seeming egocentric and to emphasize that it's about solving problems, not about visual design or aesthetics. This shift in mindset is crucial, and it resonated with me especially coming from an entrepreneurial background. Running a business teaches you about P&Ls and overall business operations, not just the discipline/craft you were trained and educated in.

Everyone wants to feel important and heard. Navigating human psychology and communication is essential, especially in a growing company. As we scaled from 18 to around 200 employees in my current role, new dynamics and executive-level politics emerged. It's crucial to ensure people feel they are a vital part of the process. Effective communication often involves changing how we present ideas and recognizing that learning is a two-way street.

Afshar: Along with your CDO role, you also contribute as a faculty member at George Brown College. Could you share your personal experience going through design school and the ways you've adapted curriculum now to best prepare students for the workforce.

Nitsopoulos: The challenge with design education is that it often lacks the involvement of active designers or studio owners who are up-to-date and producing relevant work. As a design student, it's crucial to learn from those who are currently in the industry.

In Ontario, we have the Registered Graphic Designers (RGD) association, which tries to protect the profession with guidelines against unpaid internships and spec work. However, it's hard for young, talented designers to turn down opportunities, even if they come without pay. These early career designers might not even realize that these types of practices are unethical.

Design education and the industry still have room for improvement. The key is to create an environment where active professionals can share their current, relevant experiences with students, preparing them for real-world challenges. I aim to bring honesty and practicality to my interactions with students and the portfolio reviews I participate in. The journey can be tough, but for those passionate about design, the rewards are worth it.

Afshar: Could you share some advice for design practitioners who are interested in pursuing management?

Nitsopoulos: I find design leadership fascinating because, in my opinion, titles mean little. A title that carries weight in one company might mean nothing elsewhere. Entrepreneurship has taught me to focus less on design itself and more on the business operations that tie everything together.

The real challenge is deciding whether you want to manage people or continue designing. Many designers prefer to be individual contributors (ICs) rather than people managers. One critical question to ask yourself is whether you'd be content with not designing at all (or very minimally). As a design manager, you often find yourself removed from the hands-on creative work and that doesn't jive with some designers.

Being a designer often feels like an inherent part of your identity, making it hard to separate yourself from the craft. When you're no longer actively designing, it can feel like you're losing a part of yourself. However, as a leader, your role shifts to guiding and supporting others, which is also incredibly meaningful and critical.

Achieving a balance between practical business operations and creative passion is key. Design is about problem-solving and innovation, not just aesthetics and winning awards. The industry often focuses on external validation through awards and accolades, but these don't necessarily translate to business success.

Design education and the industry have evolved, with more opportunities now, especially in product design and tech. Companies increasingly internalize design, recognizing its strategic value. The key to success is understanding the broader context of business and applying design thinking to solve real-world problems.

Another important aspect of leadership is creating an environment where your team can excel. My philosophy is similar to coaching in sports: identify each person's strengths and create the space for them to shine. By understanding each team member's strengths and fostering an environment where they can thrive, we build a collaborative and productive culture. This approach has helped me build a strong, cohesive team.

Although our design team is small, I've managed to retain everyone since day one by focusing on creating a supportive and engaging environment. Fostering a love for design and showing its value through collaboration and results can make a significant difference. Recognizing this and reframing our mindset to appreciate the impact we're making as both a design team and a unified company is essential. My goal is to ensure that design is seen as an integral part of the company's success and not just an isolated function.

CHAPTER

19

Mig Reyes
Duolingo

Mig Reyes is Head of Product Design at Duolingo, a company dedicated to crafting the best education in the world and making it universally available. Duolingo has been awarded an Apple Design Award and was named by TIME magazine as one of 2023's most influential global companies.

Previously, Mig served as a Director of Product Design at Instagram, serving as Head of Design for Instagram's Foundations team, leading managers and designers focused on accessibility, brand, design systems, notifications, emerging devices, and Instagram.com.

Jaleh Afshar: What's your career origin story?

Mig Reyes: Generally aimless after high school, I wound up going to a local art college graduating with a degree in graphic design. Raised in the Midwest as a person of color, I developed a competitive spirit with a chip on my shoulder. I wanted to prove I could be as good as the east and west coast talent I had always read about. I had a heated motivation to figure out a career and make a name for myself on my own.

I cut my teeth at small graphic design studios and had a short stint in agency life before realizing I wasn't keen on client services. My career took off once I switched in-house as one of the first fulltime interactive design hires at Threadless.com. Since then, I've transitioned from brand design to product design having led work at 37signals, Tock by Squarespace, Trunk Club by Nordstrom, Sprout Social, Instagram, and ultimately, my Head of Product Design role at Duolingo.

Afshar: How does your focus on craft influence the way you show up as a leader?

Reyes: When millions to billions of people use your product, they deserve the best. As a design leader, having a deep focus on craft is one way to signal to your teams that excellence and quality matters, down to the smallest of details. We are lucky and privileged to have the jobs we do as designers. We should sweat the little things.

Beyond steering quality, focusing on craft earns influence with one of your most important constituents as a design leader: the designers themselves. Gaining the respect of a design team means them trusting your sense of taste, wanting your feedback, and leaning on you to call out when work isn't good enough yet. Leaders with a high bar for quality inspire and attract some of the best talent, so I strive to be a leader who can articulate excellence at every level, including the pixels.

Caring about craft is about mutual trust, respect, and influence, having been through it all as a designer myself.

Afshar: That level of credibility that you have by being a builder yourself can be so helpful in managing a team. Being that leader who your team can trust: *Mig knows what he's talking about because he can roll up his sleeves and do it himself, therefore I trust him advising me on what to do.*

Now let's chat about another approach on the management spectrum—company size. Having filled both shoes, what's your take on being a senior management executive at a large corporation vs. the sole head of design at a smaller company?

Reyes: A way to think the difference is how many people you're able to positively affect and the leverage you'll have over an entire business.

As a manager and director of a big company, it's likely you'll have a specific scope with a tightly defined remit. Big companies are great if you like to go deep into specific focus areas and you're excited to learn from the world's best talent around you—often top executives from other companies. You'll have access to fine-tuned processes and an abundance of resources to ensure your teams run efficiently.

When you're head of a design at a smaller organization, by necessity your reach and responsibilities are company-wide. There aren't mature processes yet. The bar for talent is still rising. You'll be in environments where you're hands-on, and as a result you'll get to put your thumbprint on how the future of your design team takes shape in the years ahead.

Afshar: One aspect you mentioned that I'd love to dig in on a little more is when you're the head of an entire function, your peers are the top executives from each of these other departments. How do you represent design as you collaborate with these people?

Reyes: A great design leader understands the business first, with a reputation built on their high quality bar for people and the product. Before I represent design, I first try to meet every other leader where they are. I aim for fluency in the company's operating principles, key business metrics, and overall strategic direction. Only then can I do my part to represent design with other leaders.

Design makes hard things feel simple. Representing design at the company-level level means being the voice of the user in meeting rooms while having one of the most critical eyes for design work happening across the company. It also means helping the company reduce complexity not just in the work itself but suggesting ways to simplify processes of how we arrive at the work in the first place.

Afshar: When you are stuck or when you need that mentorship or guidance or leadership, where do you go?

Reyes: I seek advice from other functional heads within the company. It's likely they're wrestling with similar problems as me. I try to remember that my executive peers earned their way to their spot through their own career trials and tribulations. They've learned a lot; I'd be wise to learn from them.

I'm also very motivated to reach out to product and design executives I admire across the industry. I've developed an outreach muscle since leaving college. Design and tech are small communities and everyone has something to share. You can see some of my earliest career interviews that still stick with me to this day at humblepied.com.

Afshar: Duolingo has a distinctive brand, and is known for their mascot and even memes. Coming into an organization with such a strong brand visible throughout the product, how has that shaped the way that you think specifically about your design leadership approach?

Reyes: I often hear design interview candidates say, "I'm looking for a new job where design has a seat at the table." What I tell them is we don't have that problem at Duolingo because Design built the table. Much of Duolingo's success is attributable to design. We're the second largest function next to engineering. Design isn't just valued at Duolingo, it's part of our competitive advantage.

Duolingo's brand is a reflection of our product; our product is a reflection of our brand. To build simple, meaningful products at Duolingo, you have to understand all of the elements that make up our brand. We want to breathe life into everything we're doing.

Chapter 19 | Mig Reyes, Duolingo

Our little green owl, Duo, isn't just a graphic asset to sprinkle across different screens in our app. It's who we embody as we talk to millions of learners. Our CEO has aspirations that Duo, Lily, and our other illustrated characters reach Disney notoriety. It's a huge statement, but also an exciting mission to rally our company toward. Brand is imprinted in how we operate no matter the role you're in.

Afshar: On that note, we've heard a lot about the legacy of design that you've built at past companies and now at Duolingo. As you reflect on these bodies of work, any particular challenges you've encountered that you've had to overcome throughout your managerial life?

Reyes: In small markets like Chicago, attracting top talent had always been a big challenge. At big companies like Instagram, long-term retention for great designers was tough. One challenge I'm excited about now at Duolingo: talent development for a team with high ambitions despite not having depth in experience.

Duolingo is unique in that we invest heavily in early career talent straight out of school. When your workforce is built that way over the course of a decade, they might only be familiar with one specific way of working. My aspiration for our team is that designers have more influence, more autonomy, and more decision-making authority than they currently do. We'll get there by developing our designers' skills in craft, product, and strategy. The closer we can bring designers to the realities of the business, the more influence they'll naturally assume.

Afshar: In cases like these, where there are conflicts with how data points or outcomes are interpreted, any tips on how you diplomatically resolve situations?

Reyes: If there's a skill I encourage anyone to practice, it's active listening paired with playback. I coach my senior people on becoming excellent at this.

Whether you're meeting a new junior designer or sorting out a company-level challenge with a chief executive, aim to speak for 10% of the time while you listen to the other person share for the other 90%. Spend every second understanding someone's perspective and how they see a problem. Importantly, before leaving the conversation, run a playback and repeat what you heard. Repeat it again until you're certain both of you are on the same page.

Every piece of communication you share from there on out is tied to team and executive priorities you've uncovered. Being able to relay problems of the company by every function and level is one way to earn trust across the company.

Afshar: Outside of work, any skills, experiences, or hobbies that have shaped the way that you show up as a leader?

Reyes: Outside of work, teaching and building communities have shaped me as a leader.

I started the Chicago chapter of CreativeMornings, served as a President for AIGA Chicago, and taught design at two different schools. Bringing people together, helping people learn, and encouraging others to be better versions of themselves are critical parts of leadership. Getting to practice those outside of the work place undoubtedly sharpened my leadership skills.

Afshar: Speaking of getting to know people personally, I had a look at your website (migreyes.com), which includes your reading list. Any titles or book tidbits you'd like to share with aspiring design leaders?

Reyes: Pick up books on writing clearer and simpler. Especially if you're in leadership, where your currency takes the form of meetings, memos, and documents. Influential people get to the point very quickly and write in a way that feels like they crafted their message just for you.

Revising Prose by Richard A. Lanham was transformative. It correlates to design quite well: get to the point, get the design down to the essence.

Several Short Sentences About Writing by Verlyn Klinkenborg was a light, fun, and approachable way to learn about writing better.

Afshar: As we wind down our time together, any last words of wisdom that you'd like to share for someone who wants to follow in your footsteps and learn from your leadership philosophy?

Reyes: As you ascend in your career, keep helping everyone else around you. Invest in others as a way of working. One of the best ways to accelerate your career is to build a reputation of helping others.

Another focus area important to me is leadership development. As a leader, I'm thinking about how I'm empowering people on my team to take my job from me one day. You can learn a lot about a leader by the caliber of teams they've built and nurtured, along with their team's reputation and impact.

You can start in small ways, like simply creating the space for discussion on what leadership even means. At Instagram, I started a program called the Craft of Management (craftofmanagement.com). I brought together all Instagram's design managers, directors, and VPs where we spent an hour a month having group discussion on design leadership topics. The lesson here? If it's important to you, make space for it.

CHAPTER

20

Mohammed Adib
Intercon

Mohammed Adib is the founder of Intercon, an architecture and interior design firm. Founded in 1993 in London, Intercon is now a global firm with bases in Barcelona, Miami, Athens, and Dubai, and projects across continents.

With over 30 years of experience, Adib's expertise spans across projects of various scales and typologies. Under his leadership, Intercon has delivered over 180 projects in 15 countries with services, including interior design, architecture, product design, and signage and wayfinding.

Adib graduated from the AA School of Architecture, London, before pursuing postgraduate studies at EINA University School of Design and Art in Barcelona. Adib's creative DNA is deeply intertwined with his upbringing, with his father's construction background laying the foundation for his lifelong journey in architecture and design. Adib's relentless pursuit of excellence is evident in Intercon's diverse portfolio, reflecting a seamless blend of cultural nuances and contemporary trends. In addition to several projects across the globe, the firm is also working on coveted projects like Saudi Arabia's Qiddiya and in Obhur for SEVEN.

© Jaleh Afshar 2025
J. Afshar, *Chief Design Officers at Work*,
https://doi.org/10.1007/979-8-8688-1137-1_20

Chapter 20 | Mohammed Adib, Intercon

Jaleh Afshar: What first inspired you to pursue the field of design?

Mohammed Adib: Architects and designers are natural observers and curious people. I have been so since my childhood and always wondered how I could do things in a better way by watching and observing how people use objects and spaces. I used to accompany my father to building sites every opportunity I could and always tried to learn how to build things, a process that fascinated me and still does.

Afshar: What were the most influential moments that shaped your career?

Adib: As with any professional journey, mine has been over 35 years, there are many moments, clients, colleagues, and bosses that shape the designer and create the journey. The most important moments happen when all these factors align in a positive way and that special moment starts to shape the future outcome. One such moment when I felt that there were no limits to what we could achieve was a project that I was confident of delivering (much larger than anything we had done till then); the client blindly trusted his intuition to go with us against much more established competitors and the result was very successful, obviously none of this can ever happen without hard work and absolute dedication and belief in our abilities.

Afshar: Can you share a design project that changed your perspective or challenged your assumptions?

Adib: All projects have their particular challenges and even after 30-plus years in the industry, I still face new situations and learn new lessons. Recently, most of our projects have an added material and research aspect as modern building techniques and new materials are developed. For example, we are very actively testing carbon-neutral construction methods and trying to use as little traditional concrete as possible and have recently completed a fully "dry" project with zero use of concrete and all components were fully certified and sustainable materials. However, the biggest challenge was convincing the client to go this way and not the traditional way; all technical aspects are very easy to address.

Afshar: At Intercon, you manage a vast multidisciplinary team spanning continents, with projects across a wide variety of clients. What strategies and tools do you use to keep track of your schedule?

Adib: MS Teams is our main collaboration tool, where we share design progress for each and every project. It is a very useful tool to have all team members up-to-date with all the developments that are happening within the project, as well as keeping those in other time zones up-to-date; we share sketches, meeting minutes, client discussions, and documents received from subconsultants. However, I am old school, and I still value direct face-to-face meetings with all stakeholders involved in the design process, but I still do my daily handwritten "To Do" list every day to plan what is required.

Afshar: How do you stay current with emerging trends and learnings in your field?

Adib: The design world is getting smaller and smaller; people have access to a varied array of design inspirations and an infinite shower of images; for me, traveling is probably one of the most design-enriching experiences that any person can get, learning how designers around the world are offering solutions to their particular cultures is a very useful tool to apply in our designs. For materials and new technologies, attending events and trade fairs is where I tend to exchange knowledge with my peers and interact with manufacturers.

Afshar: What was the most challenging project you've worked on? How did you overcome its obstacles?

Adib: I think as in all projects, managing the expectations of the client is the most challenging part, understanding the vision of the client as early as possible and explaining and accompanying the client during the design process step by step is critical. As designers, we visualize what we are doing at a very early stage of the design; yet the actual visual deliverables come at a much later stage of the project; hence, the challenge is understanding what the clients want as early as possible and explaining the solution to them.

Afshar: Can you share a bit more behind-the-scenes about a situation where you've had to navigate conflicting design opinions?

Adib: Navigating conflicting design opinions can be quite challenging, especially when multiple stakeholders have strong views on what the final product should look like. The most important point is to understand the vision of the stakeholders as well as the desired demographics that will use the design. This is the critical point to achieve to be able to start the design process; also, it is paramount to separate the personal taste for the aesthetics from the functional usage of the space or object as this can be justified and explained to why a design is done in that way. Once all the clear criteria for the design are fixed and agreed on, extensive studies and benchmarking need to be done to further confirm the validity of the design, this almost never fails to convince all parties involved that the design presented is the most suitable for the task required.

Afshar: How do you integrate sustainability considerations into the design process? Have you faced challenges when convincing stakeholders to prioritize sustainability in their architecture, interior design, or landscaping?

Adib: There are two main considerations with sustainability; first of all, the design has to be efficient and the spaces correctly dimensioned and oriented for their uses and location; a Platinum-certified LEED building that is empty is the most unsustainable thing there is! No wastage of spaces, unnecessary circulation, excessive heights that need climate control, excessive sun orientation in hot climates, etc., all these have to be standard practices when designing any building. The second point relates to costs; currently, recycled materials are more expensive, more efficient MEP equipment (even though they are cheaper to run and in the long run the opex saves on the capex), modular, off-site, and pod constructions also need to be more competitive. These reductions in the capex of any project will only be achieved by more stringent legislations, once these needs become the standard, the costs will become equitable with those of traditional construction practices and all buildings will become more sustainable.

Afshar: Design can have a significant impact on society. Could you share an example where you addressed a social issue through design?

Adib: All our designs are human centric. We feel that all design needs to have human scale as a starting point, people need to use a space comfortably and need to relate to its scale. Design needs to prioritize the experience and needs of individuals rather than large groups or abstract concepts, focusing on the proportions of the buildings and the spaces; accessibility is again paramount, buildings need to be made accessible and navigable for people of all ages and abilities, ensuring that everyone can interact comfortably with the environment. The selection of materials often reflects warmth and familiarity, creating an inviting atmosphere. Natural materials or finishes can enhance the connection to the surroundings, inclusion of plants, and merging the interior with the exterior. Spaces need to be designed for daily human activities, ensuring they are practical and comfortable. This can mean creating areas for social interaction, relaxation, or productivity.

Afshar: How could design contribute to solving some of humanity's most critical challenges?

Adib: Design can facilitate and simplify the user experience and this in turn would improve the quality of life. The main challenges now are the fast pace of the modern world, the endless commuting and the overcrowding of city centers. The 15-minute city is such a solution, it's an urban planning model that aims to create cities where residents can access most of their daily necessities (such as work, shopping, education, healthcare, and leisure) within a 15-minute walk or bike ride from their homes. This idea promotes convenience, reduces reliance on cars, and fosters a sense of community, it also allows for less dense decentralized living and working areas where more importance can be given to green spaces.

CHAPTER 21

Olatunji Saliu
Interswitch

Olatunji Saliu is a multidisciplinary design leader with experience across a diverse range of clients, from startups to Fortune 500 companies. Based in Lagos, Nigeria, he currently leads the Brand Design and Multimedia departments at Interswitch, an African-focused technology company developing integrated digital payments and technological solutions for various sectors.

Jaleh Afshar: What does a typical work week involve in your role as a creative lead at Interswitch?

Olatunji Saliu: The most predictable aspect of my routine is that no two weeks are exactly the same! I juggle strategic planning, team management, stakeholder management, and hands-on design work. My typical week involves a mix of these elements: strategic thinking, partnership with various stakeholders, diving into design projects, and ensuring my team is motivated and productive.

I often liaise with stakeholders to make sure their needs are met and that our brand is well-represented. I also communicate with my team to identify and resolve any issues they might be facing, ensuring that there are no obstacles in their way, and checking in with them on their career growth and personal goals—this is very important to me.

Each week is dynamic and unpredictable, involving collaboration with cross-functional teams. We support about ten different business lines in-house, which means every day can bring new challenges and opportunities even from a pure product perspective. I work closely with product designers, front-end designers, growth marketers, and representatives from various business lines to ensure seamless operations.

Design, for me, solves two primary problems: functionality and message delivery. If a design is functional and conveys the intended message, it works. However, stakeholders sometimes prioritize aesthetics, wanting more arbitrary colors or, as many readers may have encountered, may want a bigger logo. We strive to manage these requests to achieve a win-win situation, ensuring that the final design remains effective and on-brand.

Understanding regional and market-specific design trends is crucial. It's important to know how our brand and designs resonate with different audiences and adjust accordingly to stay relevant and appealing.

In short, my routine is a blend of strategic planning, hands-on design, and team management, with a constant focus on maintaining our brand's integrity while adapting to new trends and stakeholder needs.

Afshar: What are the design trends currently emerging in Nigeria, and how are you incorporating them into your work?

Saliu: Currently, the trend in Nigeria is generative AI, which often features a distinctive visual style with lots of illustrative elements, gradients, and 3D visuals. We see a lot of AI-generated images in the market right now. However, with the rise of AI, particularly in design, there are concerns about the source of the images used. In Nigeria today, there are even laws from the Advertising Regulatory Council of Nigeria regarding Nigerian models and usage in local ads. Since it's challenging to verify the origin of AI-generated images, we've started building our own video and photography library. This way, we can ensure the authenticity and Nigerian identity of the models we use, and ensure regulatory compliance.

When it comes to trends and how they integrate into the work I do at my job, my approach is to carefully learn and explore aspects of trends first, to see if they make sense to integrate into our brand elements. For example at Interswitch, we cater to various business lines, including B2B, B2C, and B2B2C solutions. Some aspects of trends can be infused into a business line without compromising the overall style and ethos of the brand. As I navigate any trend, I strive to maintain our brand's core style and tone of voice, understanding the implications of integrating new trends.

For example, there's a resurgence of traditional African styles being blended with contemporary designs. This cultural infusion is quite prevalent and it's something that a lot of our audience resonates with, and can work quite well with our brand as well.

In essence, while we embrace new trends that might appeal to specific audience segments, we remain committed to preserving the powerful, timeless core of our brand.

Afshar: What role did your community and professional network play in your career?

Saliu: As a little background to my answer, I'll travel back in time. My first career was music. I was a professional musician playing bass guitar full time. Design was definitely not my thing back then. I was performing and my days were filled with playing instruments. However, I've always had this artistic tendency.

When I was starting out in exploring design, I had a friend whose father owned a printing press. I would visit him regularly. This friend, Oladapo Shonola, is still a designer today. Every evening around six or seven, I would go to his house to watch him work. He was incredibly skilled, and I would observe his process, asking him countless questions about graphic design. This was my introduction to the world of graphic design.

Oladapo would explain things to me and let me take over his computer when he stepped away, as I didn't have my own system. I practiced diligently, bringing my sketches to life on the computer. This experience was fascinating for me, as it allowed me to transform my drawings into digital designs.

This hands-on learning experience was how I transitioned into graphic design, combining my passion for drawing with the possibilities of digital creation. It was an exciting and pivotal time in my journey as a designer.

I also have deep gratitude to Dr. Victor Akunna, who in particular inspired much of my trajectory. At that pivotal moment in my life I was juggling those multiple interests—music, design, and architecture. I wanted to focus on design but felt uncertain about the decision. So, I sought guidance from my mentors, Dr. Victor Akunna and Benjamin Dare.

At that time, I was overwhelmed by my skill set and didn't want to be a jack of all trades. I aspired to be a master of something, to be known for one particular expertise. My dilemma was whether to choose music, architecture, or design as my primary focus.

My mentor, Dr. Victor Akunna, gave me unforgettable advice. He asked, "What is paying the bills right now?" At that moment, music was my primary source of income. Then he asked, "What would you love to be known for in the future?" My answer was design. He advised me to pursue both—let music be my main focus while continuing to develop my design skillset on the side.

I followed his advice and continued with music, incorporating design whenever I could. He predicted that, over time, I would naturally transition into design without even realizing it. That one day I could support myself through design and transition out of music. And that's exactly what happened. Gradually, as I started getting design gigs, design took center stage, and music became a secondary pursuit. The transition happened so seamlessly that I hardly noticed the shift.

He and I are still in touch, although he is presently in the United Kingdom with his family. We still often discuss various topics, and he continues to offer valuable insights, especially on career growth. His perspectives have been instrumental in shaping my career.

The other mentor, I mentioned, Benjamin Dare, is another big inspiration. He runs one of the largest printing presses (Benco Color Media) in Lagos, Nigeria. He is also a very fantastic designer. I studied his work and often visited his printing press for inspiration.

Afshar: Are there particular books, courses, or resources you recommend to those starting out in the design field?

Saliu: I watch a lot of YouTube videos. Whenever I need to learn something new, YouTube is my go-to resource. I'm also very active on LinkedIn, constantly learning from others in the field.

When I first got into design, I watched countless YouTube videos and read numerous books. One of the books that had a significant impact on me was *Steal Like an Artist*. Another influential book was *The Design of Everyday Things*. These books profoundly shaped my perspective as a designer.

My advice is to get those books—they're invaluable. Watch YouTube videos, especially those by Daniel Walter Scott and Chris Do. They are fantastic and solid in their teachings. I also watch random YouTube videos from lesser-known creators. There's always something to learn.

Afshar: What advice would you give to the next generation who are aspiring to join the creative industry?

Saliu: One thing I often say is that I'm always evolving.

If we had this interview yesterday, I may have said something different. If we had this conversation tomorrow, I may express ideas that are different because by tomorrow, I would have read some articles, started reading a new book, checked YouTube tutorials, and learned other perspectives.

The me you meet today is different from the me you will meet tomorrow.

That's who I am—always evolving every minute. I have one mantra, one main career principle, and it's simple: keep learning. I never stop learning.

I believe there is something to learn everywhere. I often listen to random conversations, not necessarily about design. I join discussions about finance, science, history, and other topics to gain different perspectives. As a designer, it's crucial to understand various stakeholders' viewpoints. A great way to build that skill is to develop connections with a circle of people in your personal life who can expose you to different perspectives and ideas.

I also recommend teaching others what you know. It helps reinforce your own understanding. Whenever I learn something new, I show someone else how to do it, and it becomes ingrained in me.

Curiosity is a powerful tool. I'm always curious, always asking questions. When you reached out to me for this interview, I checked your profile and your past publications to learn more about you. This inspired me and opened my eyes to some new topics which we were able to discuss today.

To the new generation—stay curious, keep asking questions, and always be researching. Even if a topic seems unrelated to design, there can be something valuable to learn and apply to your craft.

Stay curious and keep learning. Strive to learn new things every day.

Afshar: Can you describe your management style and the leaders you draw inspiration from?

Saliu: I'm a big fan of John C. Maxwell. His teachings on leadership resonate deeply with me. Another influential figure in my life is Pastor Sami Adeyemi, a prominent leader in Nigeria and my pastor. He's also passionate about leadership, much like Mr. Ben Dare and Dr. Victor Akunna, who are key mentors of mine.

Leadership, as I see it, differs from the conventional perspective often found in Africa, where it can sometimes be about exerting power over others in a very top-down way. I believe in a different approach: leading by example. I'm not afraid to get my hands dirty and show my team how things are done, encouraging them to follow in my footsteps, and also learn from them.

Leading a creative team presents unique challenges. Creativity is subjective, so it's essential to provide feedback that guides without stifling innovation or damaging egos. I constantly think about how to offer constructive feedback that maintains the integrity of their concepts while ensuring they stay on brand. Designers will interpret briefs in their own ways, and my role is to balance their creative freedom with brand consistency.

My focus is on nurturing my team to be the best versions of themselves while also learning from them. I want them to carry this creative freedom and discipline wherever their careers take them. My past experiences with managers who lacked this understanding constantly drives me to be a different manager. Constructive feedback is crucial to me; it should be clear and helpful without discouraging future creativity.

It's essential to cultivate innovation, even within a team that has to operate within the constraints of a brand. This balance is a rewarding challenge for me as a manager. It's about fostering an environment where creativity thrives and aligns with the business's goals.

I'm always growing and getting better at what I do. Getting better at leading is part of my everyday goal.

CHAPTER

22

Payam Tabrizian
Unity

Payam is a design leader, technologist, and spatial scientist based in San Francisco, CA. He is currently Head of Design for Consumer Products at Unity, where he empowers teams to democratize spatial design and game creation across all devices and platforms.

Previously, Payam led software design at IDEO, envisioning and launching products across media and entertainment, mobility, and digital health. He also teaches XR product design at Stanford's d.school with the aim of helping the next generation of designers and entrepreneurs create more intentional, accessible, and useful products.

Jaleh Afshar: What was your personal and professional journey to becoming a Head of Consumer Design at Unity?

Payam Tabrizian: My career had always revolved around spatial design and mapping—essentially, the world of creating and thinking about space. Despite my background in a more traditional field, I'd always had a longstanding fascination with all kinds of technology, particularly creative tools for 3D design and other tech aspects of architecture. I'm particularly passionate about mapping human needs to technological capabilities.

I began my professional career in Iran, focusing on architecture. I had been doing that for many years; however, I always wanted to poke around and understand what was happening in the world outside my realm. I really wanted

© Jaleh Afshar 2025
J. Afshar, *Chief Design Officers at Work*,
https://doi.org/10.1007/979-8-8688-1137-1_22

to pursue a master's degree in Interior Design, outside Iran. But, at the time, there was an obligation I had to stay in the country for. Men in Iran are required to complete military service. There was an exception though—if your father is over the age of 60, you're exempt, so I stayed in the country until that time. During that period, my father and I together built around 300 houses.

When I was able to leave, I went to do some interviews in Paris and Italy as I was applying to some schools. Unfortunately, in Paris, my passport and other belongings were stolen at the metro station! I was really naive—I'd never been to Europe. I didn't know how to protect myself and my things. I was so sad at the time because this situation made me miss my interview date in Italy, which was at a school for interior design.

I went back home disappointed. Shortly after though, a friend who was studying in Belgium encouraged me to explore going there. Turns out there was an urban design program at that university which presented a compelling option to me. Going all the way from interior design where you are designing the small things going inside of buildings, all the way to designing all out cities in urban design! You can imagine the massive scale shift. I said yes and went to Belgium to learn urban design. I was enamored with the whole idea of designing for people through designing large-scale environments, thinking about ecology, all the cool stuff that influences the creation of a place that people come together.

When I went back home to Iran again to begin putting these learnings into practice, I was energized to do good things for my home country and give back. But I had to be realistic and realize that, with all the limitations due to the country being governed so strictly, it means one cannot really do the things that are good for people. You always need to do the things that are imposed upon you by the policies of the government. I got really frustrated after a couple years and decided to move away permanently.

I came to the United States to continue my path in urban design. Of course, there are massive challenges in getting permanent residency here, which led to thinking deeply about whether it was reasonable in the long term to stay in this field or if there was an opportunity where I could apply my background in an adjacent field. During that shift, another hard realization I had was that, in the United States, architects and urban designers are not paid as well here, relatively. This led me to pursue a PhD in geospatial analytics and specifically publish papers highlighting innovations in that space. This was immensely helpful in my petition for a green card.

Over time, I decided to pivot entirely into product design, focusing on the user experience aspects and the intriguing challenges that come with it. In 2018, I began working with IDEO, and I moved to Unity in 2021. Interestingly, today, the day of our interview, marks my last day at Unity.

As for what's next, I'm exploring several options. I've taken a role as head of design at a startup. I'm also focusing on a course I started teaching a few weeks ago at Stanford, focused on extended realities, which is quite exciting. This period is about taking time to concentrate on giving back and planning my next steps.

Even though when I started my career journey, I could never have envisioned ending up in digital product design. If any of the conditions changed in my path, I probably would be in a different place with a different career now. I find this kind of fluidity to be common with people who immigrate and face hardship because those hardships make you find solutions and work through constraints. Just like design itself, it's about investigating what's possible, understanding people, and unlocking opportunity and inclusivity.

This journey, winding and sometimes indirect, mirrors the immigrant experience—carving out a path, navigating constraints, and designing solutions within those constraints.

Afshar: You've had a prolific career in academia, having earned a PhD focused on geospatial analytics and extensively publishing on the topics of environmental design and research. Could you tell us a bit more about your research and how your background in this focus area informs the way you approach product development today?

Tabrizian: Calculating distances, understanding erosion, articulating traffic patterns, crafting better maps, predicting flooding…these are all examples of geospatial analysis. It is very multidisciplinary, not just on the environmental side and what touches upon geography, but also when considering the layer of information beyond the natural factors. What are the cultural or economic inputs which also influence a space? How does behavioral data or population health inform us on what areas are more susceptible to certain problems? How do sociodemographic factors impact people's propensity to become more affected by certain location-based issues or diseases?

We live in a world where location and proximity impacts a lot. It's inevitable. It's part of every discipline, every domain, every industry, from military to economics, all the way to prediction of a person's own success or lifespan. It's all geospatial.

This interaction of people and space has now become a cornerstone of how I approach problem solving. It's been incredibly relevant. I've been lucky to work on the spatial fields all my career.

Much of what I'd worked on at IDEO had spatial applications. I worked on projects on the topic of mobility—how people get from a point A to B—and how to help people streamline that experience and make it more pleasant. For example, if a company like Ford wants to launch a program that helps their employees commute more efficiently, what would be the best solution or interface to design so the maps and spatial analytics are more accurate and tuned to their employee's needs?

At Unity, the focus was on the complex system of 3D modeling and software development. Specifically, how to simplify it in a way that our consumers, who may have no understanding of game development or programming, can easily program and make games. And that meant really going deep into the tools of 3D design and development and thinking about the mental map of a user who wants to create 3D information or gameplay interaction.

I now feel that it's inevitable that much of our interaction with digital information will become spatial very soon, as we see what the world of AR, VR, and XR are emerging. People inevitably interact with the information more spatially than before. Even when digital experiences were only shown on 2D interfaces, we've found that 2D interfaces have a lot of interaction design rules which follow spatial design paradigms and an understanding of relative location and depth. Coming from the background of architecture, it's always been critical to think not only about the container that houses an experience, but the behaviors of the objects in that place, and how you can arrange all of these together in a way that introduces new behaviors and helps the user, the human, in terms of what they want to achieve.

Afshar: The shift from academia to industry can be a challenge for many. Do you have advice for those who are interested in moving to industry?

Tabrizian: For many immigrants, academia serves as a gateway to entering a new country, as it can be a very effective means to facilitate residency in another place. However, for a lot of people in that situation, intentions often involve using academia as a pathway to broader success, rather than a permanent career choice. This eventually presents a duality of whether to remain in academia or venture into other industries. Major considerations in this decision are the financial prospects and work-life balance offered by each path. I have friends who stick with academia primarily because they want to work only nine months a year, and the type of work they do offers them flexibility, allowing them to travel and enjoy other pursuits for the remainder of the time.

There is undeniable value in academia—it offers the chance to teach, interact with students, and transfer knowledge, which can be incredibly rewarding. Conversely, the industry has its own appeal. It's a place where you can build things, and the potential is seemingly limitless. It offers the opportunity to be hands-on and creative, whether that's by joining a large company or crafting and selling your own products. Compared to academia, the industry might appeal more to those looking to make a significant impact. Ultimately, though, deciding whether to stay in academia involves weighing these trade-offs.

Based on my own experiences as an immigrant, establishing a foundation and creating roots in a new country were crucial. Initially, I pursued a postdoctoral opportunity vigorously. However, when the director of the innovation center I was working with informed me that they couldn't secure funding for me, I was forced to explore other options. If the funding had been secured, I likely would have stayed in the postdoc position, as academia isolated me from the outside world, more so than today since platforms like LinkedIn weren't as prominent. Had I not been forced to explore elsewhere, I wouldn't have really even known what I was missing. Nevertheless, I had the chance to explore and made a successful transition.

In retrospect, and as advice to those I mentor, I emphasize the importance of building a network early in one's academic career. Sharing your work and engaging on platforms like LinkedIn can increase visibility into the wider industry, revealing opportunities and cutting-edge developments in your field. If I had started building my network earlier, it would have greatly enhanced my career and my understanding of where technology was heading.

Unfortunately, there is a significant divide between academia and industry. While the transition of knowledge from academia to industry can be swift, especially in fields like AI where CEOs and CTOs might implement academic findings almost immediately, much of academic output may never be utilized in the real world. Some of this is simply because of the lack of practicality in how academic findings are captured and published. It took me some time to adapt my academic language to be more understandable in a professional setting, which highlights how segmented these worlds can be. This segmentation is not only unnecessary but often serves as a form of gatekeeping, maintaining a sense of hierarchy that is, in reality, entirely constructed.

Afshar: Across your past roles in software design practitioner, your career has spanned many highly technical roles. How has your hands-on expertise influenced the way you grow the skills of people in your organization today?

Tabrizian: For me, the integration of technical know-how into my design process has been transformative on multiple fronts. Take prototyping, for instance. It's not just about sketching out ideas; it's about bringing them to life in a tangible way to communicate concepts more effectively and inspire public and secure internal stakeholder buy-in. I've found that my ability to push prototypes to higher fidelity has been a game-changer and enhanced my capacity to communicate ideas effectively and mitigate risks early on in the development cycle.

Moreover, being technically savvy is important for effective collaboration with engineers and other cross-functional partners, resulting in more efficient and successful product development journeys. It's these interactions where the magic happens, where design meets functionality, and where innovative solutions emerge from the synergy of diverse perspectives.

On a more personal level, my journey in design has been guided by a deep-seated belief in human-centered innovation. Understanding the feasibility of my proposals and aligning them with user needs and technological capabilities has been my compass. It's not just about creating products; it's about crafting experiences that resonate with people on a fundamental level. This ethos has driven me to constantly seek out opportunities to bridge the gap between design and engineering, ensuring that our solutions are not only visually compelling but also deeply meaningful to those who interact with them.

Afshar: In past interview publications with your alma mater North Carolina State University, you expressed your thoughts regarding democratizing design and the significance of humanizing design tools to ensure inclusivity and simplicity in the creative process. Could you share a bit more about that philosophy?

Tabrizian: When you delve into the world of architecture and urban design, you may be surprised to learn that even today, it's still being heavily guarded by the big 'A' of architects—the people who like to wear turtlenecks, have really nice pens, and consider themselves the sole masters of creativity. These are the old guards who are really trying to control the discipline and in some cases, limit what is being formally taught. For example, during all my years of practicing architecture, I was so enamored with the openness of emerging 3D technology and all the cutting-edge, easy access tools around it. I couldn't stop wondering why it wasn't integrated into the curriculum, why one else was doing it. Why was I the only person in my class at the time who would make the 3D renderings for all the other students? Why was this not transparently taught back then? At the time I wasn't complaining—I had built a really good business around those skills back then!

Seeing that divide made me think—is it because people are not creative or because they don't have access to the tools? It immediately became apparent to me—especially through interacting with a very multidisciplinary peer group through my PhD project—that people are in fact incredibly creative; *everyone* is creative. Creation can be joyful, inherently social, and fun, but we don't always think about it that way. Some people try to gatekeep it because they want to hold onto their jobs the way they are today, and because the tools define boundaries between disciplines. But at the end of the day, much of what I'm seeing in Silicon Valley today is that these tools are evolving. In the very beginning, the first layer of most tool releases is when it's built is for the professionals of that topic. In that phase, tool creators prioritize advancing the sheer technology rather than the user experience. Think about Tesla. When Tesla first came around and gave people this amazing technology, the user experience was crap. But of course for them to have survived long term in the broader consumer market, they had to improve their user experience. Otherwise, other manufacturers who had better craftsmanship and user experience would take over their electric market more easily.

The case with creative tools is like that. Think about Instagram. Instagram came and made everyone more of a professional photographer in a sense by simply exposing people to photography tools in a comfortable and easy to access way. That's how I envision architectural tools, rendering tools, really creative tools in totality. Historically there would only be tools for professionals. Now the consumer mass market has access to use these tools at their disposal, for a wide variety of interests, and they are able to create value from it. We are now seeing the amazing creative outputs from all sorts of people. Of course this opportunity is only unlocked if you give these consumers better user experience and interaction. That was the basis of my PhD, which was a radical approach at the time. I developed a tangible interface where you could use your hands to shape sand or a physical model of a landscape and just design it intuitively, literally with your hands in a way that was very familiar to people. Showing that creating worlds can be as easy as playing with clay was powerful. You shouldn't always have to go into sophisticated GIS tools or special "jargony" interfaces where you have to know every detail about rendering. People should be able to have access to tools that allow them to work intuitively, use their hands, and be creative.

CHAPTER 23

Ruchi Batra
IBM

Ruchi Batra has over two decades of experience in the tech industry delivering large-scale design-led transformations, driving creative excellence, and operating as a trusted advisor for clients across the globe. She is currently the Chief Design Officer at IBM's iX user experience design consultancy, leading the Client Innovation Center in Delhi, India.

Jaleh Afshar: Can you share your journey to becoming a design executive at IBM? What were some pivotal moments?

Ruchi Batra: I am a self-taught designer, driven by my passion for design and fortunate enough to work with brilliant leaders and mentors who guided me along the way.

I've spent around 24 years in the design industry, starting my career as a web designer back in the early 2000s. At that time, user experience design wasn't even a concept; it was all about web design and other forms of graphic design. This marked the beginning of my journey. From there, for the first 10 to 12 years of my career, I was deeply immersed in individual contributor roles, honing my craft and becoming better at it.

Around my 12th or 13th year, I transitioned into managing and mentoring teams, helping them grow and develop their skills. As my responsibilities expanded, so did the size and reach of my teams. Throughout this period, my journey as a craftsperson paralleled my journey as a leader, often progressing together.

© Jaleh Afshar 2025
J. Afshar, *Chief Design Officers at Work*,
https://doi.org/10.1007/979-8-8688-1137-1_23

Eventually, I moved from managing teams to leading a large practice, which led me to my current role at IBM. For the past three and a half years, I've been managing a global team of about 170 designers. Our network consists of over 60 studios worldwide, making us the largest studio due to our operational scale and the diversity of talent.

Leading the IBM iX Design Studio, especially from the Client Innovation Center in India, provides a unique vantage point. Unlike market-focused studios, we engage with clients from across the world, including the Indian market. This role provides invaluable insights into global design trends and practices, enriching our engagements and allowing us to learn from various regions of the world.

Afshar: In what ways has your team's approach to product development contributed to innovation within the company?

Batra: Design at IBM is deeply embedded in everything we do. It's not just a set of practices or methods; it's a fundamental shift in mindset. This way of thinking drives us to collaborate with developers, product owners, and various disciplines across the globe, all with the mission of driving human-centered outcomes.

Our goal is to ensure that the people using our products get meaningful value. As a consulting team, we frequently work directly with IBM's clients across industries and geographies to create new products or reimagine existing products. Our engagements start with identifying and deeply understanding a business challenge. These challenges might involve creation and adoption of new products and services, taking existing products to new markets, targeting new customer segments, tackling revenue decline, or resolving customer complaints to improve NPS and overall engagement with a product.

Designers play a vital role in unpacking these business challenges, but we cannot do it alone. We partner with cross-functional peers and subject matter experts to approach these problems holistically. While different subject matter experts bring forward their unique lens to solving these problems, we concentrate in bringing forward the impact on the human experience. Combining these perspectives creates a comprehensive solution.

When my teams collaborate, they push boundaries by bringing this unique human-centered lens to every engagement. This approach allows us to create innovative and impactful products for our clients.

Afshar: How does your design team at IBM influence business strategy and product development?

Batra: As a design consulting team, we work closely with business executives from major brands worldwide. Our primary focus is to solve business problems by providing valuable insights. Practices such as design research and designing holistic customer journeys help us uncover micro and macro insights, often leading to those "aha" moments for the business.

For instance, we once worked on a project where a business had a one-size-fits-all strategy for all its customers. After speaking with various customer segments, we realized that some preferred different engagement methods, making the existing strategy ineffective. Our recommendation shifted the conversation, highlighting the need for tailored approaches rather than a single strategy. While it may be operationally simpler for a business to manage one approach, creating different value propositions for diverse customer groups is crucial for success.

We influence business strategies through our skills in research, synthesis, problem framing, and solution development. An example that illustrates this is when a company assumes they should focus on a specific demographic for their new product, potentially missing out on broader opportunities. By leaving value on the table, they risk competitors capitalizing on it.

As a design team, we open up various ways to create value, ensuring that business strategies and perspectives are well-informed and adaptable. While some organizations may consciously choose not to pursue certain opportunities, our role is to provide a comprehensive view, allowing them to make informed decisions that maximize their business value for our client's businesses.

Afshar: How has the integration of new technologies like AI and machine learning influenced the design processes at IBM?

Batra: Design for AI is not new for IBM; our journey began around 2018–2019 with the creation of the Design for AI playbook, which is an open-source resource available to the public. This playbook includes frameworks, training, and courses and is a fantastic asset we've built over the years. Through our playbook, we have outlined a unique approach to think about the relationship between humans and AI.

The recent advancements in generative AI have significantly accelerated its usage and brought new opportunities. We've been exploring and experimenting with AI for a while now. Gen AI has led to two key opportunities for designers. First, exploring avenues to reimagine the everyday tasks of designers. Designers often engage in complex tasks such as analyzing, synthesizing, and researching. We are exploring how AI can augment these tasks and automate repetitive work. For instance, design systems involve building components manually which is time-consuming and repetitive. Can AI help us accelerate or automate some parts of this process? To explore this, we've set up spaces for experimentation in our studio where we compare different AI models to see which ones work best for us while ensuring compliance with legal and client requirements.

The second area of focus is on creating AI-powered experiences. We are looking at how generative AI can be embedded in meaningful ways to enhance user journeys. Beyond just chatbots, we are thinking strategically about conversational design. Can we use AI to provide insights or make decisions for users at critical points in their journey? The goal is to integrate AI seamlessly into experiences without obstructing the user's workflow.

One exciting development is our approach to conversational UI and AI, where we aim to be more predictive and contextually aware. We envision for AI to be seamlessly integrated, enhancing the user experience while being transparent enough that users are aware of its presence without it feeling intrusive. For example, if you're investing in a financial product, the AI can gently prompt you with suggestions based on your life stage or financial goals, "Have you considered this?" or "What about that?" This guidance helps users make better decisions without the AI being intrusive.

We have also launched a design kit to design AI-driven intervention to ensure transparency. When AI makes a recommendation, we clearly indicate that it's an AI suggestion. This approach helps build trust and ensures users feel guided rather than directed.

Overall, we are excited about these developments and continue to innovate to create value for our clients and their customers.

Afshar: For those aspiring to work in a role like yours one day, what advice would you give based on the lessons you've learned?

Batra: I believe that continuous learning is crucial for all designers. Having grown in this career over many years, I can attest to the importance of diving deep into new concepts as they emerge. Lifelong learning is essential for all designers.

Another key aspect is for leaders to stay connected to their craft. While management, oversight, and strategy are important, never lose sight of your core skills. Your craft is your superpower. Whether it's UX strategy, research, or another discipline within design, remain close to it throughout your career. Strive for excellence and continuously push the boundaries of what you can achieve. There should never be a point where you feel you've reached the limit of your potential.

Additionally, designers should develop a business lens. Over the past five years, there has been much discussion about designers needing to understand business vocabulary and concepts. It's not just about recognizing their value but about integrating this knowledge into your toolkit. Treat business acumen as you would any other skill or tool.

Understanding data is another critical skill. Designers often work with various types of data, and being able to interpret and utilize this information is invaluable. You don't have to be a data expert, but having a solid grasp of the basics will enable you to engage in intelligent conversations and make informed decisions.

In summary, my advice to designers is to keep learning, stay connected to your craft, integrate business knowledge, and understand data. These additional skills will make you a more well-rounded professional. This is the guidance I consistently share with my teams.

Afshar: Could you share a project or initiative that you consider to be one of your greatest design successes?

Batra: Success in design comes from its ability to drive systemic change. While some may still view design as an act of merely making things look good, its impact goes much deeper, influencing how organizations shape their products, think about their customers, and organize themselves to deliver value.

For me, the most meaningful successes are those where we've driven significant changes within an organization. This could be in how they approach product development, engage with their customers, or structure their operations for better value delivery. These transformations represent the deepest level of impact that design can achieve.

However, these journeys of change are not always filled with successes. We've experienced our share of failures and learned valuable lessons along the way. When you delve into systemic, process, or cultural changes, mistakes are inevitable. But true success comes from making a lasting impact, despite the challenges.

For example, success could be creating something sustainable for the future or enabling a specific group of people. If I'm designing an app for a bank, success isn't just measured by commercial metrics, though those are important. It's also about driving financial literacy and awareness. Success, to me, means achieving a deeper significance and impact beyond the surface level.

Afshar: What do you find most challenging about your role as a design executive?

Batra: One of the biggest themes here has been navigating cross-functional partnership. All of us have good intentions. All of us come to work to say, hey, let's want to build something meaningful. But of course, things happen and inevitably you don't always align resulting in disjointed experiences. To help resolve that, I think it's very important to ensure that your developers, your product owners, your business experts, your data experts, and all key stakeholders are aligned to a vision, a big mission.

To accomplish this at IBM, we craft "Hill statements." These statements are a one sentence concise summary of a problem or opportunity that needs to be addressed. The goal of a Hill statement is to provide a clear and actionable direction for the design team, while also leaving room for creative solution-finding.

Each Hill statement has three components, the Who, the What, and the Wow. The Who defines the audience you are solving for. The What defines the core elements to address and solve. And the Wow is how you will differentiate your product.

When we craft those Hill statements, we try to rally all the functions around it. It's not just a design-only exercise. It's not just Design's job to build something really exceptional. Developers, marketing, product managers, testers… everybody is important and we help reinforce that importance by coming together.

Afshar: How would you describe your design philosophy? How has it evolved over the course of your career?

Batra: Over the last five years, I've seen a shift in the way I think about these experiences. Five to seven years ago, the focus was very much solely catering to the end user or the specific business that is the project's stakeholder. But in the last few years, my philosophy has evolved to making a larger, more meaningful impact.

While individual users are still crucial, and user-centered design is a great framework, it can sometimes become too focused on just one set of people, neglecting other stakeholders and resulting in unintended consequences. What has shifted for me is embracing a much more holistic approach to these problems. It brings in another dimension to explore, which is, are we sustainable? Are we driving responsible behaviors? Are we guiding these projects in a way that it's meaningful for future generations?

This means overall sustainability and timelessness of design. Bringing simplicity and removing friction, while taking into account a product's wider impact on the world at large. Considering a larger impact has become my predominant philosophy in recent years.

Reflecting on this shift, I see that this broader perspective has become much more prominent in my work. It's the lens through which I approach everything now problem spaces, and thereby creating a significant change in the nature of work we do.

Afshar: Who or what inspires you creatively, and how do you weave that inspiration throughout your life?

Batra: I definitely gain inspiration from design leaders I follow.

To start, I am a big follower of Bruce Mau and his "massive change" design principles. His work focuses on life-centered design, and I think it's a beautiful approach. His book, *MC24*, is a must-read for every designer. Originally a graphic designer, he has evolved into a change designer. His perspective on tackling large-scale problems is truly inspiring, and I deeply admire and draw inspiration from his work.

Another brilliant designer I admire is Kenya Hara. His work embodies simplicity and light, creating beautiful and thoughtful designs.

Recently, I've been fascinated by Refik Anadol's work. He combines data and AI to create stunning visualizations on a grand scale. His innovative and brilliant projects inspire me greatly.

Surrounding myself with such impactful work keeps me motivated and encourages me to think bigger and bolder. These designers not only inspire me but also push the boundaries of what I believe is possible.

CHAPTER 24

Rufei Fan
PicnicHealth

Rufei Fan is the Head of Design at PicnicHealth, a healthcare tech company focused on a suite of products and services to enable ease-of-access of medical records for patients and facilitate efficient clinical trial studies for life science customers. Fan is a research-driven designer, with an academic background from University of California Los Angeles and Carnegie Mellon, focused on cognitive science and Human–Computer Interaction.

Jaleh Afshar: How did your journey into design begin?

Rufei Fan: My encounters with design have been an evolving process that started from the very beginning of my academic career. I studied cognitive science in school, which naturally appealed to my curiosity about both psychology and computer science.

During my undergraduate years at UCLA, I worked in a research lab focused on learning and retention—essentially, understanding the best ways to teach people and help them retain knowledge. For about three years, I spent a lot of time in the lab running experiments, where I would observe students learn Swahili words presented in various randomized orders. My job was to log how well they remembered these words. It was fascinating to see how different approaches to presenting information could impact learning outcomes.

© Jaleh Afshar 2025
J. Afshar, *Chief Design Officers at Work*,
https://doi.org/10.1007/979-8-8688-1137-1_24

As I gained more job experience and learned more about edtech companies and startups in LA, I noticed a significant gap in how the learnings from scientific research could reach people. So many of the valuable insights from academic research were buried in papers, without much translation into practical applications that could genuinely change how people learn. This realization planted the first seed in my mind—was there a field or career that could bridge the gap between research and real-world application?

My first internship involved programming in C# for a VR learning environment. While I appreciated the technical challenge and the immediate sense of accomplishment that comes with solving technical problems, I quickly realized that my true passion lay in the design process—particularly in understanding how to create virtual environments that are intuitive for users. This was my very first hands-on experience with design, and I found it incredibly fulfilling.

After that, I took on yet another internship, this time focusing on product management and product design at a small startup. Here, I dove into user research, trying to understand the needs of our users—primarily professionals using an online training platform. I learned how to transform problems into tangible, software-based solutions, and this experience solidified my desire to pursue design as a career.

I began consulting with friends who were more established in the field and discovered the world of human-computer interaction (HCI), which seemed to tie together all the aspects of design I was passionate about. This led me to pursue a master's degree in HCI at Carnegie Mellon, which was a pivotal moment for me. It was during this time that I began to understand how to truly level up my design approach, using insights from research to make the things people interact with more valuable and meaningful.

After graduating, I was eager to find a design job and was fortunate to land my first position at a startup, which was here at PicnicHealth. This was my first job out of school, and it has been an incredible learning experience over the years at this company. I've grown from a junior designer to leading and building a team as Head of Design. Each phase of this journey has offered new challenges and immense opportunities for growth.

My past work on educational platforms has been particularly interesting to reapply nowadays. So much of what I did in edtech involved designing efficient processes that facilitate learning. Now, as a product designer in health tech, I focus on creating software experiences that help users comprehend and interact with data—essentially still designing experiences that facilitate learning. It is fascinating to reflect on how much of my work in design ties back to those early days in the research lab, and I'm excited to see where this path takes me next.

Afshar: What are some common design misconceptions about working in health tech?

Fan: That's a great question, and it brings up two main points that I've observed in this sector.

First, there's the idea that regulations make design more complex. While this is definitely true to some extent, I think it's important to reframe how we view these challenges. As designers, we're always working within constraints—whether those are technical, budgetary, or, in this case, regulatory. Constraints are often seen as the mother of creativity, forcing us to think more deeply and come up with innovative solutions within the given boundaries.

When designing for health tech, regulations like HIPAA play a significant role. HIPAA is designed to protect patient privacy by ensuring that personal health information (PHI) is shared only with those who have the right to access it. While this regulation might initially seem like it adds complexity, it actually provides clear guidelines that help shape our design decisions in a way that prioritizes user safety and privacy. These regulations are, in many ways, common sense—they're in place to protect individuals and ensure that their data is handled responsibly.

Another practical example is the need for electronic signatures to comply with 21 CFR Part 11, a regulation that requires electronic records to be treated with the same level of authenticity as paper documents. This regulation means that before a patient can sign a document electronically, they must go through an authentication process. This adds steps to the digital interaction, especially in something like an onboarding flow, but it also ensures the security and legitimacy of the patient's consent. Once you understand the purpose behind these regulations, it becomes clear that they don't just add complexity for complexity's sake—they enhance the safety and reliability of the entire system.

Rather than viewing regulations as a burden, I see them as a framework that guides us as design practitioners to make better, more thoughtful decisions. They help us understand the problem space more deeply and ensure that we are always designing with the user's best interests in mind. It's not about making things harder; it's about making things better and safer for the people we're designing for.

The second point I want to highlight is that the application is just one part of the user journey, especially in complex fields like health tech. It's easy to focus solely on the software interface because for many products that designers create for, the entirety of the experience exists solely in a digital world. However, for health tech, we need to remember that the patient's experience extends far beyond the app itself. Patients are navigating a complicated care journey that involves their own body, clinical visits, coordinating with various members of their care team, and managing a wealth of information across different platforms and physical locations.

For example, at PicnicHealth, we design for two primary patient journeys: one for day-to-day care management and another for patients participating in long-term clinical trials. Each of these journeys has its own set of challenges and needs. For someone newly diagnosed, their journey might involve more educational content and frequent interactions with their care team, while someone with a chronic condition might need a streamlined experience that fits into their established routine. Similarly, patients involved in clinical trials need to navigate onboarding processes, consent forms, and various study phases over several years.

To create a truly holistic experience, we can't just focus on the digital touchpoints like the app or website. We have to consider the entire ecosystem—the emails, the SMS notifications, the physical brochures, and even the interactions patients have in their daily lives that aren't directly tied to the digital product. Our goal is to make the patient's experience as seamless as possible, reducing friction and ensuring that they can access the care and information they need without added stress.

This approach is particularly important in health tech, where the stakes are high, and the user's well-being is at the forefront. We don't want patients to feel overwhelmed or burdened by our designs; instead, we want to create solutions that integrate smoothly into their lives, allowing them to focus on their health rather than the complexities of navigating the system.

While regulations and the complexity of patient journeys can seem daunting, they also present opportunities to design more thoughtfully and effectively. By embracing these challenges, we can create experiences that are not only compliant and secure but also empathetic and user-centered.

Afshar: At PicnicHealth, secure information access, such as a dashboard for patients that consolidates their medical records, is a key part of the company's mission. Can you describe a data visualization challenge you encountered, and how your design team overcame it?

Fan: Designing user experiences with medical data is tricky, especially if we are trying to standardize medical records from diverse sources—handwritten to fully digitized, from varied specialties—and at the same time create personalized views that are helpful for patients with drastically different health journeys. At Picnichealth, our patient-facing product is a medical records dashboard that acts as a "medical records concierge." It aims to centralize all medical records from every facility and doctor a patient has ever interacted with, and consolidate the data in views that are easy to use for patients.

One example challenge we faced is the complexity of laboratory data. Labs are essentially tests and results that are conducted on clinical specimens, such as blood or urine samples. Not only do labs normally come in large volumes, and it gets complex really quickly with the variability in how lab tests are named and categorized. For instance, a simple blood test could generate dozens of individual line items, and each could be referred to differently depending on the context—shorthands, full names, and variations for the same test. For example, a COVID nasal swab test has multiple names for the same procedure.

One approach is to group related data to simplify the presentation for users. By organizing the data in a way that reduces the feeling of being overwhelmed, you're making it more accessible. However, the design challenge isn't just about reducing clutter; it's about understanding what's truly meaningful to the patient and representing it in a comprehensible way. The quickest way of representing data might be to just dump all the raw data as-is on the patient. But, it may not be the most helpful for patients who need to navigate this information quickly and efficiently to get to the key points that are critical for them to know.

This brings up an important point about designing for different user personas. For example, some patients are very engaged with their health data—they track lab trends closely and want granular details. Others, however, might be more passive in their engagement, needing only the reassurance that their records are all in one place and accessible when needed. For these users, the primary value might be the peace of mind that comes from knowing their information is organized and available, rather than interacting with the data frequently.

To address these varied needs, it's essential to conduct targeted testing with high data fidelity, especially when dealing with different patient populations. At PicnicHealth, we design patient dashboards with high data fidelity with relevant data tailored to Multiple Sclerosis, Early Breast Cancer, and a couple other conditions to pressure test the design with real data. We can then conduct targeted user testing with patients living with these conditions to better understand their specific needs around navigating and using their medical records. By testing with representations of how actual patient data would look, rather than placeholder lorem ipsum texts, you can better understand how these users interact with the data and where potential pain points lie.

This approach also helps identify edge cases, such as when a patient has either a very large or very small amount of data. Designing with spreadsheets can be incredibly effective in these scenarios because it allows you to see how the data behaves in a real-world context. It's one thing to design a clean, intuitive interface; it's another to ensure that it scales and adapts to the vast variability in real patient data. When designing with complex health data, everything can be low fidelity, except for the data and content in the design.

Afshar: Continuing on the theme of personalization you mentioned, how do you approach designing a product that serves such a varied audience, spanning clinicians, patients, caregivers, and even your internal team, like PicnicHealth's own epidemiologists?

Fan: Each of these groups interacts with medical record data differently, depending on their specific objectives, whether it's making clinical decisions, conducting research, managing personal health, or optimizing operational processes.

What's particularly grounding for me is the understanding that despite these varied needs, you're ultimately working with the same fundamental material—your "pile of Play-Doh." This metaphor captures the essence of what we are doing: taking a vast, complex set of data—the different colors of Play-Doh—and shaping it into different forms to meet the diverse needs of each user.

Personally, I benefitted the most from working closely with our internal users. During my first year of designing for internal processes, I gained deep insights into our data pipeline—how medical records data is gathered, processed, and eventually packaged into different product experiences. This knowledge has undoubtedly equipped myself and the design team with a strong foundation in understanding the entire life cycle of data within the organization, which enabled us to make sustainable design decisions that (1) maximize the potential value of designing with data available and (2) elegantly fit on top of our existing systems, which is an important consideration when designing in resource and time-constrained environments.

One of the most valuable takeaways is the idea of finding universal principles within a complex system. In this case, the universal element is the data itself—how it can be organized, manipulated, and presented to various users. By understanding this underlying system and how it operates, and defining abstract processes that are reusable, you can create a solid foundation from which to design more tailored, specific experiences for each audience.

My favorite example is a flow that we have iterated multiple times for different use cases—an experience to view a set of medical documents and abstract data from it. By recognizing that the core task—working with data to make decisions—remains consistent across these different user groups, we've been able to create a flexible framework that can be adapted to meet the specific needs of clinicians, researchers, and others. This approach not only streamlines the design process but also ensures that the solutions we create are scalable and cost-effective, leveraging reusable components wherever possible.

This strategy allows the team to focus your mental bandwidth on deeply understanding the specific needs and intents of each user group. For clinicians, this might mean identifying which records are most critical for making fast, informed decisions. For researchers, it might involve surfacing data that's most relevant to their studies. By starting from a common foundation and then layering in bespoke elements based on user needs, we are able to quickly iterate and explore different design possibilities.

When faced with a complex, multi-audience design challenge, it's essential to find the common thread that ties everything together. In our case, it's the data and how it can be flexibly used across different scenarios.

Afshar: Can you describe a project where your initial concept changed dramatically during the design process?

Fan: I've been through a humbling, insightful, and challenging design pivot which taught me some fundamental lessons about what design truly entails.

When I first joined PicnicHealth, my understanding of the purpose of design was about solving problems and using design artifacts to communicate, refine, and align on solutions. Throughout my journey at PicnicHealth, I've come to realize that design is much more than just crafting solutions—it's about thoroughly understanding the problem space, questioning assumptions, and being willing to pivot when necessary.

PicnicHealth embarked on a strategic pivot after COVID, where the team aimed to create a more tech-forward, comprehensive service to run end-to-end observational clinical trial studies more efficiently. The concept of "study design" in scientific research refers to the up-front process to define methods to collect and analyze data to answer specific research questions, which can be a complex and time-consuming step requiring specialized knowledge, reviewing volumes of literature, and intensive stakeholder alignment. The idea of a study design service was promising: leverage technology, including AI, to streamline the study design process for life science companies. The initial hypothesis seemed solid—there's a clear need to reduce the time and effort involved in designing studies, and technology can indeed offer significant improvements.

However, as we engaged with potential customers and conducted initial concept testing, we encountered a reality that many designers face: the problem was real, but the dynamics of the industry meant that the solution wasn't as straightforward as it seemed. Study design, as we found out, is a strategic stronghold for our customers—life science companies. It's a process they are hesitant to work with external vendors because it's central to their competitive advantage. This is an industry that is already resistant to change to adopt new technologies. Even if we built a tool that could scientifically and technologically improve the process, there was no guarantee that these companies would adopt it, especially for this strategically critical process. The trust and control issues inherent in these companies' decision-making processes meant that our solution might never gain the traction it needed.

This realization forced me and my team to reassess the project entirely. Despite the excitement around the potential of the tool, we had to be honest with ourselves about whether this was a problem we were the best positioned to solve. It's a tough decision to pivot away from a project that has a lot of promise and team excitement, but it's a crucial part of the design process—recognizing when a solution might not fit within the broader business strategy or when external factors make it impractical.

Instead of pushing forward with a product that simply would not succeed in the market at this time, we chose to reframe the problem. Rather than building a customer-facing tool for study design, we shifted to developing an internal tool that could streamline our own processes for setting up studies. This internal tool directly addressed a need within our organization and aligned better with our capabilities and market position.

This experience underscores the importance of flexibility in design thinking. It's not just about coming up with glamorous solutions but also about understanding the broader context in which those solutions will be implemented. It's about recognizing when a promising idea doesn't align with the realities of the market or the strategic direction of the company and having the courage to pivot accordingly.

Design is as much about asking the right questions as it is about providing answers. It's about being willing to step back and reconsider an approach when new information comes to light. Ultimately, it's about ensuring that the solutions developed are not just technically innovative or creatively exciting but also strategically sound and aligned with the needs and constraints of both the users and the business.

Afshar: How do you stay motivated and inspired in your design work?

Fan: People are absolutely the biggest factor in what makes a team successful and fulfilling to work with. At PicnicHealth, I'm fortunate to work with a team of individuals who are not only talented and motivated but also genuinely care about the work we do and about each other. The camaraderie we've built is incredibly strong, and it's what keeps me going every day. We're in this together, tackling challenging problems side by side, and that sense of shared purpose is incredibly powerful.

What I find most rewarding is how we all support each other, especially when things get tough. This past year has been a real turning point for me in terms of realizing just how proud I am of my team. They're truly awesome. Last year, I was wrestling with whether leadership was the right path for me. I missed the hands-on work of design and found myself caught up in meetings, focused on ensuring everyone knew the direction we were headed, coordinating efforts, and removing roadblocks. It felt very different from what I initially set out to do in my career.

But then I looked at what our team was achieving—how deeply everyone cared about the process, how much they enjoyed working together, and how much they enjoyed working with me. That's when I realized that this role, while different, is just as fulfilling. It's motivating to see how much we can accomplish as a team, and it's clear that the mutual respect and genuine collaboration we share are what make it all possible.

Our team is a diverse mix of skills and strengths, and I often think of us as a group of Power Rangers—each of us bringing something unique to the table, ready to jump into action when challenges arise. Whether it's dealing with urgent crises or working on long-term projects, we're able to lean on each other and play to our strengths. That sense of organized chaos, where everyone is contributing their best and working together to solve problems, is what makes me excited to get up every morning and do the work we do.

CHAPTER

25

Ryan Leffel
Priceline

Ryan Leffel is a leader in user experience and product design, specializing in crafting strategic, user-centered solutions that drive growth and innovation. Currently, as the Head of Design at Priceline, Ryan is responsible for overseeing product and brand design, as well as research initiatives across web, mobile web, iOS, and Android platforms.

Motivated by his passion for addressing complex organizational and design challenges with innovative solutions, Ryan earned an MPS in Interactive Design from the Interactive Telecommunications Program (ITP) at the Tisch School of the Arts, New York University. His past roles span companies including R/GA, Yahoo!, Corra, and Pearson. Beyond his corporate success, Ryan also ventured into entrepreneurship, founding a fitness and training studio where he applied his strategic insights and leadership abilities to a new industry.

Jaleh Afshar: You began your career at the agency R/GA, where you crafted UX design and strategy for websites, kiosks, and mobile applications. What inspired your transition from agency to product company, and what did you learn from the shift?

Ryan Leffel: I started my full-time agency career after completing graduate school at NYU. I attended the Interactive Telecommunications Program and focused on design research and programming. My thesis advisor, who was also the founder of R/GA, played a crucial role in guiding me after graduation. He introduced me to a few key people at R/GA, which eventually led to what I consider my first real design job.

Prior to R/GA, I had been freelancing and did a UX design internship during my time at NYU, but R/GA marked the beginning of my formal career. I spent five years there, starting as an Associate Interaction Designer and during my tenure rose the ranks to Director. My time at R/GA was invaluable; I had the opportunity to work with some incredibly smart, creative, and talented individuals, and I was fortunate to be part of a company that was doing cutting-edge, innovative work. However, after gaining significant experience and working on a variety of projects, I was ready for a change.

At the time, I was still early in my career and felt it was important to gain experience outside the agency world. Otherwise, I risked becoming typecast indefinitely as an "agency designer." I'm grateful for the foresight to recognize that, and I'm glad I made the switch.

Working at Yahoo was a completely different experience. I was focused on a single product: their ad-serving platform. This was a stark contrast to agency life, where I worked on various accounts, some for extended periods, but still moved from project to project and participated in pitches. At Yahoo, I got to dive deeply into one core thing, really getting to know the product and the business behind it. It also exposed me to a different type of collaboration, with a new set of stakeholders and a different set of best practices. The growth I experienced there was significant, and it allowed me to gain a deeper understanding of product design and development in a corporate setting.

Afshar: Can you share some of those best practices you gained from working in both agency and product environments?

Leffel: The biggest takeaway I've found working at an agency is the appreciation for process. In an agency, you're constantly juggling different clients, each with unique timelines and evolving needs. This requires you to be adaptable with your processes. It becomes crucial to think creatively about how to produce smart, well-thought-out work within shorter time frames because deadlines are non-negotiable. Working in an agency teaches you to constantly tweak and streamline your processes to work more efficiently while maintaining quality. It fosters a deep sense of adaptability, which is a valuable skill in any fast-paced environment.

One of the major aspects of agency life that I truly value, and something I always recommend to designers early in their careers is the discipline you develop in presenting your work. In an agency, you're constantly selling design ideas to clients who are paying for the work, so being able to effectively communicate and sell your decisions is critical. You can be an excellent designer, but if you can't explain and justify your decisions, it won't matter. I've noticed that when designers come from the product-only side, they often struggle with articulating why they made certain choices when presenting to executives. On the agency side, however, you're trained to pitch your ideas effectively because that's a large part of the job.

In my experience on the product side, whenever we've hired designers with agency backgrounds, they've excelled in pitching ideas and have a solid grasp of process rigor. They've been through the wringer when it comes to presenting work, communicating with clients, and delivering under pressure. This experience is invaluable when it comes to pitching internally, especially in product companies, where you need to get buy-in from multiple stakeholders.

On the product side, however, you get to dive deeper into a single focused area. You get to live and breathe that product every day, learning how it works inside and out. This depth of experience is different from agency life, where you might move between clients frequently, unless you're assigned to one account for an extended period. In a product company, you're interacting daily with people who are just as invested in the product as you are, and you develop a different type of collaboration with internal stakeholders compared to agency clients.

Another significant difference on the product side is the exposure to C-suite executives. When working within a brand, I've had more opportunities to interact directly with the C-suite, whereas in an agency, you're usually pitching to other agency counterparts or mid- to senior-level stakeholders representing the client. This exposure to the C-suite in product companies has helped me develop "executive presence"—the ability to effectively influence top-level leadership through communication—which is an important skill that product designers tend to develop earlier on than agency designers.

One area where product design has evolved, particularly in recent years, is in the use of design systems. At Priceline, where I've been for nearly five years, we rely heavily on a polished, sophisticated design system. This system completely changes the design process because we're working more with high-fidelity components rather than starting from scratch. In contrast, when I worked at agencies, we had UX designers working closely with visual designers, taking wireframes and bringing them to life. Now, on the product side, there's more reliance on predefined components, which shifts the focus to high-level execution rather than starting from a blank slate.

Working in a product company also means you're part of multidisciplinary teams, often collaborating with engineers, product managers, data analysts, and marketers. This level of cross-functional collaboration is something you might not experience as deeply in an agency, depending on your role. In my experience, whether at Priceline or earlier at Yahoo, having a diverse group of stakeholders involved from the beginning leads to better outcomes. Everyone has a stake in the product's success, and this shared investment means that when it comes time to push something forward, you face fewer roadblocks.

At Yahoo, I learned the value of design sprints, where cross-functional teams would come together for three to five days to focus on a specific problem. Everyone, from account managers to engineers, would collaborate, sketch, and brainstorm together, resulting in a solution that everyone had a hand in shaping. This collaborative process was key to delivering better outcomes because everyone was invested in the solution, reducing the pushback and friction you might encounter later on.

In an agency, the collaboration model is often different. There can be more negotiation between design and development teams, especially around timelines and budgets. Looking back, I realize that had we brought everyone together in a room to workshop solutions more often, we might have avoided some of the back-and-forth over timelines and costs.

One thing I've come to appreciate on the product side is the shared sense of purpose that comes from working toward a common mission. For example, at Priceline, we have a clear mission: to be the best travel dealmakers in the world. Our CEO reiterates this mission in every weekly update, and it serves as a rallying point for the entire team. When everyone is aligned around a shared mission, it makes collaboration smoother and more focused. In an agency, you're working with clients who have their own missions, but it's not the same as being part of a company with a unified purpose.

Both agency and product work have their strengths, and I believe it's important for designers to experience the two sides. Agency work sharpens your adaptability, pixel-level presentation polish, and ability to work under tight deadlines, while product work gives you a deeper understanding of how to develop and evolve a product over time. Each environment teaches you something different, and combining those experiences can make you a stronger, more versatile designer.

Afshar: What trends do you see across the design industry that impact how you approach your work at Priceline?

Leffel: The obvious answer right now is AI—how we, as designers and researchers, can leverage it effectively. Priceline is all in on AI. It's a big and important piece of our product experience. On the Design and Research team, AI is something we fully embrace. We are still experimenting with how we will use AI within our craft—and we're really excited about what that future looks like. AI is a tool we need to get comfortable with and skilled at using, and I'm excited to see how AI evolves to truly assist designers and researchers in their workflows.

From a leadership perspective, especially in today's environment, teams are often leaner than they've been in the past. This ties back to what we discussed about agency work—you need to be creative with your processes. Even when you're working with a smaller team, the workload remains the same. Figuring out how to adapt and modify processes is essential. I often think of process like building a product: you're testing new approaches, listening to feedback, and constantly adapting. The key is to avoid getting locked into a rigid process where every step must be completed in order. Sometimes, you can skip ahead or modify the sequence if it makes sense, allowing you to move faster without sacrificing quality.

Creativity and efficiency in processes are critical, especially when leading a team or trying to get things done quickly and well. It's important to stay flexible and continually evaluate what's working and what isn't. Talk to other teams involved, identify gaps, and make adjustments where needed. That way, you can keep moving forward without being bogged down by unnecessary steps.

Another crucial element is understanding the business side of design. Designers need to go beyond talking about design; they should also understand how the product they're working on makes money and how the business as a whole operates. Many times, decisions are made that frustrate the team, but if you step back and understand the business rationale behind those decisions, it becomes easier to accept them.

For instance, at Priceline, we have designers working on a variety of products—hotels, flights, rental cars, insurance, and even fintech and AI products. Each of these has its own KPIs and business drivers. Understanding those details allows designers to make smarter, more informed decisions. It's not just about creating something visually appealing but about understanding how that product needs to perform, where the supply comes from, and how it generates revenue.

I've seen a significant shift in this mindset over the years. While understanding business has always been important, it's now more critical than ever, given the complexity of the products we're designing. Back in the early 2000s, when I was at R/GA, we were primarily designing for larger screens. Now, we're dealing with mobile experiences, responsive design, apps, and small interfaces, all existing across a variety of channels. Designers today need to think not only about what they see in front of them but also how their decisions impact the broader landscape.

The more designers can understand the business context of their work, the better they can navigate the complexities of modern design and make choices that drive both user satisfaction and business success.

Afshar: Can you share any surprising insights you've learned across your various consumer product roles?

Leffel: One of the more surprising lessons I've learned in my career came from my experience working on e-commerce projects. During my time at R/GA, I was heavily involved in e-commerce, and then, two jobs ago, I spent over five years overseeing design and strategy at a digital agency focused on e-commerce solutions. We worked primarily with companies using platforms like Shopify and Magento, helping businesses develop and implement their e-commerce strategies. There was a strong emphasis on optimization, research, and understanding how consumers shop, particularly in the fashion, beauty, and lifestyle sectors.

What I found interesting is that when I transitioned from those industries to the travel e-commerce space at Priceline, many of the principles that had worked well in fashion and beauty didn't translate directly. Many of the triggers that work in fashion, lifestyle, and apparel don't apply directly to how consumers shop in a travel experience—especially a company like Priceline, which is truly focused on deal making, and the inventory isn't an actual physical product.

That shift taught me a valuable lesson: when you move into a new industry, it's crucial to take the time to understand the specific customer you're now serving. You can't simply apply the same e-commerce strategies from one sector to another because the product and consumer behavior vary widely. E-commerce isn't just a one-size-fits-all formula—it requires a deep understanding of the particular vertical you're working in.

At the core of e-commerce, no matter the industry, you're delivering a message and motivating the consumer to take action, whether it's making a purchase or engaging in some other way. However, the way that message resonates and the triggers that drive action can differ significantly depending on the vertical. Recognizing and adapting to those differences is key to creating effective strategies across different industries.

Afshar: In the midst of your design career, you made a pivot to start a gym. Could you share more about that story?

Leffel: Around the time Yahoo let go of their New York design team, I had an unexpected opportunity to help start a gym from the ground up. It's a long story, but the short of it is a promising chance was there, and I had always been interested in fitness and entrepreneurship. It seemed like the perfect time, and my instinct was telling me to go for it. I thought it would be easy—I had severance from Yahoo, so I figured I could get the gym up and running within a year, and it would start making money. In my mind, I'd have this business on autopilot while getting back into design work, with the gym running in the background.

What I quickly learned is that being an entrepreneur is incredibly difficult. It took about three and a half years to get the gym to a place where it was somewhat stable, with a trustworthy team running the day-to-day operations. Even then, it wasn't financially successful, but I discovered something unexpected—there were other rewarding aspects to it. Seeing someone lose weight, reach their fitness goals, improve their health, and change their life in a positive way was incredibly fulfilling. That kind of impact made me realize how rewarding it can be to help someone grow, whether it's in fitness or in their professional career. As a leader, helping others progress and reach their goals became a valuable lesson for me.

However, the financial side wasn't working out, and I needed to return to design, which I had been doing for years. I thought it would be easy to re-enter the field—after all, I had a solid portfolio, having worked at R/GA and Yahoo, and I had a master's degree from NYU in design. But after three and a half years out of the industry, no one wanted to hire me. I kept hearing "no" because people saw me as a "gym person." They couldn't see the connection between my design background and what I had been doing at the gym.

I remember going to one of my first interviews, and they asked me about responsive design—a concept that had evolved while I was running the gym. I didn't know much about it because I hadn't been following the industry closely, and I was completely thrown off. That moment made me realize how out of touch I had become with the latest trends in UX, so I took the time to get up to speed, which helped in subsequent interviews. Still, people were hesitant to take a chance on me.

Eventually, I got lucky. Someone I had worked with at R/GA was leading a creative team at another large agency, and he pulled me in to do freelance work. That helped me rebuild my portfolio, and things started to get a little easier. However, whenever the gym came up in interviews, I struggled to talk about it. At the time, I'd say things like, "I did a lot of marketing and helped design the space," thinking it was a decent answer. But in hindsight, I realized I had gained so much more from that experience.

Running the gym was essentially like getting an MBA. I learned an immense amount about business that I wouldn't have learned otherwise—everything from managing finances and working with suppliers to dealing with contractors—the trainers—and handling customer service. With a few hundred members, I had to navigate complaints, even over the smallest issues, and that taught me the value of patience and communication. All those lessons were incredibly valuable, but it took me a while to understand how to frame that experience in a way that made sense to potential employers in the design world. Learning all these facets of how a business works made me a better designer. This understanding of business helped when it came to communicating with clients and understanding how a product should work.

Afshar: What lessons from entrepreneurship influence the way you approach leadership today?

Leffel: I've learned so much from my time running the gym that made me a better designer and, ultimately, a stronger leader. The biggest lesson I took away, which I think has really shaped how I approach things today, is that success wasn't about having the best equipment or the trendiest fitness programs—it was about building a community.

The gym started as a modest 24-hour facility offering small group training. Eventually, we added CrossFit, which quickly became our primary focus as it started to take off. Looking back, there was a key moment when I realized that it wasn't just about fitness anymore. People weren't coming in just for the workouts; they were coming because they enjoyed being part of something bigger—a community of like-minded individuals all working toward similar goals.

Without even fully recognizing it at the time, I started to focus on fostering those connections. I realized that if I could create an environment where people felt connected, they'd keep coming back. It wasn't just about the exercise; it was about the friendships. So, we started doing things like hosting pizza nights or happy hours after workouts. We would bring in bagels in the morning as a treat after sessions, and people would stick around to hang out, chat, and bond. Over time, a core group of people became really tight-knit, and even after I sold the gym, many of them stayed because of the community that had formed. There were even a number of former members who went on to get married!

That experience taught me a lot about community building, and it's something I've carried with me into my design career. Whether it's designers, researchers, or anyone really, people thrive when they feel like they're part of a community of like-minded individuals. I think that's something I became really good at during that time, and it's helped me immensely in other areas of my career.

For example, when I moved to a previous company, part of my role there involved helping to stabilize a team that needed support. Even though I was only there for a short time, I was able to help build a more cohesive and supportive design community. I've done the same at Priceline, where building culture and a sense of belonging has been key to fostering a productive and engaged team.

When I think about how to build culture and community in a workplace today, I realize much of what I'm good at stems from what I learned while running that gym. It's funny how those skills translate across such different industries, but building community is universal.

Afshar: Could you share the inspiration behind your podcast "That Pivotal Moment of Change", and the kind of conversations you have with your guests?

Leffel: I've noticed that people really resonate with behind-the-scenes conversations, like the one we're having now! I believe it's because these kinds of discussions tap into something real and relatable. When we're vulnerable and open about our experiences, it often helps others who are going through similar situations. I've found myself focusing more on the idea that it's not always about what you do, but how you got here. Everyone has twists and turns in their journey, and that's the one thing that's truly unique to each of us—our individual path.

I do a lot of mentoring with designers working on their portfolios, and I always start by asking them to tell me about themselves. Every time, they have these fascinating, personal stories. But then we look at their portfolio, and it's just project after project, like a checklist. I always tell them, "You need to weave your story into your portfolio. That's what's going to make you stand out next to someone else showing similar work." No one else will have your exact same background or story about who you are. What is it from that background that makes you passionate about getting into design? That is what can truly differentiate one's portfolio.

I love asking questions that dig into someone's journey, like, "How did you get through a challenge?" or "Can you share a setback that turned into an opportunity?" It's important to learn what lessons people have taken from their career and what advice they would pass on—whether to someone just starting out or to more seasoned leaders. Those kinds of conversations hold so much value because they provide insight and inspiration for anyone, regardless of where they are in their career.

I've kicked off this podcast project at pivotalmomentspod.com where I am interviewing people and recording these kinds of conversations. It's been a great experience so far, and I'm excited about the potential they have to help others navigate their own paths. The idea is really just to get people talking about how they got to where they are, with the hope that there will be nuggets of wisdom in there for those trying to figure things out. Whether it's someone just starting in design or a leader looking to learn from other leaders, these stories can be incredibly powerful.

CHAPTER

26

Saurabh Soni

Razorpay

Saurabh Soni is the Head of Design at Razorpay, a full-stack financial solutions company serving over 5 million businesses, 300 million end-consumers and processing payments worth $150bn USD annually operating in India and Malaysia. Saurabh's team spans product design, communication design, user research, and the UX writing function across verticals, including online payments, in-store payments, business banking, payroll, lending, and many other fintech products. Prior to Razorpay, Saurabh also led teams at an early stage startup and Housing.com.

Jaleh Afshar: Let's start off with a classic question—what's the story of how you got into design?

Saurabh Soni: I've always had the soul of a designer, even before I knew what design was. Growing up in a middle-class family in a small city in Rajasthan, India, I was deeply influenced by two aspects of my childhood that steered me toward design.

First, I was a born tinkerer. From a young age, I found joy in experimenting with the objects around me—be it toys, furniture, or electronics. I would break and rebuild them into something better. I have a memory of once dismantling a solar-powered toy to build a table lamp that turned on automatically when it got dark. This innovative spirit was something I inherited from my father, who was always fixing or improving things around the house.

© Jaleh Afshar 2025
J. Afshar, *Chief Design Officers at Work*,
https://doi.org/10.1007/979-8-8688-1137-1_26

Second, my mother taught me the importance of empathy from a young age. She taught me to understand and consider what others might be thinking and feeling. This lesson stayed with me and influenced my approach to design. Whenever I created something, I was keen to see how others reacted and what they felt, often picking up on unspoken feedback. The intersection of my love for making things and the joy of making others happy formed the foundation of my designer DNA.

When I was about 12, we got our first computer at home. This was before the Internet became a thing in India. My habit of tinkering met a new world to experiment with. Instead of playing games, I was more interested in creating them. I used to build custom themes and share with friends. Soon I discovered tools like Microsoft FrontPage and Macromedia Flash. With the scarcity of tutorials, I spent hours figuring out what each button did and learning through trial and error. Eventually, I built many games for my friends and interactive demos for my school projects, one of which was presented at a national level event.

High school introduced me to programming, which I loved immensely. It allowed me to build larger and more complex projects. The logical structure and creative potential of coding captured my imagination. However, the idea of design as a career was still foreign to me. The common career aspirations were becoming a doctor, engineer, scientist, or securing a government job.

When it was time for college, I chose computer science, as it seemed to align best with my interests. During my college days, I learned to design and develop websites and apps for college events and startups incubated in college. It was during an internship that I had an epiphany: the realization that designing and developing were distinct roles. Up until then, I had been doing both. I saw that designing something and developing it required different skills and mindsets and I was passionate about designing.

Even though it was a niche field with no role models for me at the time, this realization led me to pursue a career in design. Today, I'm glad I chose this path. I thoroughly enjoy what I do, and it feels incredibly meaningful.

Afshar: How did you land your current role at Razorpay?

Soni: I joined Razorpay in 2016. Back then, it was a young fast-growing startup in the nascent Indian startup ecosystem. I was the third designer in the company of 50 people. In the first few months, I invested significant time in understanding the big picture—the business and the customers—and soon I was driving major projects.

The fast growth also came with several challenges: hiring the right design talent, improving design culture, bridging collaboration gaps between designers and others, and prioritizing among various customer needs—while we build delightful products or communication for complex business-finance problems.

Whenever these challenges arose, I eagerly took them on, never drawing boundaries around my role. I approached these problems with a designer's mindset—by empathizing with everyone to understand the problems, experimenting with solutions and aiming to create exceptional experiences.

For example, to improve collaboration between designers and engineers, I interviewed many of them individually to learn that last-minute design changes used to upset engineers and designers were having trouble predicting all cases leading to such last-minute changes. So we experimented with *design-together workshops*, iterating upon the workshops' formats and eventually solving collaboration challenges significantly.

Toward the end of my second year at Razorpay, my role evolved into leading a team of ten talented designers. While the experience was exciting, balancing my passion for creating great products with growing managerial responsibilities was challenging. Hence in my third year, I moved to a new vertical with a small team of three designers, to build a *Business Banking* product from zero to one. This shift gave me much-needed focus to sharpen my design craft, build a strong team culture, and create a world-class product.

In the subsequent years within this new vertical, I played a pivotal role in creating a collaborative work culture that seamlessly brought design, engineering, and product teams together. I introduced many rituals, such as the *Design-Engineering-Product Office Hours*, which enabled deep collaboration and mutual understanding between these teams. I launched *Design Demo Hours* to present completed designs to the entire team, ensuring transparency and alignment. I helped organize cross-functional customer calls and established forums like *KYC (Know Your Customer)* for sharing valuable insights and deepening customer empathy. I took ownership of the monthly *Townhall* event for the vertical and re-imagined it to celebrate our mission and reinforce a shared sense of purpose. This boundaryless approach not only helped me grow as a leader but also aligned my team with cross-functional teams creating a cohesive working culture.

In the next four years, as the *Business Banking* vertical grew and my team increased to around 30 people, I learned to delegate and coach my team to take on my previous responsibilities, allowing me to focus on bigger challenges. I had achieved what I had set out for—sharpening my design craft, building a strong team culture, and creating a world-class product.

Around the time I completed six years at Razorpay, recognizing my contributions and growth, the leadership team promoted me to the role of Head of Design and for the last year and a half, I have been leading a team of 70 brilliant designers.

Reflecting on my journey, several key skills and attitudes have helped me do well: a boundaryless thought process, a high sense of agency, a continuous learning attitude by drawing inspiration from diverse sources.

I firmly believe that magic happens at the intersection of multiple fields. By immersing myself in areas like product management, strategy, business, and marketing beyond design, I could develop more holistic and impactful solutions. Embracing a high-agency mindset helps me tackle problems with confidence and energy. With a continuous learning attitude, I celebrate progress over perfection which gives me the motivation to continuously improve. And lastly, inspiration can be found anywhere—always be looking for it.

Afshar: How would you define your responsibilities as a design leader at Razorpay?

Saurabh Soni: My role as the Head of Design at Razorpay has evolved significantly as our team and company have grown. When I was managing a smaller team of 10–20 designers, it was feasible to personally review each project. Now, with about 70 designers and a total of 3000 employees, we often run between 50 and 100 projects simultaneously. Direct oversight of each project isn't practical; instead, my focus has shifted toward creating the right culture and systems that help Razorpay succeed. However, my approach to operating without boundaries continues and I spend significant time beyond design.

A few things that top my chart include inspiring cross-functional teams I work with so that they can do great work and push their boundaries. I achieve this via one-on-one conversations, design events, and multiple cross-functional forums. I also make sure we are structured well. This includes hiring the right talent and ensuring that each member is placed in a role where they can add the most value.

I also focus on making sure everyone at Razorpay understands and values design and product experience. By teaching other departments about design's important role in our success, I help our designers get involved in major projects and decisions.

Beyond that, I'm heavily involved in key decisions about our products and design, like managing how our products are structured, evolving our Design System, experience of platform products and defining the bar of design excellence.

Afshar: You've previously hosted a panel discussion on designing for revenue and achieving profitability. Could you share an overview of your thoughts on that topic?

Soni: The following two topics elicit strongly divergent responses.

The first question I'll address is—how do designers contribute to revenue and profitability?

Design's contribution to revenue and profitability is twofold. The first aspect is widely recognized: designers enable the creation of user-friendly products that enhance user experience. This improves acquisition through better funnel conversions and customer retention through ease of use.

The second part is less obvious but even more important. It's about how people perceive a product. Does it evoke the right emotions? People might forget the features of a product but how it made them feel leaves a lasting impression, which can keep bringing them back.

Consider this: are you simply attracting customers, or are you creating fans? Products designed intentionally for a certain emotion can create irrationally loyal fans who are deeply committed to the brand. This is a significant contribution that design makes to a company's success, though often impossible to measure and difficult to experiment with. The insight and priorities of design leaders and executives who recognize this can drive significant differentiation to such organizations, much like Apple. They don't just have users; they have passionate fans.

At Razorpay, we build products with this philosophy. We want our customers to perceive and realize that managing money doesn't have to feel boring, intimidating, and complicated. Razorpay makes it simple and delightful. We absorb the complexity for our customers. To achieve that, we work very closely with our customers to build products and understand the nuances really well. And with that, we have customers who have Razorpay as their default choice for any finance problem.

Now I'll address the second question—does focusing on revenue and profitability in design inherently conflict with a customer-first approach?

Not at all. In fact, these two aspects—focusing on revenue and maintaining a customer-first approach—are fundamentally aligned. A business operates on a simple principle: provide something valuable that customers want, and in return, they pay you for it. This mutual exchange does not inherently create conflict.

In the long term, a business can only sustain its revenue and profitability by prioritizing its customers. Occasionally, companies might face decisions that seem to require a short-term trade-off against a customer-first approach, but such decisions often risk damaging both revenue and long-term customer trust and enough of such instances open the door to disruption by competitors.

But the financial viability of a business is crucial, hence it requires making smart financial decisions without compromising customer trust.

For example, consider the tactic of adding a small fee to a transaction. If done transparently—explaining to customers why this fee is necessary to maintain service quality—it can be acceptable. On the other hand, if this fee is added secretly, customers may feel deceived once they discover it, which can damage their trust in the brand and, ultimately, hurt the business.

Afshar: Given your experience as an executive leader, what advice would you give designers who are looking to make a shift into management?

Soni: When I first started to take up people management responsibilities, I felt out of my comfort zone. But this one idea suddenly brought it to my comfort zone. I compared the manager role to a designer role and drew parallels. As a manager, the problem scope expands from user problems to team and organizational problems and the solution canvas expands from the screen to the entire world—encompassing tactical, physical, and psychological aspects.

With this thought, transitioning into a managerial role became exciting as it allowed my creativity to operate on a much larger scale. For instance, when tackling the problem of growing designers in the team, I approached it as a design problem. I conducted 'user research' to understand what designers seek, experimented with small solutions, and iterated based on feedback. Similarly, for internal *Town Hall* sessions, I continuously refined the approach based on floor readings and feedback to keep everyone excited and engaged.

I often talk to designers who are unsure about transitioning into management. It's common for designers to hesitate because they love their craft and fear losing touch with it. I encourage them to critically evaluate whether their reluctance is due to a genuine love for the craft or discomfort with stepping into a new role. If it's the latter, it might be worth embracing the discomfort to learn something new and grow.

Transitioning into management doesn't mean abandoning the craft; it means expanding the influence and applying design thinking to larger, more complex problems. This broader perspective can be incredibly fulfilling and can lead to a significant impact both for the team and the organization.

Another significant change that occurs when moving from an individual contributor to a managerial role is that one may no longer create designs themselves. So it's important to realize that *knowing what constitutes great design* and *the ability to create great designs*, are two different skills. As a manager, one should focus on the former and inspire their team to enable them to do the latter.

And finally, a vital lesson I learned is that great designs come in many versions. Someone else's design solution may not align with your own equally great design. It's essential to appreciate it without being attached to a specific version.

CHAPTER 27

Temilola Oyenuga
Spazio Ideale

Temilola Oyenuga serves as the Head of Design at Spazio Ideale, an interior design firm based in Lagos, Dubai, and Johannesburg. She spearheads an innovative team delivering exceptional spaces for organizations, including Ernst & Young (EY), Paystack, Moniepoint, Kuda, and SoFresh. Temilola also serves as the Team Lead for the Construction and Architecture team at Slum2School Africa, an NGO empowering underserved children in Africa. Prior to Spazio Ideale, Temilola held architectural and interior design roles at Housessories Limited, Grant Quartermaine, Jamescubitt Architects, and FMA Architects.

She holds a bachelor's degree as well as a master's degree in Architecture from Covenant University, and was recognized with the prestigious 2016 FAN (Female Architects of Nigeria) Best Student in Nigeria award. Temilola is very passionate about sustainability, affordable housing, education, and leadership. Temilola believes design is not merely a commercial endeavor but a cultural expression that speaks to the essence of human existence.

Jaleh Afshar: For our readers who may be less familiar with the role of Head of Design within an interior design firm, could you share a glimpse of your role and responsibilities?

Temilola Oyenuga: Spazio Ideale is a multidisciplinary, full-service interior design firm with a primary focus on connecting people to spaces through creative design, experiential spaces, and excellent execution. We handle turnkey interior fit-outs from design ideation to execution for various building types—commercial, hospitality, residential, education, and so on. While our main focus is on interior fit-outs, we also take on some exterior fit-out works, curating a positive experience in both interior and exterior environments.

As for how my role as Head of Design fits into things, I have a mix of responsibilities from the creative direction to team management and administrative tasks.

My main responsibility is providing creative leadership. I set the tone for our designs and establish the creative vision for our department. This means defining how our designs should look fundamentally, setting the standards our company upholds, and ensuring that our clients know what to expect from us. It's all about maintaining that design standard while continually fostering a culture of innovation and creativity within the team to allow for evolution.

As a team leader, I also manage the team from a people perspective, offering guidance and mentorship, conducting performance reviews, giving feedback, and supporting the professional growth of my reports.

Another key part of my job is project oversight. I review and approve designs for our projects, especially as a project moves into its most significant milestones. I make sure the concepts and presentations we share with clients meet our quality standards, are error-free, and align with showcasing the client's objectives clearly. I also keep an eye on timelines, budgets, and other project parameters to ensure everything stays on track.

Building and managing client relationships is another crucial aspect of my role. I work closely with clients to understand their design preferences, ensure we're on the same page, and maintain a strong relationship that helps with negotiations and other aspects of the project. I also spend a lot of time sharing our design concepts with them, walking them through the ideas we've developed.

In addition, I'm involved in shaping the design strategy for our department. This often means collaborating with our marketing and sales teams to ensure we're moving forward in the right direction from a brand perspective.

Quality control on our interior design deliverables is another important responsibility. I visit project sites to ensure that our designs are being properly implemented in the real world, and that the craftsmanship meets our standards—sometimes external artisans can on some occasions take creative liberties with how they interpret a project contract, so it's important to ensure everything is executed as planned.

Operational efficiency is also key. I make sure the team is functioning well, has the right tools and training needed, and that our processes are up-to-date and effective. This includes managing resources and budgets.

Beyond these core duties, it's personally important to me to stay up-to-date with industry standards and trends, continuously learning to keep both myself and the team moving forward. I attend industry events and speaking engagements, collaborating with others in the field.

I'm grateful for this dynamic position that allows me to contribute meaningfully to the spaces we create.

Afshar: How do you structure your schedule? What is your day-to-day like?

Oyenuga: A successful schedule requires planning. To ensure my day and week go smoothly, I rely heavily on organization tools like calendars and to-do lists. I use Google Calendar extensively, with separate calendars for personal and work-related tasks. I also prefer the traditional approach of writing down my daily to-do list, which allows me to physically check off tasks and have a clear view of what needs to be done.

In my organization, we operate with a hybrid work model. About 90% of the time, I work from home, with occasional days spent on-site, meeting with clients, or working from the office. My day usually starts around 6 a.m., with the first three hours dedicated to personal activities like prayer, bible study, and other routines.

Work typically begins at 9 a.m. Mondays are especially busy, as they are our primary meeting days. We regularly have a start-of-week meeting that covers project overviews for the entire organization, where we review the status and updates of each workstream. Following that, I hold a separate meeting with my direct team to touch base on individual deadlines, workloads, and tasks for the week, ensuring everything aligns with our scheduled timelines.

My day-to-day involves a mix of meetings, collaboration, design reviews, and hands-on work. As the week progresses, I update my calendar as new tasks and meetings arise. This rhythm helps me stay on track and ensures that everything runs smoothly.

Afshar: Can you share an example of how collaboration with a client led to a unique design outcome?

Oyenuga: Collaboration with clients is a key part of our process. Whenever we come up with new design ideas, we share them with our clients, who then provide their feedback. It's a back-and-forth exchange where they might say, "We love this!" or ask, "Can we tweak this?" or "What if we tried that?"

It's tough to single out just one instance, but there's a particular recent project that stands out in my memory. We presented a design to the clients, and they absolutely loved it. Their excitement was clear, and they were full of ideas to build on top of our concept, saying things like, "Oh, can we add this?" or "Wouldn't it be fun to include that?"

One unique feature we incorporated into their interior design was an interactive music access QR code system placed on the walls. This is sort of like the Spotify Code brandable scannable barcode that links to a specific music playlist. They loved this idea so much that they asked if we could include their office playlist, which they all listen to regularly. This wall feature allowed anyone in the office to access and update the playlist, adding a personal and interactive touch to the space. We placed this on the door of one of the work booths, and the client was thrilled.

This small addition really brought the space to life and made it more meaningful and personalized to the vibe of that office. We've had several instances where clients suggest playful or creative ideas like this, which ultimately add more depth and personality to the design. It's always exciting to see how these collaborations can infuse a space with more character and fun.

Afshar: Starting from your academic background and spanning your entire career thus far, you've always focused on the design of structures and spaces. What event or experience ignited your passion for this subject?

Oyenuga: I believe that, for many people, their choice of study and career path is often sparked by interests that emerge in childhood. My own journey is no different.

Looking back, I can trace my passion for design to two key aspects of my early years. The first is my love for creating things—art, to be specific. I've always enjoyed working with my hands, whether it was drawing, building, or crafting. The second is my passion for problem-solving. From a young age, I was drawn to the idea that spaces could be better organized and more functional. Whenever I saw something out of place, I felt compelled to fix it, to make it better.

As a child, I spent countless hours playing with LEGO and plasticine—which is like a type of moldable clay. I loved pulling things apart to see how they worked, then trying to put them back together. My parents were very supportive of my creative inclinations. I think I inherited my artistic side from my mom, who is a fashion designer. She creates beautiful things with fabric. My problem-solving nature, on the other hand, comes from my dad, who, while working as a pharmacist, is also a technical thinker.

One of my earliest "projects" was constantly rearranging the furniture in our living room. We had this modular L-shaped sofa, and almost every week, I would change its configuration, trying to find the perfect layout. I was always experimenting with how the space could be improved.

When I got to secondary school in Nigeria, which is equivalent to American high school, my interest in design became more focused. I started drawing a lot and took up technical drawing as a subject. This involved creating engineering and architectural drawings, which I found both challenging and exciting. I had two technical drawing teachers who really saw potential in me. They would often encourage me, saying things like, "You did this so well! Have you considered studying architecture?" At that time, I didn't even know what architecture was, but their guidance was instrumental in opening my eyes to the field. They kind of took me under their wing, providing mentorship that fueled my interest further.

Around the same time, my family took our first trip to Dubai. This was long before Dubai became the ultra-modern city it is today, but even then, it was filled with impressive tall buildings. I was fascinated by the stark contrast between the skyscrapers in Dubai and the buildings we had in Nigeria. Seeing those structures on that trip ignited a new level of passion in me.

Later in secondary school, we had a requirement to do a short work experience. My dad suggested I spend it with an architect friend of his. Those ten days were absolutely eye-opening. I got a firsthand look at what architecture involves and how it can genuinely impact people's lives. That experience solidified my decision to pursue architecture in college.

Afshar: How do you envision the role of architects evolving in the next decade?

Oyenuga: There are three major ways in which architecture, like many other industries, is evolving: through technology, sustainability, and societal shifts.

The rapid pace of technological advancement is influencing every industry, including architecture. We're seeing more integration of AI, VR, and AR in architectural design. These tools allow clients to experience and visualize spaces before they're even built, creating a more immersive and informed design process. Technology is making architecture more dynamic and responsive, with innovations that enhance both the design and construction phases. We're already seeing that in architecture now. There are designers who specialize in augmenting spaces, ensuring that you can try out an interior design through AR, feeling like you are in the space but virtually. Many clients love that they can already imagine a space, even if it has not actually been brought to life yet physically.

Regarding sustainability, in today's world, everyone must be sustainability-conscious, and architecture is no exception. The role of architects is evolving to include a greater focus on the environmental impact of buildings. We're seeing the rise of sustainability experts who specialize in assessing how a building interacts with its environment and advising on measures to minimize negative impacts. This means considering the human factor, that is, the social impact, the environmental, and economic impact, to ensure that buildings are responsible and sustainable.

I also believe societal shifts play a significant role. As cultures and societal norms continue to change, architecture must adapt to these shifts. This includes a move toward more integrated design processes, where architects collaborate more closely with other stakeholders in the built environment, such as engineers, contractors, and sustainability experts. It's about creating a holistic approach to building design.

One aspect of this evolution is the increased focus on community engagement. Architects are increasingly involving communities in the design process, especially for public spaces such as parks, community centers, and so on. This might involve the skills of Community engagement facilitators to facilitate workshops and consultations, ensuring that the needs and voices of the community are reflected in the final design.

Another critical area the role of Architects will evolve in is resilience and adaptation. These professionals will ensure that buildings are being designed with greater flexibility to adapt to societal changes, climate shifts, and other external factors, ensuring that structures are not only durable but also capable of evolving alongside the communities they serve.

Afshar: What are some architectural challenges you foresee emerging in the future?

Oyenuga: The first major challenge we might face is regarding the climate crisis. Right now, we're seeing more frequent and severe climate events—floods, tornadoes, and other natural disasters. Unfortunately, many of our existing buildings aren't designed to withstand these crises. In Nigeria, our climate is generally more stable compared to some other regions of the world; however, even Nigerians can't afford to be complacent. Take Lagos, for example—a city surrounded by water. Despite its relatively stable climate, Lagos is vulnerable due to its geography, especially in areas where land has been reclaimed from the ocean and artificial islands were constructed. While these developments may seem beneficial now, they could have serious repercussions in the future. It's crucial that we put measures in place to ensure that our buildings can withstand whatever climate challenges lie ahead. Above all, we must prioritize human safety by designing more resilient structures that protect people from potential disasters.

Another critical issue I foresee is regarding urbanization and population density. Many countries, including Nigeria, are grappling with overpopulation in urban areas. Planning for this requires us to think ahead about how cities can accommodate growing populations without compromising quality of life. Affordable housing is particularly close to my heart. The housing crisis isn't just a Nigerian problem; it's a global issue. We need to develop more cost-effective solutions to address the shortage of affordable housing and ensure that everyone has access to a safe place to live.

Technological integration is also a growing challenge, particularly in developing countries. While more developed nations are already incorporating advanced technologies into their built environments, it's essential for countries like Nigeria to catch up. This includes ensuring that our buildings and infrastructure are in harmony with technological advancements, making our cities more efficient and interconnected.

Social and cultural shifts are another area where architecture must adapt. As societies evolve, our buildings need to reflect these changes by being inclusive and accessible to all. This means designing spaces that cater to people with disabilities, whether they are wheelchair users, visually impaired, or have hearing impairments. It also means creating environments that are safe and user-friendly for all ages, from children to the elderly.

Resource scarcity is another significant future challenge which ties into sustainability. We need to devise means to manage our resources—water, materials, and energy—more efficiently. This involves using energy-efficient lighting, optimizing power sources, and ensuring that buildings are designed with sustainability in mind.

Health and well-being are also increasingly important considerations in architecture. The way a building is designed can significantly impact the health, productivity, and overall well-being of its occupants. Hence, if not taken into consideration from the inception of architectural projects, it can prove detrimental to the quality of life of people. This ties into the third Sustainable Development Goal (SDGs), which emphasizes good health and well-being as a key factor in enhancing quality of life.

Transportation and infrastructure present ongoing and future challenges. Our cities need to be more dynamic, inclusive, and technologically integrated, ensuring that urban areas are interconnected and that infrastructure supports the needs of a growing population. This is particularly urgent in Nigeria, where efficient and effective infrastructure is critical for the future.

These challenges we face require us as design practitioners to rethink how we develop our environments, and hopefully ensure we are supportive of human well-being.

Afshar: What do you believe is the most important quality of a successful architectural design?

Oyenuga: For me it's empathy. It's a word I try to live by, and I believe it's the number one quality that designers need to embody. In design, particularly architectural design, truly understanding and prioritizing the needs and experiences of the users is critical. It's about ensuring that every aspect of the design process takes into account the people who will interact with the space so it's actually livable and usable.

This empathetic approach extends beyond just the users to also include the environment and the context of the architectural space. You have to consider the city it's in, how the building will impact the community around it, and how it fits into the broader environment. Sustainability and ecological impact are also critical. Designers need to be mindful of resource usage—minimizing waste, conserving power, and making choices that reduce the environmental footprint.

Empathy also involves being attuned to the social and community aspects of a project. It's about understanding and responding to the needs of the community, keeping them engaged and involved in the design process, especially for public or community buildings. This engagement ensures that the final design is not only functional but also resonates with the people who will use it.

Moreover, empathy in design includes a deep consideration for the emotional and psychological well-being of the users. Design is not just about aesthetics and functionality; it's also about how spaces make people feel and influence their behavior. The design has to answer the question, "Are the users able to connect to the space on a deeper level?" The psychology of design plays a crucial role in affecting well-being, and it's essential to incorporate factors that promote a positive, supportive environment.

Afshar: What are your favorite structures in the world?

Oyenuga: Number one for me is *Fallingwater* by Frank Lloyd Wright. This architectural masterpiece left such a strong impression on me during my studies in school when I was first introduced to it. The way the building integrates with nature is truly remarkable. The cantilevered structure over the flowing water, the steps that blend seamlessly with the surrounding landscape, and the overall design that merges indoor and outdoor spaces—it all creates a harmonious connection with the environment. When you're inside, it feels like you're still part of the natural world outside. I love how simple yet profound the design is. It doesn't overwhelm the inhabitant, instead, it respects the environment and promotes a sense of integration, peace, and well-being.

The second building that has always stood out to me is the Taj Mahal. It is, of course, a world-renowned monument, but what really captivates me is the love story behind it. The Taj Mahal was created as a tribute by an emperor for his beloved wife, and that deep emotion is captured in the architecture. The symmetry, the graceful curves, the soaring height—all of it reflects the profound connection he felt for her. It's not just a building; it's a dynamic expression of love and loss, and that emotional depth is what makes it truly special to me.

I'm hoping to one day visit both amazing structures in person.

Afshar: What personal passions or hobbies bring you inspiration?

Oyenuga: When I was younger, I used to draw and paint quite a bit. My drawings and paintings back then were mostly in pencil, crayon, and watercolor, just playful, childish creations that I enjoyed. As I entered secondary school, I started drawing more and realized that I had a real knack for it. But when I moved on to university and began studying architecture, my passion for drawing took a backseat. My focus shifted entirely to designing buildings, interiors, and the technical aspects of architecture.

However, after graduating and starting my career, I found that my passion for drawing and painting started to resurface. It's funny how something you're passionate about never really leaves you—it just waits for the right moment to re-emerge in your life. Now, I've returned to painting, and it's become a significant part of my life again. Although it started as more of a hobby, I'm gradually developing it further alongside my design career.

I also get inspiration from my love for nature. The kind of art I create and resonates with me are those that incorporate breathtaking natural scenery. I also do nature photography as a hobby, capturing serendipitous scenes with animals or humans as my main characters, and stunning scenery that naturally occur in our everyday life. Writing thought-provoking poems is another passion of mine that I recently took up.

I make it a point of duty to share my ideas and creations with the world through these art forms, solely to contribute to impacting people's lives positively. I currently share them on Instagram @temilola.creates and @lolashotit. These personal passions not only bring me inspiration, I hope they inspire others as well.

CHAPTER 28

Uday Shankar
Perforce

Uday Shankar is the Global Head of Product Design for Perforce. His team supports a product line of more than 30 tools and services for engineering automation, DevOps, mobile and web application testing automation, and IP and application lifecycle management, which are used by 75% of Fortune 100 companies.

Past projects include developing Nokia Symbian OS features, Yahoo Mail, Yahoo's ad quality tools, SaaS marketplaces, flight & cruise management software, various enterprise products, a crypto derivatives trading platform, version control systems, and IP management tools. Uday resides in Minneapolis, Minnesota.

Jaleh Afshar: Can you describe your experience managing global teams, and the strategies you employ to ensure effective collaboration?

Uday Shankar: The team I lead at Perforce works across seven time zones, which presents an ongoing challenge in figuring out how to collaborate effectively. Even within the United States, we have people spread across three different time zones. We've tried several approaches, failed a few times, and ultimately found what works best for us.

Initially, when the team was smaller, we attempted a Design-wide stand-up meeting. However, as the team grew, especially with members in Europe and India, this quickly became unsustainable. For them, any meeting with US-based colleagues falls during their evening, which often conflicts with their engineering or product stand-ups, not to mention personal time like dinner. I try to avoid adding unnecessary meetings to people's calendars, especially when they can be avoided.

After many trials, the best solution was to split the team into smaller groups, with members located closer to each other geographically. Each group focuses on a set of products and reports to a design manager responsible for those products. A typical design manager oversees three to five products. This structure works well, and while there is still a bit of matrixed cross-collaboration between teams, in our model, design managers are responsible for managing expectations across the leadership chain. They ensure that product managers and directors are fully aware of what's happening, and that the VPs know the designers working on their products. General managers also receive quarterly updates. However, as designers began working across multiple domains, complexities arose. While this is primarily a leadership issue, we've managed to make it work by keeping communication clear and responsibilities aligned.

The challenge now is dealing with dotted-line reporting, where one designer may work under multiple general managers. We're trying to avoid situations where a single person has to give updates or manage expectations for two different general managers. This is an issue I'm still working on with my leadership team. What is important to me during this phase though is to ensure that the Design team members are insulated from these leadership-level complexities. My aim is for our designers to continue collaborating closely without unnecessary blockers to their work. They have regular check-ins, which are scheduled during their daytime hours only, ensuring minimal disruption.

One tool that has been incredibly helpful is AI-driven meeting technology. Transcripts from meetings are now automated and highly accurate, which saves our managers from having to summarize discussions or send updates manually. Once a meeting is done, Zoom provides an automated transcript that captures everything, often with eerie accuracy!

I'm also focused on making sure the designers' work experience is as seamless as possible. Our senior leadership handles any challenges that arise so the designers can focus on their work. We've set cross-organizational goals to encourage collaboration across smaller teams, outside of their regular roadmap commitments. For example, we're currently running an AI-centric initiative that involves designers and principal engineers from different teams coming together to create a unified set of AI design principles. With 25 products all implementing AI in different ways, it's easy for efforts to become fragmented. This initiative ensures consistency in key areas like data privacy, customer assurance, and PII handling.

These cross-functional initiatives have been running for over a month, with participants meeting weekly to whiteboard ideas, take on tasks, and collaborate. It's a low-pressure way for designers and engineers to work together, get to know one another, and foster a positive environment of collaboration.

Afshar: What drives your passion for executive management?

Shankar: There are two primary reasons why I'm here today. The first is the responsibility and opportunity to influence and shape the careers and lives of fellow designers. It's a humbling challenge, knowing that we play a significant role in their growth, and I take great pride in that. In the early stages of my career, before there were established design education programs in the mainstream, I used to recruit individuals from engineering colleges who had a creative inclination and guide them into the world of design. Some thrived, while others realized it wasn't for them. However, those who found their passion in design often went on to pursue further formal education as the field expanded. Many of them are now in leadership roles at companies like Meta, Airbnb, and Asana. When I see their profiles and recognize that some of them have achieved more than I have, it fills me with pride.

As you climb the career ladder, the ability to impact the lives of fellow designers becomes one of the most rewarding perks. It's both a responsibility and an opportunity that I'm incredibly grateful for, especially because my own managers paved the way for me in this regard.

The second reason spawns from something I've observed in the design industry, which is that designers naturally tend to obsess over craft. While this is admirable, once they reach higher roles, such as sitting at the leadership table, they often continue to focus solely on the craft and user experience, unable to see the bigger picture. I've spoken to many of my peers, and one of the things I've realized is that because they report to design leadership, their focus remains deeply rooted in user experience, which is important, but it limits their perspective.

When you step into a chief design or head role, your responsibilities expand, and you begin to see the broader context. Sitting at the table with leaders from other departments—such as VPs of product—has been incredibly enlightening. These leaders are facing challenges like losing customers or dealing with financial impacts that could create a $300 million dent in the company's revenue. Understanding these pressures changes the way I approach my work and prioritize tasks.

Earlier in my career, I would get frustrated when scope changed or good ideas were de-prioritized. Now, I understand the pressures that leadership faces—from the board and from revenue officers—and I see things differently. This has become the second reason I feel so drawn to executive management and broader leadership roles. It's an education in itself, realizing that while

UX is crucial, there is a whole world beyond it that we need to take into account. We must stop being narrow-minded and recognize how UX can contribute to the larger picture, while also understanding that sometimes, we need to think beyond just UX. This expanded perspective is something I truly enjoy and value as part of my role.

Afshar: Are there any skills or knowledge you wish you had acquired earlier in your management career?

Shankar: I'm truly grateful for the managers who mentored me early in my career. They didn't just hand me a self-help book and say, "Read this and become a manager." Instead, they took the time to coach me, allowed me to make mistakes, and supported me when I made big blunders. They helped me correct my course and guided me in the right direction, which was invaluable to my growth.

In terms of skill development, as I moved into senior executive leadership, one thing I wish I had been better at from the start is being comfortable with numbers. As a student, I was never into math. I was the quintessential "creative" person. But now, in my current role, a significant portion of my time is spent looking at sales figures, revenue numbers, user adoption metrics, operating costs, and so on. I've had to learn to be comfortable with these numbers, and I need to have them at my fingertips.

It's not that I need numbers to design better, but when I'm at the leadership table, I need to speak in a way that others take seriously. For instance, if I'm proposing an overhaul of a product, I need to justify it with data. I can't just show up with a Figma file. Sure, showing off design concepts has a place. But to even have my ideas considered, I need to present Excel sheets with projections and numbers. This was something I had to learn on the job.

At first, I thought, "We're all working toward the same goal—the success of the product. So, if I, as the designer, come to you with a solution, why wouldn't you just trust me? You hired me for this." But I quickly learned that's not how it works. For others to trust me, I need to speak their language—numbers. I need to talk about sales, operating costs, and annual recurring revenue (ARR) to effectively pitch my ideas. Without that, some stakeholders won't even entertain my proposals.

In addition to numbers, learning marketing and business terminology has been crucial. I have an MBA, but that was from a very long time ago. I've been in the design industry for 25 years now. Terms like ACV (annual contract value), ARR (annual recurring revenue), and understanding that "new logos" in the jargon of business talk is referring to a set of newly minted clients is all important to understand. I'm constantly interacting with salespeople and support teams. Even if I'm not directly negotiating with them, I need to understand what's being discussed. When a salesperson celebrates closing a new ACV deal with balloons and fanfare, I need to know what we're celebrating for it to be genuine.

Maintaining relationships with people across the organization, especially those selling our products or engaging with our customers, requires understanding their world. Learning the business language helps build rapport, and it's an essential part of being effective in this role.

Afshar: Can you share your process for designing tools that integrate with existing engineering workflows?

Shankar: One of the key things about working at any enterprise company is that we're building a product that's just one piece in a much larger puzzle—the software infrastructure that our users rely on every day. Users are constantly juggling multiple tools to get their tasks done. This is true across roles. For instance, even as designers, we use at least two or three different products just to complete our work. Engineers, on the other hand, have an even higher number of tools they interact with, and it becomes more complex for management.

When someone new joins the team, we ensure they're given time—about two to three months—to regularly meet with subject matter experts (SMEs), who are often technical product managers. Many of these product managers have come from the customer side, so they bring a wealth of knowledge not just about the domain but also about the pain points and frustrations customers face while using our product. It's crucial to have these conversations early on because learning the domain is vital.

Of course, no matter how much effort we put in, new team members can't fully absorb what product managers have learned over five or ten years of industry experience in just a few weeks or months. So, the best approach is to have consistent check-ins with product managers and engineering reviews. At Perforce, one challenge we face is that our products are built by engineers, for engineers. This creates a strong sense among the engineering community that they already understand the user personas and don't need any additional insights or education about the design process.

For designers, this means navigating a delicate balance. Our job isn't to antagonize engineers but to listen carefully to their viewpoints and find ways to integrate their feedback into our designs. Every designer who joins us is prepped for this dynamic. We tell them, "Engineers will have strong opinions about features, so don't dismiss their input. Take it in, write it down, and then we'll brainstorm as a design team before coming back with more refined proposals." This process may add to our design iterations, but it's beneficial because it fosters collaboration without compromising design integrity.

Another unique challenge is that we're designing highly complex tools for engineers, which means we can't always anticipate how the tools will be used. For instance, in version control systems, the tools we're familiar with as designers—like GitHub or Figma branching—are fairly simple compared to more advanced features in engineering-focused systems like Helix Core

Version Control, which has far more complexity under the hood. It's unrealistic to expect designers to fully understand this complexity in just a couple of years.

That's why we mandate research and data-backed justification for every design decision, even when it involves well-known design patterns. For example, if we're dealing with something as common as Single Sign-On (SSO), I still encourage my designers to research how SSO is designed for engineering products compared to how it functions in tools like Figma or Atlassian. Understanding these nuances can make a significant difference in the final design and user experience.

We ensure that our designers are prepared for the complexities of working with engineers, prioritize research-driven decisions, and maintain constant communication with technical experts. This approach helps us build more effective products while fostering a collaborative environment across disciplines.

Afshar: What methods do you use to gather user feedback and iterate on design concepts?

Shankar: One of the fortunate aspects of managing a portfolio with over 25 products is that many of our own employees, who are subject matter experts (and often former clients of our products), haven't used the other products in our portfolio. This means finding "newbie" users within the same demographic is relatively easy internally.

For example, one of our products is JRebel, a coding tool and IDE plugin for Java developers. Despite having many Java developers in the company, many of them have never even heard of JRebel, let alone used it. This isn't due to a lack of internal "dogfooding" (which we do aggressively), but because we're continuously acquiring companies, and therefore new teams come in every few months. As a result, it's easy to find someone internally who hasn't used a specific product before, making it simple to recruit them for user testing.

However, relying solely on internal users isn't enough, so we also reach out through our sales and support channels to connect with our direct customers. One of the benefits (and sometimes challenges) of having an enterprise customer base is that we know exactly who our users are. We're not targeting a generic demographic—we have their names, roles, and contact details in our database. This allows us to work with our touchpoints on the customer side to open up channels of communication and set up times for interviews or usability tests.

Many of these customers come into the conversation with a list of frustrations, and they're often eager to vent during the initial call. We take all that feedback, internalize it, and then set up a follow-up meeting where we come back with a clearer understanding of their pain points. From there, we conduct more focused usability tests and interviews to dive deeper into specific aspects of the product.

In addition to this, we have a program called the Design Partnership Program, which involves offering our customers incentives to participate in research and testing. Our sales team will often bring this up when closing deals, asking if the client is interested in working with us on research. This program acts as a data pool for us to recruit highly targeted users for testing, offering a more refined approach than simply having an open signup on our website.

We have sponsor users for each of our products, so we know exactly who to reach out to at different stages of the development cycle. For example, if we're conducting ideation research, we might reach out to senior company members who are more aspirational and submit wish list ideas. For evaluative research, we target "champion users"—those who have reported the most bugs or use our platform extensively. We have our own filtering mechanisms to identify the best users for each research phase.

Our product VPs also have quarterly check-ins with CIOs, CEOs, and CPOs of our customer organizations through customer and product advisory boards. These high-level connections are incredibly effective. When they reach out to customers, they can easily get 20 responses with just one email from a top executive, compared to the five responses we might get from sending out an email to 200 people. It's far more impactful and efficient to leverage these relationships at the top of the chain for insights and feedback.

To support all of this, we now have three full-time researchers within the design organization whose sole focus is running design and research studies. They utilize tools like Dovetail, Zoom, and sometimes Usertesting.com in the cases where we need to recruit users from a more general demographic.

The research process we've developed is quite robust, allowing us to gather specific, hyper-targeted feedback. However, it's still a work in progress. When I started here three years ago, this system didn't exist. In the first year, we focused on stabilizing the team and only then moved toward building this comprehensive research program. What I've described is something we've only gone through for two cycles so far, so it's still maturing, but we're learning and evolving as we go.

Afshar: Where do you see the field of automation tools headed in the next five years? How do you plan to contribute to this evolution?

Shankar: Unlike in the 1990s, when users were still in awe of computers, and the early 2000s, when people were fascinated by the Internet, today's users—whether in consumer Internet applications or enterprise—have grown up with both. They've used the Internet and multiple devices at home, school, and work, and as a result, they are far less tolerant of bad UX than previous generations.

Back in the day, my generation was just grateful for anything that worked, even if the user experience was clunky. For example, 25 years ago, booking train tickets online, even if it meant refreshing the page a dozen times, was still preferable to standing in line for hours at the railway station. Today, users' expectations are much higher. They've been exposed to a wide variety of products, and they have little patience for poor design.

In the early 2000s, there wasn't a standardized way to discover applications or services, so users mostly stuck with what they were trained to use. The general public, especially those in enterprise companies, had limited exposure to the tools they used daily. But today, consumer products have set such a high bar for user experience and engagement that even the enterprise world is playing catch-up. For a long time, enterprise software was tolerated because "it worked," even if the experience was frustrating. But now, that's no longer acceptable, because every enterprise product has competitors in the startup ecosystem that are laser-focused on UX and design.

In the startup world, most companies try to get their UX and product design right early on. Once they gain traction, they prioritize refining the UX because they understand that it's crucial for adoption. As I look at the enterprise landscape, many of the competitors have only a small fraction of the features that the larger enterprise products have, but their UX is vastly superior. This becomes particularly important when trying to attract trial users. These users aren't going to take the time to explore every feature or workflow. They're judging the product based on the first couple of screens and flows they interact with, and if the experience isn't good, they'll move on.

This is a tough problem to solve because it's difficult to justify the ROI of a UX overhaul. Convincing leadership to put all roadmap commitments on hold for six months and focus entirely on UX improvements can be a hard sell. We've done this at Perforce a couple of times, but only because we were able to show, through research, that customers were actually complaining about UX issues, even when, at first glance, their feedback sounded like they were complaining about a feature being missing. By cutting through the noise and identifying UX as the core problem, we were able to make a strong case for modernization.

In one instance, customers were threatening to pull the plug on multi-million dollar contracts. During a sales cycle, when the conversation was close to ending, the sales team showed some early mockups for a version that was planned for release in 2026. That single move changed the entire conversation, and the sales team walked out with a pending multimillion dollar deal, contingent on a proof of concept. We ended up pushing the modernization effort forward by a year and delivered it in December, proving that UX improvements can make a huge difference.

This experience demonstrated the power of modernization and how it can directly impact sales and adoption. Now, we're constantly thinking about how new users will adopt the product vs. how expert users will use it. We have to strike a balance with every feature we build, focusing not just on functionality but on delivering a great user experience for all types of users.

Afshar: How do you balance simplicity with functionality in tool design?

Shankar: I really like this question because it directly relates to how I approach onboarding for every designer who joins the team. One of my favorite examples, which I heard from a friend, involves the cockpit of a passenger airplane. The cockpit is packed with buttons, switches, lights, and gauges, which can be intimidating and overwhelming at first glance. However, every one of those controls is necessary to ensure the plane can take off, fly, and land safely.

If a designer at Honeywell or Boeing had tried to simplify that interface to make it look "cleaner" or less complex, it could have had serious implications for passenger safety. This illustrates "necessary complexity"—the idea that every design can be simplified to a point, but not beyond that.

This concept is crucial for most of the products we build, especially in the DevOps space. Even for newbie users, our target audience is still technical at its core. As a result, there's a certain level of complexity that must remain in our product because our main focus is on productivity and efficiency. If we try to make the product overly simple and, in the process, reduce its functionality or force users to navigate through multiple screens to get the same information, we aren't doing our jobs right.

I first internalized this philosophy when I was working in my last job in the crypto derivatives space, building a trading UI. At the time, one of our go-to comparisons was Robinhood, which did an excellent job of simplifying a stock trading interface to be user-friendly and visually clean. We aspired to create something like that, but soon realized that derivative trading is entirely different from stock trading. In derivatives, users need a lot of detailed information to make well-educated risk decisions.

Trying to simplify the screen for the sake of visual clarity would only make users less informed, increasing the likelihood of them making poor decisions and potentially losing large sums of money. Safeguarding the user's money from unintended mistakes became our top priority, so everything in our design had to ensure that they could accurately interpret the constantly changing data. This meant having all relevant information visible not just on the market screen but also on the order placement screen, so users knew exactly what they were committing to before hitting the "confirm" button.

This lesson has been incredibly valuable and has shaped my approach to many of the products we work on at Perforce. While simplicity is important, we also have to recognize when complexity is necessary for the user's success and safety. Balancing these needs is a core part of the design process.

Afshar: Where do you see the field of automation tools headed in the next five years? How do you plan to contribute to this evolution?

Shankar: Over the past two years, I've spent a lot of time reading industry analysis and Gartner reports to stay on top of tooling trends. The one recurring theme, which may sound a bit cliché, is AI. However, when I talk about AI, I don't mean getting caught up in the current hype around tools like ChatGPT. Today, whenever people mention AI, they often jump straight to conversational prompts and how they can get AI to do tasks for them via commands. But AI has been around far longer than ChatGPT.

In fact, my earliest memory of what could be characterized as widespread consumer AI is Clippy from Microsoft Word in the 1990s. Clippy would pop up and say, "Are you drafting a letter?" That, to me, was one of the first indications of a system attempting to understand user intent without explicit instructions. It was the system trying to predict what you were doing based on your actions. Similarly, products like Apple's intelligent background processes have been doing this quietly for years.

Now, with AI models like ChatGPT, OpenAI, and even products like Apple's Intelligence and Gemini, AI has become more mainstream and has been given names. Interestingly, even kids are noticing this. My 12-year-old daughter recently asked me, "I see Meta AI on both Instagram and WhatsApp. Does that mean these products are made by the same company?" It's fascinating to see how AI is now cross-pollinating different platforms and products in ways that are becoming more apparent to everyday users.

For me, AI is really about figuring out user intent. In the enterprise world, most of our products are about converting manual business processes into something more efficient. Right now, we've done that halfway, but it still requires a lot of human intervention—like setting things up, configuring tools, and making decisions. I envision a future where the tool can automatically understand user intent based on the environment it's installed in.

Imagine a tool that, once installed, can look around its ecosystem, detect the other systems it's connected to, and figure out what the user is likely trying to accomplish. It could then prompt the user by saying, "Is this what you're trying to do?" The user simply confirms, and the tool generates a basic framework or boilerplate. From there, the human can step in and make the necessary customizations.

This kind of AI, which can predict user intent without explicit prompts, is the next big challenge for AI. It's easier to implement in enterprise products than in consumer ones because in the enterprise space, we often have the permissions, trust, and legal frameworks like NDAs which allow us to explore these possibilities.

That's where I believe the real opportunity for AI lies: enabling tools to understand and predict user needs more intuitively, making processes smoother and more efficient without the user having to explain everything up front.

Afshar: What trends across creative careers concern you, and how do you think they can be addressed?

Shankar: What I've observed in the design community over the past eight to ten years is that there's been a significant shift. Around a decade ago, there was a push for companies to hire full-stack designers instead of focusing on specialized roles like visual designers or interaction designers. As a result, many designers have been trying to be jacks-of-all-trades rather than diving deeply into any one craft.

The outcome of this shift is visible everywhere. If you browse Behance or Dribbble, you'll notice that many designs look very similar. The same thing happens when reviewing resumes—they all seem to follow the same formula. You'll see a portfolio with one enterprise product, one crypto wallet, and a set of tools used being listed. Designers can have a tendency to be more focused on making things look pretty rather than truly thinking about the user experience or rethinking design patterns. There's a tendency to reuse existing patterns even if they are not optimal for the user problem at hand, rather than innovate because no one has the time to go back to basics and deeply focus on their craft.

Instead of focusing on improving core design elements like accessibility, hierarchy, or user flow, many are simply applying new skins or colors. We used to see experiments like the ones from *CSS Zen Garden*, which was revolutionary for those of us learning CSS back in the beginning of the 2000s. This was a platform which provided a base HTML markup as a resource for designers to fully experiment with the frontend, which showcased the flexibility which could be accomplished with applying design fundamentals creatively to the presentation layer. But now, with the rush to cover the entire design stack, we're not seeing as much of that experimentation or dedication to craft.

The full-stack designer trend began when the lines between the presentation layer and the backend were more abstracted, and designers were also handling HTML and CSS. At that time, the need for full-stack designers made sense because there was a demand for designers who could work across the entire spectrum, from UX research to visual design to frontend code. But the world has changed since then. We now have full-stack engineers who rarely touch the HTML and CSS delivered by designers, since frontend ecosystems have become far more complex than they were 20 years ago.

What I hope to see is a return to recognizing the value that specialized designers bring. Visual designers, interaction designers, and user researchers each bring something unique to the table. By giving them the space to focus on their craft and collaborate rather than expecting everyone to be a jack-of-all-trades, we'll see better designed products and richer user experiences. I believe this is the way forward, but it's something we haven't seen much of in recent years, even though we did see it back in the 1990s.

Today, the business world hasn't changed much in other ways, but this convergence toward "safe" design has created a culture where everyone turns out the same thing. A "safe" design portfolio might be enough to get hired at a particular company, but it doesn't push the boundaries of design as a field overall. We're missing out on the next phase of design's evolution. With AI entering the picture, there's a real risk that mediocrity will rise even more as AI takes over many basic design tasks.

Afshar: How do you feel about the reliance on technical tools to generate ideas in the product development process? Is there a risk of designers becoming too focused on learning tools rather than the fundamentals of design itself?

Shankar: I do observe designers becoming overly obsessed with tools like Figma. While Figma is a fantastic tool, and it has provided designers with the robust ecosystem we've long needed, there's a trend toward focusing on mastering Figma's features rather than focusing on the fundamentals of design. Many designers now spend more time exploring what Figma can do, rather than working on solving deeper information architecture questions, refining user flows, or having meaningful conversations about the people-centric aspects of a potential solution.

As design leaders, we need to encourage our teams to think beyond Figma. Figma is just a tool—it was built for designers, and it does everything we could have hoped for in terms of design collaboration. But it's still just a tool. Great design doesn't come from any one specific tool, it comes from understanding core principles like hierarchy, information architecture, typography, and color.

Powerful tools can create a false sense of accomplishment because what you produce may look polished on the surface, but the thinking behind it might be shallow. The essence of being a successful, timeless designer isn't about mastering a software tool—it's about mastering the fundamentals that make the design meaningful and effective. That's something we need to bring back to the forefront of our practice.

CHAPTER 29

Wendy Owen
Meta

Wendy Owen is the VP and Head of Design for Facebook, leading a team of product and content designers, design engineers, and design operations leads for one of the most downloaded apps in the world. Previously, Owen founded the strategy group at the San Francisco design agency Hot Studio where she partnered with Google, YouTube, AT&T, and other leading companies. She also ran her own design and research firm and held several product executive positions within startups in the Bay Area.

Wendy's career reflects a demonstrated track record and passion for helping companies create compelling online experiences driven by customer needs.

Jaleh Afshar: Could you share more about your career path and what led you to your current role as a VP of Design?

Wendy Owen: My journey is nonlinear and I am self-taught. As a kid, I knew I would do something which involved creativity and business. I also knew fairly early in my career that I wanted to go into tech because it seemed like a way to blend creativity, problem-solving, and creating valuable things for people. I did not imagine being a VP of Design, but I always imagined helping to lead large efforts and teams.

On the academic side, I studied English literature and gender studies in college and was heavily involved in arts. This spanned both fine arts, such as ceramics, and also performing arts, including theater, film, and dance. I went to a school called Wesleyan where there was a lot of rigor across academics and arts and emphasis on joining the two. In the time immediately following college, I was very focused on photography and video. My focus was experimental documentaries and had them shown in a number of festivals.

My most pivotal role in the early years of my career was at Wired Digital, which was the digital side of Wired Magazine and one of the first tech startups in San Francisco. At that time, we were creating one of the first news sites, chat engines, DIY coding tools, and immersive entertainment experiences. We had world class designers from the graphic design world partnering with very creative engineers. I left a full-time job with benefits and a promotion to be a front-end engineering intern because I was truly excited by the idea of being at a company that was building the Internet before most people really understood what that was. I got a book about HTML and crammed for the interview over the weekend and then called them every day until they finally hired me. The truth is I wasn't a very good front-end coder and thus found myself more drawn to developing the design system and the user research lab. This experience gave me firsthand learnings on how to turn customer insights into product improvements. But regardless, being responsible for pushing code live every day taught me a lot about designing a system. I ended up working for a lot of startups where I was responsible for owning the entire system. That work is really in my DNA.

Following that, I had the fun, yet simultaneously hard, experience of running my own design and research firm in San Francisco with my husband. That gave me the experience to later join Hot Studio, a creative firm also based San Francisco which eventually got acquired by Meta.

Meta has been my favorite job. There is nothing like designing at scale. It is definitely the hardest and most interesting job that I have ever had and I feel very fortunate to get to do what I do. At Meta, I have led the Monetization team and now Facebook—the product I am focused on today.

The thread that weaves through all of my jobs is a focus on people and a determination to figure out what will add value to their life experience through the products they use.

Jaleh Afshar: Can you describe your current role and the team you lead?

Wendy Owen: I lead design for Facebook. This means my team is responsible for designing the user experience for the app. My team includes all of the product, communication, and content designers for Facebook as well as the design program managers. In this role, I sit on the executive leadership team for the app.

Afshar: What are some of the most surprising ways users have interacted with the Facebook platform?

Owen: I am surprised at the variety of usage you see within Facebook. It is one app but supports people from all over the world with very different needs. Of course many come to the app to connect with friends and family as well as to go deeper on a wide range of interests. Some come daily to engage in a community through groups. Some come to buy and sell on Marketplace and others come to engage with our dating app. So I think the most surprising thing is that the app serves very different purposes for different people.

Afshar: What do you hope your legacy will be at Facebook and the design community at large?

Owen: I am inspired by adding value to people's lives through design. I hope Facebook will continue to evolve, and across its future evolutions continue to bring even more value to people, and continue to serve a wide variety of needs globally.

Afshar: What are the key elements that make a successful design culture?

Owen: When I evaluate the health of design teams in particular, there are four fundamental factors I always look for.

First, I consider whether there is a strong focus on both innovation and craft. I firmly believe that to raise the bar in any design work, you need to prioritize these two elements simultaneously. Innovation requires understanding the value you're providing to users and identifying where there's room to expand that value even further. Craft, on the other hand, ensures that the quality and execution of the design match the ambition behind it. So, I ask myself: is there an opportunity to innovate and to elevate the craft at the same time?

Secondly, I believe that a deep focus on the customer's needs is crucial. You can't create great design, or product as a whole, without centering on what people need. For me, it's important to see if this customer-first mentality is deeply ingrained in the leadership team and woven into the culture of the team. It's something I always assess when considering a professional opportunity.

The third critical element is a team that embraces a growth mindset. This can show up in a variety of ways, from how a team initiates new product ideation to how they approach testing and experimentation. I look for a culture that sees testing not just as a box to tick, but as a key tool for evolving a product. Equally important is how much the team values *individual* growth—whether there's space for people to try new things, even if they don't always work out. A healthy approach to failure, where trying and learning from mistakes is rewarded, is essential for innovation. I always check to see if this mentality is truly embedded in the culture.

And last but not least, across any type of team for any discipline, inclusivity is non-negotiable for me. It's not just about creating inclusive products, but also about building diverse and inclusive teams. A culture that actively promotes inclusivity in both design and team dynamics is one that's primed for success.

Afshar: Can you share a moment when you've had to ask for help or support in your career? What prompted you to reach out and what was the outcome?

Owen: The story begins when I was working at Hot Studio as a principal and opened up the Facebook Hot Studio account. At that time, a newly formed team at Facebook was kicking off with a leader named Margaret Stewart, and Hot Studio embedded a small team within Facebook to assist with that effort. I led the team, helping with the overall design process and providing creative direction.

At the time, I had never worked for a large company and didn't think it was the right fit for me. However, I remember being incredibly inspired by the Facebook team, the company culture, and the challenges we were facing. I came home one day and told my husband, "Wow, I really love working there. If I ever were to work for a large company, this could be the one."

But I had already committed to taking a different job offer at a startup, so a few months later, I left Hot Studio to begin that role. Six months after I left, Hot Studio was acquired by Facebook. While I was thrilled for the founder Maria Giudice and the team, I felt a deep sadness—I knew I had missed out on an amazing opportunity. I realized then that I wished I had been part of the acquisition and stayed on with the team.

I went through a period of soul-searching and even talked with some of my girlfriends about the FOMO I was feeling. They encouraged me to be upfront about what I really wanted and reminded me that I hadn't necessarily missed my chance to work at Facebook.

A few days after one of those conversations, I happened to run into Maria, who was now at Facebook after the acquisition. She asked how I was doing, and I had one of those pivotal moments where I could've just said, "Everything's fine." But instead, I was honest and told her, "Actually, I'm not doing that great. I'm really sad about missing out on this opportunity." Maria responded with, "Okay, we're getting together in the next 24 hours."

We met, and I shared my thoughts with her. Within a few weeks, I was interviewing at Facebook and eventually joined the company. This journey was truly thanks to the support of women leaders—my girlfriends who pushed me to be honest about my desires, Maria Giudice who helped me see the opportunity was still there and helped open a door for me, and Margaret Stewart who brought me into the company.

This story is meaningful to me because it highlights the importance of being honest about your hopes and dreams, and leaning on other women leaders in tech as a support network.

If I can get even more vulnerable and go one step deeper, I additionally had to come to terms with the fact that the startup role I had pursued during that interim period was not the right fit for me. As a naturally positive and optimistic person, I tend to believe there's always a path forward in any situation. But sometimes, the best career decisions come when we're really honest about what we want and don't want in a job. Staying true to that helps you find a role that aligns with your skills, interests, and values.

Being happy and successful in your role isn't just about hard work—it's about finding a position that truly aligns with what you want to learn and experience. And that requires a lot of honesty with yourself.

Afshar: How do you balance the demands of a high-profile job with your personal life?

Owen: There are a few key things that are really important to me when it comes to finding balance and inspiration.

First, spending time in nature and stepping away from technology brings me a lot of clarity and joy. It recharges me, allowing me to return to work with renewed energy, ready to offer inspiration or guidance to others. I believe that being outdoors and staying active are essential parts of my creative process and personal balance.

Another thing that's crucial, and has evolved over time, is getting clear on my non-negotiables. For me, one of those is being home for dinner. As a mom, prioritizing family time, especially being present for meals, is vital to maintaining a sense of balance, both for myself and for my family. I've made this a priority because it helps me feel more grounded, stable, and happy. When I'm able to keep that commitment, I bring that sense of stability into my work as well.

Additionally, I'm a big believer in planning ahead, especially when it comes to taking time off for myself, my family, and friends. I always remind people that work will always be there, and there's rarely a "perfect" time to take a vacation. So, it's important to intentionally schedule that time off to recharge. When we return, we're more focused, with a fresh perspective, which ultimately enhances the quality of our work and creativity.

A

Acknowledgments

This book simply would not have been possible without the many kind and generous people supporting me behind the scenes.

Heartfelt thanks to everyone who introduced me to incredible design leaders:

- **Dana Bright**
- **Sandra Chen**
- **Alisa Olmsted**
- **Bona Kim**
- **Tina Kong**
- **Amanda George**
- **Joseph Reni**
- **Sherry Xue Ding**
- **Bryce Li**

My sincere appreciation also goes out to **Tan Ma** for the crucial research and review expertise.

I'm indebted to the team at **Apress**, for their enthusiastic commitment in making this book a reality.

And of course, deepest gratitude to **Leonardo Tozzi** for all the encouragement.

© Jaleh Afshar 2025
J. Afshar, *Chief Design Officers at Work*,
https://doi.org/10.1007/979-8-8688-1137-1

Index

A

A/B testing, 94, 148
Accountability, 94, 95, 157, 162
Ace Hardware, 49, 51
Action-oriented leaders, 120
Adobe, 13, 17, 22, 23, 26
Agile dev process, 28
Agile transformations, 51
AI-driven intervention, 194
AI-driven meeting technology, 236
AI playbook, 193
AI-powered experiences, 193
AI-powered solutions, 5
Analytical thinking, 41
Android app, 28
Annual contract value (ACV), 238
Annual recurring revenue (ARR), 238
APAC design team, 57
Apple, 69, 102, 137, 167, 244
Applied artists, 8
Approachability, 121
Architects, 55, 87, 174, 188, 229, 230
Architecture
    climate crisis, 230
    ecological impact, 232
    empathy, 231, 232
    health and well-being, 231
    societal shifts, 230
    sustainability, 229, 232
    transportation and infrastructure, 231
Artificial intelligence (AI), 5, 73–75, 83, 138, 178, 213, 246
Associates, 81, 99, 127
Autodesk, 13, 17, 19
Automation, 5, 83, 235, 243
Automotive industry, 102, 103

B

Batra, R., IBM
    craftsperson, 191
    experiences, 196
    global team, 192
    web designer, 191
Behavioral wealth management, 40
Bill of Materials (BOM), 73
Black Lives Matter movement, 149
Brands, 19, 57, 102, 103, 133, 192
Brenner-Bruzgis, B., Twitch, 35
    change management, 40
    communications, 36
    contributions, 38
    cost-saving measures, 38
    department head, 36
    design program managers, 37
    experiences, 37, 40

© Jaleh Afshar 2025
J. Afshar, *Chief Design Officers at Work*,
https://doi.org/10.1007/979-8-8688-1137-1

Index

Brenner-Bruzgis, B., Twitch (*cont.*)
    sense of community, 42
    skills, 39–41
    team's meetings, 39
Brown, C.A., CarMax, 79
    Capital One, 80
    career journey, 79
    challenges, 81
    conversations, 81
    design operations, 82–84
    experiences, 80
    integrated producer, 80
    responsibilities, 80
    roles, 82
Brugnoli, G., TomTom
    consumer electronics retailer, 103
    design approach, 101
    design philosophy, 101
    design student, 100
    digital ecosystems, 101
    digital transformation, 103
    freelancer, 100
    frog, 100
    project challenges, 104
    research team, 100
Budget strategy, 110
Business analyst, 8, 40
Business challenges, 192
Business environment, 2, 102
Business Operations, 118, 152, 163–164
Business Resource Groups (BRG), 77
Business strategies, 102, 192, 193
Butler, A.P., Strava
    design and writing, 26
    design classes, 26
    ECD, 32
    HTML/emails, 26
    and junior designer, 33
    one-on-one meetings, 32
    roles, 31

C

Calibration processes, 145
California College of the Arts (CCA), 108, 114
Capital One, 79, 80, 82
Carbon-neutral construction methods, 174
CarMax, 79, 82
Change management, 35, 40, 50, 51
Chatbots, 193
Chicago, 49, 56, 78, 107, 170, 171
Chief design officer (CDO), 1, 36, 37, 55, 159, 191
Chinese automakers, 102
Chinese brands, 102
Chinese consumers, 102
Chinese market, 103
Chris No, Demand.io
    business goals, 64
    designers, 66, 67
    design-focused people, 64
    Head of Design, 63
    learning patterns, 62
    partners, 63
    personal goal setting, 64
    VR, 65
C-level, 30
C-level leaders, 95
Client Innovation Center, 191, 192
Clients, 26, 49, 79, 100, 102, 192, 211, 240
Clinicians, 203, 204
Collaboration, 7, 37, 72, 80, 83, 105, 154–156, 206, 227, 246
Collaboration model, 119, 212
Commerce, 17
    aspect, 19
    connections, 18, 19
    direct consumer-to-buyer version, 18
    human activities, 18
    important realization, 17
    misconceptions, 18
    online shop, 18
    technical aspects, 18
Community engagement, 230
Companies, 8, 9, 64, 103, 124, 165, 200
Companies shift, 101
Comprehensive approach, 84

Comprehensive research program, 241
Constructive feedback, 111, 181
Consumer design team, 31
Consumer electronics retailer, 103
Consumer experience, 75, 101, 102
Consumer-focused companies, 41
Continuous learning, 194, 221, 222, 227
Corporate environment, 73, 77, 144
Craft, 6, 108, 171, 194, 249
Craft of Management program, 171
Creative block, 48, 96
Creative life, 10, 11
Creative practitioner
    craft, 6
    expression, 6
    market, 6
Creativity, 10, 100, 181, 213
Critical thinking, 14, 130, 146
Cross-disciplinary leadership, 79
Cross-functional collaboration, 105, 117, 135, 211
Cross-functional partnership, 195
Cross-functional teams, 109, 111, 178, 222

D

Daily human activities, 176
Data, 4, 28, 75, 109, 194, 200–205, 238
Data analytics, 36
Day-to-day operations, 214
Deadlines, 47, 64, 210, 212
Decision-making, 3, 95, 112, 115, 205
Design
    AI era, 20
    digital spaces, 19
    evolution, 19, 20
    executive function, 15
    head of design, 15, 16
    history, 20
    products, 20
    rocket ship, 20
    skills, 23
    traditional aspects, 20
    value, 14
Design consulting team, 192
Design decisions, 3, 49, 109, 201, 204
Design education, 113, 124, 164, 165
Design-Engineering-Product Office Hours, 221
Designers, 13, 14, 23, 24, 43, 104, 174
    acknowledgement, 7
    AI, 83, 197
    aim, 104
    business challenge, 192
    business lens, 194
    challenges, 175
    communication, 170
    content designers, 69, 70, 74, 75
    continuous learning, 194
    craft, 7
    data, 194, 197
    engagement methods, 193
    expression, 6
    fast-paced environment, 95
    graphic, 196
    industrial designers, 8
    junior, 33
    learning, 175
    managing team, 191
    mentoring team, 191
    portfolios, 217
    post-production, 79
    product designers, 95
    products, 213
    promotions, 31
    responsibilities, 97
    role, 6, 8
    self-taught, 191
    skills, 8, 85, 170, 193, 195
    tasks, 193
    tools, 26
    user empathy, 9
    vocabulary and concepts, 194
Design executive, 15, 117, 159, 169, 195
Design exploration, 112
Design-forward
    companies, 30
Design industry, 67, 83, 137, 191, 212
Design interview candidates, 169
Design language, 3

Design leaders, 17, 57, 126, 169, 196, 237, 246
Design leadership, 57, 76, 113, 156, 164, 169, 237
Design managers, 77, 143, 164, 236
Design operations, 35, 84, 151–153, 155
    See also User experience (UX) operations)
Design opinions, 175
Design Partnership Program, 241
Design philosophy, 101, 196
Design principles, 9, 82, 104, 124, 148, 196, 236
Design program management, 40
Designs, 191, See also Designers
    AI, 193, 194
    and business, 101
    business side, 213
    challenges, 100, 176, 203, 204
    consulting team, 192
    consumer team, 31
    content design, 69–73, 76
    decisions, 204
    emails, 26
    financial side, 215
    functional usage, 175
    Gen AI, 193
    graphic, 86, 191
    health tech, 201, 202
    holistic experience, 202
    HTML, 26
    human scale, 176
    IBM, 192
    impact, 196
    impact on society, 176
    interaction design, 70
    issues, 175
    legacy, 170
    management, 29
    management roles, 26
    material selection, 176
    opinions, 175
    patients, 203
    product background, 27
    purpose, 205
    regulations, 201, 202

representation, 169
research, 192
stages, 175
studies and benchmarking, 175
success, 195
sustainability considerations, 175
and tech, 169
trends and learnings, 175
UX, 176, 202
value, 104
workspace, 89
Design school, 2, 125, 126, 160, 163
Design system, 1, 28, 35, 38, 82, 101, 130, 211, 222
Design teams, 9, 74, 80, 101, 168, 193
Design thinking, 99, 110, 133, 137, 206
Developers, 82, 163, 192, 196, 240
Development cycle, 71, 103, 187, 241
Digital ads, 27
Digital art, 22, 74, 89
Digital ecosystems, 101
Digital interface, 103
Digital marketing, 27
Digital markets, 27, 102
Digital technology, 89
Digital transformation, 103
Diversity, 21, 112, 114, 134, 192
Diversity, equity, and inclusion (DEI), 144, 149
DNA products, 28
Duolingo, 169, 170

E

E-commerce, 17, 19, 28, 29, 213, 214
E-commerce company, 4
E-commerce projects, 213
Efficiency, 16, 38, 130, 138, 213
Electric vehicles (EVs), 129
Electronic signatures, 201
Email campaign, 27

Emotional intelligence, 116
Employee/manager partnership, 122
Employee Resource Groups (ERG), 78
Engagement methods, 193
Engineering counterparts, 121
Engineering, product, and design (EPD), 37
Entrepreneur, 17, 162–164, 209, 214, 215
European Accessibility Act (EAA), 37, 42
Executive Creative Director (ECD), 32
External design agency, 57

F

Facebook, 94, 124, 151, 247–250
Facebook Hot Studio account, 250
Face-to-face meetings, 174
Fallingwater, 232
Fan, R., PicnicHealth, 199
    customers/concept testing, 205
    design job, 200
    educational platforms, 200
    experiences, 200
    internships, 200
Fashion industry, 108
Feedback, 3, 108, 143–145, 213, 239–242
Figma, 47, 91, 158, 238, 240, 246
Financial-focused companies, 41
Financial literacy, 195
Financial product, 142, 147, 194
Fine-tuned processes, 168
Four-directional D-pad, 147
Freelancer, 100
Fremon, C., Asana, 69
    connecting people, 71
    content design, 70
    experiences, 73
    heads-down time, 72
    interaction design, 70
    meeting, 77
    processes/approaches/attitudes, 77
    severe warning messages, 70
    team meeting, 72
    team members, 76
    workplace, 78
frog, 100
Functional assessments, 81
Future resilience, 41
Future resistance, 41

G

Gamers, 148
Generative AI, 130, 178, 193
Google, 22, 69, 94, 124, 144, 247
Google Calendar, 227
Graphic design, 86, 108, 109, 179, 191
Graphic design environment, 93
Graphic designer, 62, 109, 196
Graphic design studios, 167
Group Ride, 129

H

Health tech, 200–202
Hill statements, 195, 196
Human-centered design, 16, 128
Human-computer interaction (HCI), 92, 199, 200
Human connection, 80

I

IBM iX Design Studio, 192
Ideal process, 3
Indian market, 192
Individual contributors (ICs), 38, 121, 135, 164, 224
Individual Objectives and Key Results (iOKR), 117
Industrial automation, 5
Industry leaders, 59, 118
Instagram, 141, 170, 171, 244
Integrated producer, 80
Interactive Telecommunications Program (ITP), 209
Internet, 17–19, 24, 26, 220, 241, 248

Internship-type program, 62
Investors, 16, 95, 96, 162
Irizarry, B., Sony Pictures Entertainment, 45
    architectural diagram, 52
    clients, 49
    colorful diagrams, 48
    community work, 46
    craft, 52
    creative spark, 48
    drawing circles, 48
    flamenco, 53
    Gantt charts, 47
    inspiration, 48
    poetry book, 47
    priorities, 47
    projects, 46, 50
    roles, 46
    and Rowley, R., 47
    sculpture, 48
    sprints, mapping, 48
    stories, 52
    storyteller, 53

J
Jha, A., Miko, 1
    challenges, 2
    creative activities, 1
    designing cars, 2
    design school, 2
    flagship products, 3
    product development process, 2
    team members, 4

K
Know Your Customer (KYC), 221

L
Labs, 202
Lagos, 177, 180, 230
Leadership, 10, 51, 76, 165, 171, 206
Leadership development, 171
Leadership team, 51, 96, 113, 221, 248
Lee, G., Statsig, 91
    challenge, 93
    companies, 96
    experiences, 92
    Facebook, 94
    GPA, 92
    graduate program, 94
    human behavior, 92
    internship, 93
    products, 96
    programs, 93
    skills, 93
    UX, 92
Leffel, R., Priceline, 209
    agency life, 210
    agency/product work, 212
    AI, 212
    collaboration model, 212
    community building, 216
    connections, 216
    conversations, 216, 217
    entrepreneurship, 215
    experiences, 215
    internship, 210
    interviews, 215
    leadership perspective, 212
    podcast project, 217
    process appreciation, 210
    product design, 211
    product side, 211
    R/GA agency, 209, 210, 213
    travel dealmakers, 212
    Yahoo, 210, 212
Life-centered design, 196
Lifestyles, 5, 6
Local customization, 127
Local market strategies, 127
Logistic decisions, 72

M
Mahoney, J., Breadfast
    business, 134
    business decisions, 135
    companies, 135
    creative inspiration, 138
    cultural factors, 136
    decision-making, 140
    design, 137
    design community, 135
    design thinking and design practices, 137

geographic trends, 136
solving problems, 139
working, 134
Management style, 181
Managing Transitions, 51
Market-focused studios, 192
Material Design, 28
Media, 1, 4, 42, 45, 46, 180, 183
Medical documents, 204
Medical records data, 204
MEP equipment, 176
Mergers & acquisitions (M&A), 40
Micromanagement, 110, 120
Microsoft FrontPage, 220
Mobile, 20, 27, 36, 57, 102, 142, 149, 209, 213
Mobile phone brands, 102
Mobile revolution, 101
Mockups, 3, 242
Modern building techniques, 174
Mohammed A., Intercon, 173
   design opinions, 175
   MS teams, 174
   professional journey, 174
   projects, 174
   sustainability issues, 175
Multidisciplinary team, 87, 100, 174, 211
Multimedia, 56, 100, 177
Multitasking, 148

N

Naming programs, 73
Networking, 38
Networks, 17, 57
Nitsopoulos, M., Thentia
   business cultures and processes, 162
   businesses, 161
   business mechanisms, 162
   career, 160
   CINDERBLOC, 160
   design and tech industry, 161
   entrepreneurship's mechanisms, 162
   environment, 165
   human psychology and communication, 163
   institutionalized businesses, 161
   long sales cycles, 161
   operational culture, 163
   problem-solving, 163

O

One-on-one approach, 81
One-on-one meetings, 32
Operational efficiency, 38, 227
Operational model, 125
Operations practitioners, 80, 81
Original equipment manufacturer (OEM), 50
Owen, W., Meta
   academic side, 247
   creative engineers, 248
   customer's needs, 249
   design, 249
   Facebook, 249
   growth mindset, 249
   high-profile job, 251
   work and creativity, 251
Ownership, 97, 111, 114, 122, 135, 221
Oyenuga, T., Spazio Ideale
   architectural challenges, 230
   client relationships, 226
   collaboration with clients, 227
   interior fit-outs, 226
   leadership, 226
   managing resources and budgets, 227
   passions/hobbies, 233
   scannable barcode, 228
   schedule, 227
   social and cultural shifts, 231
   technological advancement, 229

P

Parr, L.S., Personio
   complex projects, 154
   Design Ops, 152
   facilitator, 154
   issues, 156
   Meta, 153
   qualities, 157

Parr, L.S., Personio (*cont.*)
    resource allocation, 154
    tools, 158
Passive management, 145
People Operations, 152
Pergament Home Centers, 49
Persistence, 32
Personal health information (PHI), 201
Photography, 22, 178, 188, 248
Photoshop, 21–23, 26
PicnicHealth, 199, 202, 203, 205, 206
Printing press, 179, 180
Problem-solving, 38–40, 112, 130, 157, 228
Process documentation, 38
Processes/Programs, 152
Product as a system concept, 100
Product company, 209, 211
Product design, 13, 28, 62, 109, 123, 168, 200, 235, 242
Product development, 96, 192, 195
Product development cycle, 71
Product/digital organization, 36
Product management, 8, 64, 102, 139, 154, 200, 222
Product manager, 28, 52, 126, 156, 211, 236, 239
Product-org-wide mentorship program, 119
Product redesign, 150
Professionals, 83, 146, 157, 187–189, 230
Programmers, 54, 85, 87
Project challenges, 104

Q
QR codes, 57
QR code system, 228
Quality control, 226

R
Recycled materials, 176
Registered Graphic Designers (RGD), 164
Research team, 4, 100, 133, 212
Resilience, 32, 41, 118, 120, 162, 230
Resource-constrained environments, 155
Resource scarcity, 231
Return on investment (ROI), 146
Reyes, M., Duolingo, 167
    craft, 168
    Craft of Management program, 171
    design head, 168
    graphic design studios, 167
    leadership development, 171
    management spectrum, 168
    teaching and communities, 171
    website, 171
Room for creativity, 74
Routines, 36, 38, 39, 227

S
Sakai, D., teamLab
    experiences, 90
    human robotics, 85
    outcomes, 88
    restructuring, 87
    rules and hierarchy, 88
    unpredictability, 87
Sales cycle, 161, 242
Saliu, O., Interswitch
    business lines, 178
    creative team, 181
    generative AI, 178
    problems, 178
    professional network, 179
    routine, 177
    YouTube videos, 180
Selflessness, 120
Self-taught designer, 61, 138, 191
Seo, H., DoorDash
    career opportunities, 119
    career path, 116
    connections, 113, 114
    core values, 118
    craftsmanship, 107
    cultural adjustment, 114
    customer problem, 109
    feedback, 108, 117, 122

guiding principles, 110, 111
IPO impact, 117
leadership, 114
management career, 110
responsibilities, 117, 119
skills, 120
success, 118
team building, 119
user types, 118

Service design, 82, 99, 101, 136

Severe warning messages, 70

Shankar, U., Perforce
AI design, 236
consumer products, 242
feedback, 239
goal, 238
Java developers, 240
leadership-level, 236
products and reports, 236
responsibility and opportunity, 237
software infrastructure, 239
zones, 235

Shopify, 13, 17, 18, 214

Simplicity, 88, 104, 147, 188, 243

Single Sign-On (SSO), 240

Skill assessments, 81

Societal expectation, 11

Sociology, 22, 23

Software architect, 8

Soni, S., Razorpay
challenges, 221
customers, 223
design system, 222
managerial role, 224
responsibilities, 221
role, 220
skills, 221

Spreadsheets, 203

Stakeholder management, 36, 135, 177

Stakeholders, 3, 6, 9, 71, 72, 104

Startup, 45, 46, 97, 133–135, 200, 220, 242

Store operations, 27

Studios, 160, 167, 192

Study design, 23, 205, 206

Subject matter experts (SMEs), 36, 192, 239, 240

Sum, L., Samsung
academic background, 142
customer feedback, 143, 144
interviews, 143
partnerships, 146
projects, 142, 143
vision, 145

Supersonic designer, 58

Supply chain functions, 9

Sustainability, 16, 108, 129, 175, 225, 229, 232

Sustainable Development Goal (SDGs), 231

T

Tangible business goal, 29

Team culture, 30, 31, 155, 221

Teams, 3, 19, 38–40, 101, 148, 174, 211–213, 238

Teamwork, 113, 121

Tech industry, 109, 114, 124, 153, 191

Technical constraints, 154, 155

Technological integration, 231

Technologies, 21, 23, 24, 193, 205, 231

10-foot UX, 147

3D printing, 3

Time management, 66

Traditional hierarchical systems, 88

Transformations, 10, 51, 101, 191, 195

Trends, 83, 96, 118, 173, 212, 244

True excellence, 115

Typography, 6, 56, 57, 124, 246

U

Uber Moto, 127

Uber Share, 129

Ultra Subjective Space, 89

Urbanization, 230

Urban planning model, 176

Index

User-centered design, 100, 101, 104, 196
User experience (UX), 20, 92, 103, 191
    designer, 69
    design peers, 71
    emotion, 70
    hardware, 75
    tempo, 70
User experience (UX) operations
    CDO, 36
    composition, 36
    cost-saving measures, 38
    creative teams, 37
    EAA regulations, 42
    high-profile projects, 36, 37
    legal implications, 42
    legal resources, 37
    levels, 37, 38
    networking, 38
    positioning, 37
    roles, 36
    routines, 38, 39
    service, 36
    stakeholder management, 36
    tools, 38
User experience research (UXR), 36
User interface (UI) design, 16, 67, 69, 92, 141

V

Virtual environments, 200
Virtual reality (VR), 61, 65, 186, 200, 229
Visual design, 58, 83, 93, 109, 163, 211, 245

W

Web-based applications, 39
Wiki, 76
Wired for Story, 52
Wongwattanasilp, C., Bank of Singapore
    advertising, 56
    flexibility, 58
    leadership, 60
    MFA, 57
    QR codes, 57
Workplaces, 136
World Wide Web, 100
Writing briefs, 40
Wu, J., Uber
    agency experience, 124
    AI, 131
    challenges, 130, 131
    design function, 128
    design influenced, 128
    fieldwork, 126
    graduation, 124
    leadership experience, 124
    management roles, 125
    research skills, 126
    safety features, 128

X

Xiaomi car, 103

Y, Z

Yahoo, 210–212, 214, 235
YouTube, 45, 46, 180, 247

GPSR Compliance

The European Union's (EU) General Product Safety Regulation (GPSR) is a set of rules that requires consumer products to be safe and our obligations to ensure this.

If you have any concerns about our products, you can contact us on

ProductSafety@springernature.com

In case Publisher is established outside the EU, the EU authorized representative is:

Springer Nature Customer Service Center GmbH
Europaplatz 3
69115 Heidelberg, Germany

www.ingramcontent.com/pod-product-compliance
Lightning Source LLC
LaVergne TN
LVHW010338260326
834688LV00036B/773